# Hacking Web
# Intelligence

# Hacking Web Intelligence
## Open Source Intelligence and Web Reconnaissance Concepts and Techniques

**Sudhanshu Chauhan**

**Nutan Kumar Panda**

AMSTERDAM • BOSTON • HEIDELBERG • LONDON
NEW YORK • OXFORD • PARIS • SAN DIEGO
SAN FRANCISCO • SINGAPORE • SYDNEY • TOKYO

Syngress is an imprint of Elsevier

Acquiring Editor: Chris Katsaropoulos
Editorial Project Manager: Benjamin Rearick
Project Manager: Punithavathy Govindaradjane
Designer: Matthew Limbert

Syngress is an imprint of Elsevier
225 Wyman Street, Waltham, MA 02451, USA

**Notices**
Knowledge and best practice in this field are constantly changing. As new research and
experience broaden our understanding, changes in research methods, professional practices,
or medical treatment may become necessary.

Practitioners and researchers must always rely on their own experience and knowledge
in evaluating and using any information, methods, compounds, or experiments described
herein. In using such information or methods they should be mindful of their own safety and
the safety of others, including parties for whom they have a professional responsibility.

To the fullest extent of the law, neither the Publisher nor the authors, contributors, or editors,
assume any liability for any injury and/or damage to persons or property as a matter of
products liability, negligence or otherwise, or from any use or operation of any methods,
products, instructions, or ideas contained in the material herein.

ISBN: 978-0-12-801867-5

**British Library Cataloguing in Publication Data**
A catalogue record for this book is available from the British Library

**Library of Congress Cataloging-in-Publication Data**
A catalog record for this book is available from the Library of Congress

For Information on all Syngress publications
visit our website at store.elsevier.com/Syngress

Working together
to grow libraries in
developing countries

www.elsevier.com • www.bookaid.org

# Contents

# Preface

It was just another day at work, as usual we were supposed to configure some scans, validate some results, and perform some manual tests. We have been working with our team on some pentesting projects. Unlike many other jobs pentesting is not that boring, honestly who doesn't enjoy finding flaws in someone's work and get paid for it. So following the process we did some recon and found some interesting information about the target. We started digging deeper and soon we had enough information to compromise the target. We finished the rest of the process and send out the reports to the clients, who were more than happy with the results.

Later that evening we were discussing about the tests and realized that most of the information, which allowed us to get a foothold in the target was actually public information. The target has already revealed too much about itself and it was just a matter of connecting the dots. It ended here and we almost forgot about it. Another fine day we were working on some other project and the same thing happened again. So we decided to document all the tools and techniques we were aware of and create a shared document, which we both could contribute to. Anytime we encountered some new method to discover public information, we added it to the document. Soon we realized that the document has grown too long and we need to categorize and filter it.

Though the topic has been known and utilized in pentesting and red team exercises widely yet when we tried to find documented work on it, we didn't find anything substantial. This is where we started thinking of converting our document into a book.

While researching about the topic we understood that there is too much public information, which is easily accessible. Most of it might not seem very useful at first glance but once collected and correlated, it can bring phenomenal results. We also realized that it is not just pentesting where it is of prime importance to collect information about the target, but there are many other professions, which utilize similar methods, such as sales reps find information about prospective client, marketing professionals collect information related to market and competition. Keeping that in mind we have tried to keep the tone and flow of the book easy to follow, without compromising on the technical details. The book moves from defining the basics to learning more about the tools we are already familiar with and finally toward more technical stuff.

## WHAT THIS BOOK COVERS

Hacking Web Intelligence has been divided into different sections according to the complexity and mutual dependency. The first few chapters are about the basics and dive deep into topics most of us are already familiar with. The middle section talks about the advanced tools and techniques and in the later portion we will talk about actually utilizing and implementing what we discuss in previous sections.

While following the book it is suggested to not just read it but practice it. The examples and illustrations are included to understand how things work and what to expect as a result. It is not just about using a tool but also understanding how it does so as well as what to do with the information collected. Most of the tools will be able to collect information but to complete the picture we need to connect these dots. On the other hand like any tool, the ones we will be using might be updated, modified, or even depreciated and new once might show up with different functionality, so stay updated.

## HOW DO YOU PRACTICE

A desktop/laptop with any operating system. Different browsers such as Mozilla Firefox, Chrome or Chromium, and internet connectivity. Readers will be assisted to download and install tools and dependencies based on the requirement of the chapter.

## TO WHOM THIS BOOK IS FOR

The book would focus mainly on professionals related to information security/intelligence/risk management/consulting but unlike "from Hackers to the Hackers" books it would also be helpful and understandable to laymen who require information gathering as a part of their daily job such as marketing, sales, journalism, etc.

The book can be used in any intermediate level information security course for reconnaissance phase of the security assessment.

We hope that as a reader you learn something new which you could practice in your daily life to make it easier and more fruitful like we did while creating it.

**Sudhanshu Chauhan**
Principal Consultant, Noida, India

**Nutan Kumar Panda**
Information Security Engineer, Bangalore, India

# About the Authors

## SUDHANSHU CHAUHAN

Sudhanshu Chauhan is an information security professional and OSINT specialist. He has worked in the information security industry, previously as senior security analyst at iViZ and currently as director and principal consultant at Octogence Tech Solutions, a penetration testing consultancy. He previously worked at the National Informatics Center in New Delhi developing web applications to prevent threats. He has a BTech (CSE) from Amity School of Engineering and Diploma in cyber security. He has been listed in various Hall of Fame such as Adobe, Barracuda, Yandex, and Freelancer. Sudhanshu has also written various articles on a wide range of topics including Cyber Threats, Vulnerability Assessment, Honeypots, and Metadata.

## NUTAN KUMAR PANDA

An information security professional with expertise in the field of application and network security. He has completed his BTech (IT) and has also earned various prestigious certifications in his domain such as CEH, CCNA, etc. Apart from performing security assessments he has also been involved in conducting/imparting information security training. He has been listed in various prestigious Hall of Fame such as Google, Microsoft, Yandex, etc. and has also written various articles/technical papers. Currently he is working as Information Security Engineer at eBay Inc.

# Acknowledgments

## SUDHANSHU CHAUHAN

I would like to dedicate this book to my family, my friends, and the whole security community, which is so open in sharing knowledge. Few people I would like to name who have encouraged and motivated me through this journey are Shubham, Chandan, Sourav da, and especially my mother Kanchan.

## NUTAN KUMAR PANDA

I would like to dedicate this book to my parents and my lovely sister for believing in me and encouraging me. My friend, well-wisher, and my coauthor Sudhanshu for all the help and support during this book writing process, and last but not the least all my friends, colleagues, and specially Somnath da and the members of Null: The Open Security Community for always being there and giving their valuable suggestions in this process. Love you all.

# Foundation: Understanding the Basics

## INFORMATION IN THIS CHAPTER

- Information overload
- What is internet
- How it works
- What is World Wide Web
- Basic underlying technologies
- Environment

## INTRODUCTION

Information Age. The period of human evolution in which we all are growing up. Today internet is an integral part of our life. We all have started living dual life; one is our physical life and the other is the online one, where we exist as a virtual entity. In this virtual life we have different usernames, aliases, profile pictures, and what not in different places. We share our information intentionally and sometimes unintentionally in this virtual world of ours. If we ask ourselves how many websites we're registered on, most probably we won't be able to answer that question with an exact number. The definition of being social is changing from meeting people in person to doing Google hangout and being online on different social networking sites. In the current situation it seems that technology is evolving so fast that we need to cope up with its pace.

The evolution of computation power is very rapid. From an era of limited amount of data we have reached to the times where there is information overload. Today technologies like Big data, Cloud computing are the buzzwords of the IT industry, both of which deal with handling huge amount of data. This evolution certainly has its pros as well as cons, from data extraction point of view we need to understand both and evaluate how we can utilize them to our advantage ethically. The main obstacle in this path is not the deficiency of information but surprisingly the abundance of it present at the touch of our fingertips. At this stage what we require is relevant and efficient ways to extract actionable intelligence from this enormous data ocean.

Extracting the data which could lead toward a fruitful result is like looking for a needle in a haystack. Though sometimes the information which could play a game changing role is present openly and free to access, yet if we don't know how to find it in a timely fashion or worse that it even exists it would waste a huge amount of critical resources. During the course of this book we will be dealing with practical tools and techniques which would not only help us to find information in a timely manner but also help us to analyze such information for better decision making. This could make a huge difference for the people dealing with such information as a part of their daily job, such as pentesters, due diligence analysts, competitive intelligence professionals, etc.

Let's straightaway jump in and understand the internet we all have been using for so long.

## INTERNET

Internet, as we know it has evolved from a project funded by DARPA within the US Department of Defense. The initial network was used to connect universities and research labs within the US. This phenomenon slowly developed worldwide and today it has taken the shape of the giant network which allows us to connect with the whole world within seconds.

## DEFINITION

Simply said the internet is a global network of the interlinked computers using dedicated routers and servers, which allows its end users to access the data scattered all over the world. These interconnected computers follow a particular set of rules to communicate, in this case IP or internet protocol (IP) for transmitting data.

## HOW IT WORKS

If you bought this book and are reading it then you must be already knowing how internet works, but still it's our duty to brush up some basics, not deeply though. As stated above, internet is a global network of interconnected computers and lots of devices collaboratively make the internet work, for example, routers, servers, switches with other hardware like cables, antennas, etc. All these devices together create the network of networks, over which all the data transmission takes place.

As in any communications you must have end points, medium, and rules. Internet also works around with these concepts. End points are like PC, laptop, tablet, smartphone, or any other device a user uses. Medium or nodes are the different dedicated servers and routers connected to each other and protocols are sets of rules that machines follow to complete tasks such as transmission control protocol (TCP)/IP. Some of the modes of transmission of data are telephone cables, optical fiber, radio waves, etc.

## WORLD WIDE WEB

World Wide Web (WWW) or simply known as the web is a subset of internet or in simple words it's just a part of the internet. The WWW consists of all the public websites connected to the internet, including the client devices that access them.

It is basically a structure which consists of interlinked documents and is represented in the form of web pages. These web pages can contain different media types such as plain text, images, videos, etc. and are accessed using a client application, usually a web browser. It consists of a huge number of such interconnected pages.

## FUNDAMENTAL DIFFERENCES BETWEEN INTERNET AND WWW

For most of us the web is synonymous to internet, though it contributes to the internet yet it is still a part of it. Internet is the parent class of the WWW. In the web, the information and documents are linked by the website uniform resource locators (URLs) and the hyperlinks. They are accessed by browser of any end device such as PC or smartphone using hypertext transfer protocol (http) and nowadays generally using https. HTTP is one of the different protocols that are being used in internet such as file transfer protocol (FTP), simple mail transfer protocol (SMTP), etc. which will be discussed later.

So now as we understand the basics of internet and web, we can move ahead and learn about some of the basic terminologies/technologies which we will be frequently using during the course of this book.

## DEFINING THE BASIC TERMS
### IP ADDRESS

Anyone who has ever used a computer must have heard about the term IP address. Though some of us might not understand the technical details behind, yet we all know it is something associated with the computer address. In simple words, IP address is the virtual address of a computer or a network device that uniquely identifies that device in a network. If our device is connected to a network we can easily find out the device IP address. In case of Windows user it can simply be done by opening the command prompt and typing a command "ipconfig". It's near about the same for a Linux and Mac user. We have to open the terminal and type "ifconfig" to find out the IP address associated with the system.

IP address is also known as the logical address and is not permanent. The IP address scheme popularly used is IPv4, though the newer version IPv6 is soon catching up. It is represented in dotted decimal number. For example, "192.168.0.1". It starts from 0.0.0.0 to 255.255.255.255. When we try to find out the IP address associated with our system using any of the methods mentioned above, then we will find that the address will be within the range mentioned above.

Broadly IP address is of two types

1. Private IP address
2. Public IP address

Private IP address is something that is used to uniquely identify a device in a local area network, let's say how our system is unique in our office from other systems. There are sets of IP address that is only used for private IP addressing:

10.0.0.0–10.255.255.255
172.16.0.0–172.31.255.255
192.168.0.0–192.168.255.255

The above mentioned procedure can be used to check our private IP address.

Public IP address is an address which uniquely identifies a system in internet. It's generally provided by the Internet Service Provider (ISP). We can only check this when our system is connected to the internet. The address can be anything other than private IP address range. We can check it in our system (despite of any OS) by browsing "whatismyipaddress.com".

## PORT

We all are aware of ports like USB port, audio port, etc. but here we are not talking about hardware ports, what we are talking about is a logical port. In simple words, ports can be defined as a communication point. Earlier we discussed how IP address uniquely identifies a system in a network and when a port number is added to the IP address then it completes the destination address to communicate with the destination IP address system using the protocol associated with the provided port number. We will soon discuss about protocol, but for the time being let's assume protocol is a set of rules followed by all communicating parties for the data exchange. Let's assume a website is running on a system with IP address "192.168.0.2" and we want to communicate with that server from another system connected in the same network with IP address "192.168.0.3". So we just have to open the browser and type "192.168.0.2:80" where "80" is the port number used for communication which is generally associated with http protocol. Ports are generally application specific or process specific. Port numbers are within the range 0–65535.

## PROTOCOL

Protocol is a standard set of regulations and requirements used in a communication between source and destination system. It specifies how to connect and exchange data with one another. Simply stated, it is a set of rules being followed for communication between two entities over a medium.

Some popular protocols and their associated port numbers:
- 20, 21 FTP (File Transfer Protocol): Used for file transfer
- 22 SSH (Secure Shell): Used for secure data communication with another machine.
- 23 Telnet (Telecommunication network): Used for data communication with another machine.
- 25 SMTP (Simple Mail Transfer Protocol): Used for the management of e-mails.
- 80 HTTP (Hyper Text Transfer Protocol): Used to transfer hypertext data (web).

## MAC ADDRESS

MAC address is also known as physical address. MAC address or media access control address is a unique value assigned to the network interface by the manufacturer. Network interface is the interface used to connect the network cable. It's represented by hexadecimal number. For example, "00:A2:BA:C1:2B:1C". Where the first three sets of hexadecimal character is the manufacturer number and rest is the serial number. Now let's find MAC address of our system.

In case of Windows user it can simply be done by opening the command prompt and typing a command either "ipconfig/all" or "getmac". It's near about the same for a Linux and Mac user. We have to open the terminal and type "ifconfig-a" to find out the MAC address associated with the system. Now let's note down the MAC address/ physical address of our network interface of our system and find out the manufacturer name. Search for the first three sets of hexadecimal character in Google to get the manufacturer name.

## E-MAIL

E-mail is the abbreviation of electronic mail, one of the widely used technology for digital communication. It's just one click solution for exchanging digital message from sender to receiver. A general structure of email address is "username@domainname.com". The first part which comes prior to @ symbol is the username of any user who registered himself/herself for using that e-mail service. The second part post @ symbol is the domain name of the mail service provider. Apart from all these, nowadays every organization which have website registered with a domain name also creates mail service to use. So if we work in a company with domain name "xyz.com" our company e-mail id must be "ourusername@ xyz.com". Some popular e-mail providers are Google, Yahoo, Rediff, AOL, and Outlook, etc.

## DOMAIN NAME SYSTEM

Domain name system (DNS) as the name suggests is a naming system for the resources connected to the internet. It maintains a hierarchical structure of this naming scheme through a channel of various DNS servers scattered over the internet.

For example, let's take google.com it's a domain name of Google Inc. Google has its servers present in different locations and different servers are uniquely assigned with different IP addresses. It is different for a person to remember all the IP address of different servers he/she wants to connect, so there comes DNS allowing a user to remember just the name instead of all those IP address. In this example we can easily divide the domain name into two parts. First part is the name generally associated with the organization name or purpose for which domain is bought as here Google is the organization name in google.com. The second part or the suffix part explains about the type of the domain such as here "com" is used for commercial or business purpose domain. These suffixes are also known as top level domains (TLDs).

---

**SOME EXAMPLES OF TLDS:**

- net: network organization
- org: non-profit organization
- edu: educational institutions
- gov: government agencies
- mil: military purpose

One of the other popular suffix class is country code top level domain (ccTLD). Some examples are:

- in: India
- us: United States
- uk: United Kingdom

---

DNS is an integral part of the internet as it acts as yellow pages for it. We simply need to remember the resource name and the DNS will resolve it into a virtual address which can be easily accessed on the internet. For example, google.com resolves to the IP address 74.125.236.137 for a specific region on the internet.

## URL

A URL or uniform resource locator can simply be understood as an address used to access the web resources. It is basically a web address.

For example, http://www.example.com/test.jpg. This can be divided into five parts, which are:

1. http
2. www
3. example
4. com
5. /test.jpg

The first part specifies the protocol used for communication, and in this case it is HTTP. But for some other case other protocols can also be used such as https or ftp. The second part is used to specify whether the URL used is for the main domain or a subdomain. www is generally used for main domain, some popular subdomains are blog, mail, career, etc. The third part and forth part are associated with the domain name and type of domain name which we just came across in DNS part. The last part specifies a file "test.jpg" which need to be accessed.

## SERVER

A server is a computer program which provides a specific type of service to other programs. These other programs, known as clients can be running on the same system or in the same network. There are various kinds of servers and have different hardware requirements depending upon the factors like number of clients, bandwidth, etc. Some of the kinds of server are:

Web server: Used for serving websites.
E-mail server: Used for hosting and managing e-mails
File server: Used to host and manage file distribution

## WEB SEARCH ENGINE

A web search engine is a software application which crawls the web to index it and provides the information based on the user search query. Some search engines go beyond that and also extract information from various open databases. Usually the search engines provide real-time results based upon the backend crawling and data analysis algorithm they use. The results of a search engine are usually represented in the form of URLs with an abstract.

Apart from usual web search engines, some search engines also index data from various forums, and other closed portals (require login). Some search engines also collect search results from various different search engines and provide it in a single interface.

## WEB BROWSER

A web browser is a client-side application which provided the end user the capability to interact with the web. A browser contains an address bar, where the user needs to enter the web address (URL), this request is further sent to the destination server and the contents are displayed within the browser interface. The response for the request sent by client contains of raw data with associated format for the data.

Earlier browsers had limited functionality, but nowadays with various features such as downloading content, bookmarking resources, saving credentials, etc. and new add-ons coming up every day, browsers are becoming very powerful. The advent of cloud-based applications has also hugely contributed in making browsers the most widely used software.

## VIRTUALIZATION

Virtualization can be described as the technique of abstracting physical resources, with the aim of simplification and utilization of the resources with ease. It can consist of anything from a hardware platform to a storage device or OS, etc. Some of the classifications of virtualization are:

Hardware/platform: Creation of a virtual machine that performs like an original computer with an OS. The machine on which the virtualization takes place is the host machine and the virtual machine is the guest machine.

Desktop: Concept of separating the logical desktop from the physical machine. The user interacts with the host machine over a network using another device.

Software: OS level virtualization can be described as hosting of multiple virtualization environments within a single OS instance. Application virtualization is hosting of individual applications in an environment separated from the underlying OS. In service virtualization the behavior of dependent system component is emulated.

Network: Creation of a virtualized network addressing space within or across network subnets.

## WEB BROWSING—BEHIND THE SCENE

So now as we have put some light on some of the technological keywords that we will be dealing with in later chapters, let's dive a little deeper and try to understand what exactly happens when we try to browse a website. When we enter a URL in a browser it divides the same into two parts. Let's say we entered "http://www.example.com". The two parts of this URL will be (1) http and (2) example.com. The reason for doing so is that to identify the protocol used and domain name to resolve it to an IP address. Let's again assume that the IP address associated with the domain name example. com is "192.168.1.4" then browser will process it as "192.168.1.4:80" as 80 is the port number associated with protocol HTTP.

From paragraph which contains details about DNS we already came across that it is used to resolve the domain name into IP address but how? It depends whether we are visiting a site for first time or we often visit this site. But still for both the case the procedure remains quite same. First DNS lookup starts with browser cache to check if there is some records present or not or checks whether we visited this site earlier or this is the first time. If the browser cache does not contain any information the browser does a system call to check whether OS is having any DNS record in its cache or not. Similarly if not found then it searches the same DNS info in router cache if not found the ISP DNS cache then finally if not found any DNS record in these places starts a recursive search from root name server to top level name servers to resolve the domain name. The thing which we need to think about is that some domain names are associated with multiple IP addresses such as google.com in that case also it returns with only one IP address based on the geographic location of the user who intent to use that resource. The technique is also known as geographic DNS.

In above paragraph we understood how DNS lookup searches for information from browser cache but that is only for sites which are static, because dynamic sites contains dynamic contents that expires quickly. However, the process is quite same for both the cases.

After DNS resolution, browser opens a TCP connection to the server and sends a hypertext request based on the protocol mentioned in the URL as it is HTTP in our case browser will send an HTTP GET request to the server through TCP connection. Then browser will receive an HTTP response from the server with status code. In simple words, status codes define the server status for the request. There are different types of status codes, but that is a huge topic on its own; hence just for our understanding I will include some of the popular status codes that a user might encounter in browsing

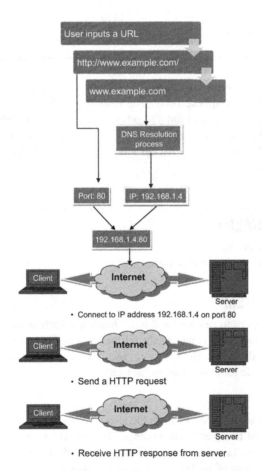

**FIGURE 1.1**

Web browsing—behind the scene.

> ### HTTP STATUS CODE CLASSES
> They lie between 100 and 505 and are categorized as different classes according to its first number.
> - 1xx: Informational
> - 2xx: Successful
> - 3xx: Redirection
> - 4xx: Client-error
> - 5xx: Server-error
>
> Some popular status codes:
> - 100: continue
> - 200: ok
> - 301: moved permanently
> - 302: found
> - 400: bad request
> - 401: unauthorized
> - 403: forbidden
> - 404: not found
> - 500: internal server error
> - 502: bad gateway

If browser gets any error status code then it fails to get the resources properly if not then it renders the response body. The response body generally contains html codes for the page contents and links to other resources, which further undergo the same process. If the response page is cacheable it will be stored in cache. This is the overall process takes place in the background when we try to browse something in internet using a browser.

## LAB ENVIRONMENT

As we have discussed the basic concepts, now let's move ahead and understand the environment for our future engagements.

## OPERATING SYSTEM

For a computer system to run we need basic hardware such as motherboard, RAM, hard disc, etc. but hardware is worthless until there is an OS to run over it. An operating system basically is a collection of software which can manage the underlying hardware and provide basic services to the users.

### Windows

One of the most widely used OS introduced by Microsoft in 1985. After so many years it has evolved to a very mature stage. The current version is Windows 8.1. Though it has had its fair share of criticism yet it holds a major percentage of the market share. The ease of usability is one of the major features of this OS which makes it widely acceptable.

Though during the writing of this book we were using Windows 7 64 bit, any version above 7 will also be fine and would function more or less in similar fashion.

### Linux

Popular as the OS of geeks, this OS is available in many flavors. Mostly it is used for servers due to the stability and security it provides, but is also popular among developers, system admins, security professionals, etc. Though it surely seems a bit different as well as difficult to use for an average user, yet today it has evolved to a level where the graphical user interface (GUI) provided by some of its flavors are at par with Windows and Mac interfaces. The power of this OS lies in its terminal (command line interface), which allows to utilize all the functionality provided by the system.

We will be using Kali Linux (http://www.kali.org/), a penetration testing distribution during this book. It is based on Debian, which is a well-known, stable flavor of Linux. Though, other flavors such as Ubuntu, Arch Linux, etc. can also be used as most of the commands will be similar.

### Mac

Developed by Apple this series of OS is well known for its distinctively sleek design. In the past it has faced criticism due to the limited options available at software front, but as of today there is a wide range of options available. It is said to be more secure as compared to its counterparts (in average use domain), yet it has faced some severe security issues.

Mac provides a powerful command line interface (GUI) as well as CLI which makes it a good choice for any computing operation. Though we were using Mac OS X 10.8.2 during the writing of this book, any later version will also be fine for practice.

Most of the tools which will be used during the course of this book will be free/open source and also platform independent, though there will be some exceptions which will be pointed out as and when they come into play. It is recommended to have a virtual machine of a different OS type (discussed above) apart from the base system.

To create a virtual machine we can use the virtualization software such as VirtualBox or VMware Player. Oracle VirutalBox can be downloaded from https://www.virtualbox.org/wiki/Downloads. VMware Player can be downloaded from http://www.vmware.com/go/downloadplayer/.

## PROGRAMMING LANGUAGE

A programming language is basically a set of instructions which allows to communicate commands to a computing machine. Using a programming language we can control the behavior of a machine and automate processes.

### Java

Java is a high-level, object-oriented programming language developed by Sun Microsystems, now Oracle. Due to the stability provided by it, it is heavily used to develop applications following client–server architecture. It is one of the most popular programming language as of today.

Java is required to run many browser-based as well as other applications and runs on a variety of platforms such as Windows, Linux, and Mac.

The latest version of Java can be downloaded from: https://www.java.com/en/download/manual.jsp

### Python

A high-level programming language, which is often used for creating small and efficient scripts. It is also used widely for web development. Python follows the philosophy of code readability, which means indentation is an integral part of it.

The huge amount of community support and availability of third party libraries makes it the preferable language of choice for most of the people who frequently need to automate small tasks. Though this does not mean that Python is not powerful enough to create full-fledged applications and Django, a Python-based web framework is a concrete example of that. We will discuss Python programming in detail in later chapter.

The current version of Python is 3.4.0, though we will be using the version 2.7 as 3.x series has had some major changes and it is not backward compatible. Most of the scripts we will be using/writing will be using the 2.7 version. It can be downloaded from https://www.python.org/download/releases/2.7.6/

## BROWSER

As discussed above, a browser is a software application which is installed at the client's end and allows to interact with the web.

### Chrome

Developed by Google and it is one of the most widely used browser. First released in 2008, today this browser has evolved to a very stable release and has left the competition way behind. Most of its base code is available online in form of Chromium (http://www.chromium.org/Home).

Today Chrome is available for almost all devices which are used for web surfing, be it a laptop, a tablet, or a smartphone. The ease of usability, stability, security, and add-on features provided by Chrome clearly makes it one of the best browsers available. It can be downloaded from https://www.google.com/intl/en/chrome/browser/.

### Firefox

Firefox is another free web browser and is developed by Mozilla Foundation. The customization provided by Firefox allows to modify it to your desire. One of the greatest features of Firefox is the huge list of browser add-ons, which allows to tailor it for specific requirements. Similar to Chrome it is available for various platforms. It can be downloaded from https://www.mozilla.org/en-US/firefox/all/.

In this book we will mainly be using Chrome and Firefox as our browsers of choice. In a later chapter we will be customizing both to suit our needs and will also try out some already modified versions.

So in this chapter we have understood the basic technologies as well as the environment we will be using. The main motivation behind this chapter is to build the foundation so that once we are deep into our main agenda i.e., web intelligence, we have a clear understanding of what we are dealing with. The basic setup we have suggested is very generic and easy to create. It does not require too much installations at the initial stage, the tools which will be used later will be described as they will come into play. In the forthcoming chapter we will be diving deep into the details of Open source intelligence.

# Open Source Intelligence and Advanced Social Media Search

## 2

## INFORMATION IN THIS CHAPTER

- Open source intelligence (OSINT)
- Web 2.0
- Social media intelligence (SOCMINT)
- Advanced social media search
- Web 3.0

## INTRODUCTION

As we already covered the basic yet essential terms with little details in the previous chapter, it's time to move on to understanding the core topic of this book, that is open source intelligence also known by its acronym OSINT, but before that we need to recognize how we see the information available in public and up to what extent we see it.

For most of us internet is limited to the results of the search engine of our choice. If we talk about a normal user who wants some information from the internet he/she directly goes to a search engine; let's assume it's one of the most popular search engine Google and puts a simple search query. A normal user unaware of advanced search mechanisms provided by Google or its counterparts puts simple queries he/she feels comfortable with and gets a result out of it. Sometime it becomes difficult to get the information from search engine due to poor formation of the input queries. For example, if a user wants to search for a *windows blue screen error troubleshoot*, he/she generally enters in the search engine query bar "my laptop screen is gone blue how to fix this," now this query might or might not be able to get the desired result in the first page of the search engine, which can be a bit annoying at times. It's quite easy to get the desired information from the internet, but we need to know from where and how to collect that information, efficiently. A common misconception among users is that the search engine that he/she prefers has whole internet inside it, but in real scenario the search engines like Google have only a minor portion of the internet indexed. Another common practice is that people don't go to the results on page two of a search engine. We all have heard the joke made on this that "if you want to hide a dead body then Google results page two is the safest place." So we want all our readers to clear their mind if they also think the same way, before proceeding to the topic.

## OPEN SOURCE INTELLIGENCE

Simply stated, open source intelligence (OSINT) is the intelligence collected from the sources which are present openly in the public. As opposed to most other intelligence collection methods, this form does not utilize information which is covert and hence does not require the same level of stealth in the process (though some stealth is required sometimes).

---

OSINT comprises of various public sources, such as:
- Academic publications: research papers, conference publications, etc.
- Media sources: newspaper, radio channels, television, etc.
- Web content: websites, social media, etc.
- Public data: open government documents, public companies announcements, etc.

---

Some people don't give much heed to this, yet it has proven its importance time and again. Most of the time it is very helpful in providing a context to the intelligence provided from other modes but that's not all, in many scenarios it has been able to provide intelligence which can directly be used to make a strategic decision. It is thought to be one of the simplest and easiest modes by many if not most, yet it does has its difficulties; one of the biggest and unique out of all is the abundance of data. Where other forms of intelligence starve for data, OSINT has so much data that filtering it out and converting it into an actionable form is the most challenging part.

OSINT has been used for long time by government, military as well as the corporate world to keep an eye on the competition and to have a competitive advantage over them.

As we discussed, for OSINT there are various different public sources from which we can collect intelligence, but during the course of this book we will be focusing on the part which only uses internet as its medium. This specific type of OSINT is called as WEBINT by many, though it seems a bit ambiguous as there is a difference between the internet and web (discussed in Chapter 1). It might look like that by focusing on a specific type we are missing a huge part of OSINT, which would have been correct few decades earlier but today where most of the data are digitized this line of difference is slowly thinning. So for the sake of understanding we will be using the terms WEBINT and OSINT interchangeably during this book.

---

## HOW WE COMMONLY ACCESS OSINT
### SEARCH ENGINES

Search engines are one of the most common and easy method of utilizing OSINT. Every day we make hundreds of search queries in one or more search engines, depending upon our preference and use the search results for some purpose. Though the results we get seem simple but there is a lot of backend indexing goes on based on complex algorithms. The way we create our queries make a huge difference in the accuracy of the result that we actually seek from a search engine. In a later chapter we will discuss how to craft our queries so that we can precisely get the result that we desire. Google, Yahoo, and Bing are well-known examples of the search engines.

Though it seems like search engines have lots of information, yet they only index the data which they are able to crawl through programs known as *spiders* or *robots*. The part of the web these spiders are able to crawl is called as the surface web, the rest of the part is called as the dark web or darknet. This darknet is not indexed as it is not directly accessible via a link. Example of darknet is a page generated dynamically using the search option on a web page. We will discuss about darknet and associate terms in a later chapter.

## NEWS SITES

Earlier the popular mediums of news were newspaper, radio, and television; but the advancement in the internet technology has drastically changed the scenario and today every major news vendor has a website where we can get all the news in a digital format. Today there even exist news agencies which only run online. This advancement has certainly brought news at the touch of our fingertips at anytime, anywhere where there is an internet connection available. For example, bbc.com is the news website for the well-known British Broadcasting Corporation.

Apart from news vendors, there are sites run by individuals or a group as well and some of them focus on topics which belong to specific categories. These sites are mainly present in form of blogs, online groups, forums, or IRCs (Internet Relay Chat), etc. and are very helpful when we need the opinion of the mass on a specific topic.

## CORPORATE WEBSITES

Every major corporation today runs a website. It's not just a way to present your existence but also interact directly with customers, understand their behavior, and much more. For example, www.gm.com is the corporate website for General Motors. We can find out a plethora of information about a company from its website. Usually a corporate website contains information like key players in the organization, their e-mails, company address, company telephone, etc. which can be used to extract further information.

Today some of the corporate websites also provide information in the form of White Papers, Research Papers, corporate blogs, newsletters subscription, current clients, etc. This information is very helpful in understanding not only the current state of the company but also its future plans and growth.

## CONTENT SHARING WEBSITES

Though there are various types of user-generated content out there which contains an amalgam of text as well as various different multimedia files, yet there are some sites which allows us to share a specific type of content such as videos, photo, art, etc. These types of sites are very helpful when we need a specific type of media related to a topic as we know exactly where to find it. YouTube and Flickr are good examples of such sites.

## ACADEMIC SITES

Academic sites usually contain information to some specific topics, research papers, future developments, news related to a specific domain, etc. In most cases this information can be very crucial in understanding the landscape for current as well as future development. Academic sites are also helpful in learning traits which are associated to our field of interest and also understand the correlation in between.

The information provided in the academic sites is very helpful in understanding the developments that are taking place in a specific domain and also to get a glimpse of our future. They are not only helpful in understanding the current state of development but also generating ideas based upon them.

## BLOGS

Weblogs or blogs started as a digital form of personal diary, except they are public. Usually people used to write blogs in a simply way to express their views on some topics of interest, but this has changed in the past decade. Today there are corporate blogs, which talk about the views of the company and can reveal a lot about its pursuits; there are blogs on specific topics which can be used to learn about the topic; there are blogs related to events, etc.

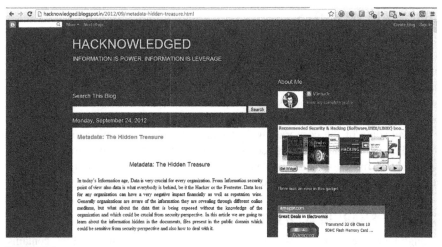

**FIGURE 2.1**

A blog on bylogger.in.

Blogs reveal a lot about not just the topic written about, but also about its author. In many job applications it is desired to have a blog for the applicant as it can be used to understand his/her basic psychological profile, communication skills, command over the language, etc.

## GOVERNMENT SITES

Government sites contain a huge amount of public data. This includes not just information about the government but also about the people it is serving. Usually there are government sites which contain information about registered companies, their directors, and other corporate information; then there are sites which contain information about specific departments of the government; there are also sites where we can complain regarding public issues and check the status on it; etc.

From geopolitics perspective, government sites can be a good source of information for the development of a country, current advancements, its future plans, etc.

So now this is how we usually interact with the internet today, but it was not always like this. There were no blogs, no social media, no content sharing, etc. so how did we got here, let's see.

## WEB 2.0

Earlier websites used to be mainly static, there was not much to interact with. Users simply used to open the web pages and go through the text and images and that was pretty much it. Around the late 1990, the web started to take a new form. The static pages were being replaced by user-generated content. The websites become interactive, people started to collaborate online. This was the advent of Web 2.0.

Web 2.0 drastically changed the way the web was interacted with. Earlier the content shared by the webmasters was the only information one could access, now people could post data on the web, opinions were being shared and challenged. This changed the way information was generated; now there were multiple sources to confirm or discredit a piece of data. People could share information about themselves, their connections, their environment, and everything they interacted with.

Now people were not just the viewers of the content of the web but the creators of it. The feature to interact and collaborate allowed people to create new platforms for information sharing and connecting around in the virtual reality. Platforms like content sharing portals, social networks, weblogs, wikis, etc. started to come into existence. Virtual world slowly started to become our second home and a source of plethora of information, which would have not existed earlier.

This virtual world is now our reality. The ability to create content here allows us to share whatever information we want, our personal information, our professional information, our feelings, our likes/dislikes, and what not. Here we can tell others about ourselves and at the same time learn about others. We can share our views about anything and understand how other people perceive those issues. It allows us to interact with the whole world by sitting in a nook of it.

Today on these social platforms of ours it's not just individuals who exist, but there is much more. There are people in form of communities and/or groups; there are pages of political parties, corporates, products, etc. Everything we used to deal with in real life is being replicated in the virtual world. This certainly has brought the world closer in a sense and it does affect our lives.

The web at its current stage is not only a part of our life but it also influences it. By sharing our feelings, desires, likes/dislikes online we let others to know about us, understand our personality, and vice versa. Similarly the content posted online plays a huge role in our decision making. The advertisements we see online are personalized and depend upon our online behavior and these ads influence what we buy. Be it a political hashtag on Twitter or a viral video on YouTube we daily process a lot of online data and it does make a difference in our decisions.

Today the web has evolved to a level where there is abundance of data, which is a good thing as it increases the probability of us finding the answers to our questions. The issue with this is how to extract relevant information out of this mammoth and this is exactly what we will be dealing with in this book, starting from this chapter.

## SOCIAL MEDIA INTELLIGENCE

Social media is an integral part of the web as we know it. It is mostly where all the user-generated content resides. Social media intelligence or SOCMINT is the name given to the intelligence that is collected from social media sites. Some of these may be open, accessible without any kind of authentication and some might require some kind of authentication before any information is fetched. Due to its partially closed nature some people don't count it as a part of OSINT, but for the sake of simplicity we will be considering it so.

Some social media types are:
- Blogs (e.g., Blogger)
- Social network websites (e.g., Facebook)
- Media sharing communities (e.g., Flickr)
- Collaborative projects (e.g., Wikipedia)

As now we have a clear idea about OSINT as well as social media from its perspective, let's move on to understand one of the integral part of social media and a common source of information sharing, i.e., social networks.

## SOCIAL NETWORK

A social network website is a platform which allows its users to connect with each other depending upon their area of interest, location they reside in, real life relations, etc. Today they are so popular that almost every internet user has a presence on one or more of these. Using such websites we can create a social profile of our own, share updates, and also check profiles of other people in which we have some form of interest.

Some of the common features of social network websites are:
- Share personal information
- Create/join a group of interest
- Comment on shared updates
- Communicate via chat or personal message

Such websites have been very helpful in connecting people over boundaries, building new relations, sharing of ideas, and much more. They are also very helpful in understanding an individual, their personality, ideas, likes/dislikes, and what not.

## INTRODUCTION TO VARIOUS SOCIAL NETWORKS

There are several popular social network sites where we are already registered, but why so many of these different social network sites, why not just couple of them? The reason is different social network focuses on different aspects of life. Some focus on generic real life relations and interests like Facebook, Google+, etc. Some focus on its business or professional aspect like LinkedIn and some on microblogging or quickly sharing of views like Twitter. There are lot more popular social networks with different aspects but in this chapter we will restrict to only these some of the popular ones, which are:

- Facebook
- LinkedIn
- Twitter
- Google+

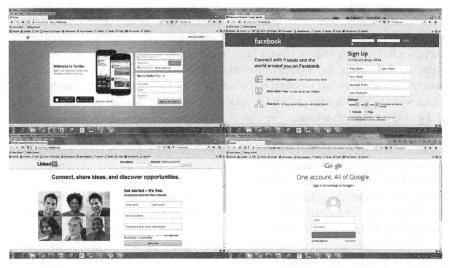

**FIGURE 2.2**

Social network sites.

### Facebook

Facebook is one of the most popular and widely used social network sites. It was founded on February 4, 2004 by Mark Zuckerberg with his college roommates. Initially Facebook was restricted among Harvard University students, but now it's open for all to register and use Facebook whose age is above 13, though no proof is required. Among all other social network sites it contains the most wide-age group audience due to some of its popular features and generic aspects. Currently it has over a billion active users worldwide and adds over half a petabytes of data every 24 h.

It allows creating a personal profile where user can provide details like work and education, personal skills, relationship status, add family member details, add basic information like gender, date of birth, etc.; contact information like e-mail id, website details, etc.; and also life events. It also allows creating a page for personal or business use which can be used as a profile. We can also create groups, join a group of his/her interest, add other Facebook users based on relations or common interest, and categorize the friends. Like something we like, comment on something, share what we feel as status, check in where we were, share what we are doing right now, add pictures and videos. We can also share messages with someone or in a group publicly or privately and chat with someone. Adding notes, creating events, and playing games are some of its other features.

Now you might be thinking that why are we sharing all this information, because as a Facebook user most of us are aware of all these things. The reason to put a light on these features is it will help us in OSINT. As we discussed earlier, Facebook adds over half a petabyte data every 24 h, it has more than a billion active user and it allows users to share almost everything, combining all these three above statements we can say Facebook contains petabytes of structured data of over billion users like what a user likes, a user's basic information such as his/her name, age, gender, current city, hometown, work status, relationship status, current check-ins where he/she visited recently, everything which is a treasure hunt for any information gathering exercise. Now though mostly we don't use Facebook for hardcore intelligence purposes but still we use its search facility sometime to search for some person or page, etc. Like some day we remembered a school friend and we want to search for him/her in Facebook, so we search his/her name in Facebook or we search his/her name with the school name to get the result. Other option that can be used is if there is a group for the schoolmates, we can directly go there and search for the friends. Based on our preferences, location, studied school, college, colleagues, and friends, Facebook also recommends us some friends with people you may know option. This option also helps a lot to search someone in Facebook. We will cover advanced ways of searching in Facebook in an upcoming topic.

Facebook does allow setting privacy in most of the things mentioned above, like whom you want to share this information with, whether public, friends and friends of friends, only friends or only me. It also allows users to block inappropriate content or users, report spam and inappropriate content. But guess what most of us are unaware of these functionalities or simply ignore them.

### LinkedIn

If you are a job seeker, jobholder, job provider, or business person, LinkedIn is the best place to stay active. It can be called as professional network where people are mostly interested in business-oriented stuffs. It has more than 259 million members in over 200 countries and territories.

LinkedIn allows us to register and create a profile. The profile basically consists of name, company name, position, current work location, current industry type, etc. Here we can also add details about our work like job position and responsibilities, add educational details, honor and award details, publications, certificates, skills, endorsement, projects undertaken, languages known, almost our complete professional life. Apart from that LinkedIn also allows us to add personal details such as date of birth, marital status, interests and contact information, which are a concern for certain employers.

Like Facebook it also allows us to connect with other users of similar interest or with whom we have some level of relationship. To maintain professional decorum LinkedIn restricts us to invite others if we have got too many of responses like "I don't know" or spam for our connection requests. Similar to Facebook there are also different groups present in LinkedIn where we can join to share common interest. It also provide feature to like, comment, and share whatever we want and also to communicate with other connections via private message. The one simple yet rich feature of LinkedIn over Facebook is that in Facebook we can only see the mutual friends between two users, but in LinkedIn it will show us how we are connected with a particular user just by visiting his or her profile. It also shows what are the things common between two of us so that we can easily understand on what and up to what extent the other user is similar to us. Other major thing is that in LinkedIn if we sneak into someone's profile, that user will get to know that someone has viewed his/her profile. Though this can be set to partial anonymous or full anonymous using privacy settings but still it's a very good feature in terms of professional network. Let's say we are a job seeker and some recruiter just sneaked into your profile, then we can expect a job offer. Like Facebook, LinkedIn also allows us to set privacy policy on almost everything.

LinkedIn is a great place for job seekers as well as job providers. The profile can be used as bio-data/resume or CV where recruiter can directly search for candidate based on the skill set requirement. Other than that it also has a job page where we can search or post jobs. We can also search for jobs based on his current industry type or company followed by him/her. Job seeker can search job based on location, keyword, job title, or company name.

Now from an OSINT perspective like Facebook, LinkedIn also has a lot of structural information or we can say structural professional information about a particular user and company such as full name, current company, past experience, skill sets, industry type, company other employee details, company details, etc. and using some advanced search techniques in LinkedIn we can collect all those information efficiently which we will discuss soon.

### Twitter

Twitter is a microblogging service type social network. It allows us to read the short 140 character (or less) based messages as known as tweets without registration but after logging in we can both read as well as compose tweets. It is also known as SMS of the internet.

Unlike other social network sites Twitter has a user base which is very diverse in nature. Nowadays Twitter is considered as the voice or speech of a person. Tweets are considered as statements and are parts of news bulletin, etc.

The major reason why it is considered as voice of a person is because of its verified accounts. Verify account is a feature of Twitter which allows celebrities or public figures to show the world that it is the real account, though sometimes they also verify their account just to maintain control over the account that bears their name.

Like other social networking sites when we get registered in Twitter, it allows us to create a profile, though it contains very limited information like name, Twitter handle, a status message, website detail, etc.

A Twitter handle is like a username which uniquely identifies us in Twitter. When we want to communicate with each other we use this Twitter handle. Twitter handle generally start with a "@" sign and then some alphanumeric characters without space, for example, @myTwitterhandle. It allows us to send direct message to another user privately via messages or publicly via tweets. It also allows us to group a tweet or topic by using hashtag "#". Hashtag is used as a prefix of any word or phrase such as #LOL which is generally used to group a tweet or group a topic under funny category.

A word, phrase, or topic that is tagged mostly, within a time period is said to be a trending topic. This feature allows us to know what is happening in the world. Twitter allows us to follow other users. We can tweet, or simply share someone's tweet which is also known as retweets. It also allows us to favorite a tweet. Like other social network sites it also allows us to share images and videos (with certain restrictions). Tweets visibility is by default public but if a user wants then he/she can restricts their tweets to just their followers. Twitter is nowadays popularly used for announcement or giving verdict, statement, or replying to something online. The tweets of the verified account are taken as direct statement of that person. Corporates use this for advertising, self-promotion, and/or announcements.

Unlike the two social networks we discussed earlier Twitter does not contain much personal or professional data, yet the information it provides is helpful. We can collect information about social mentions, such as if you want to search details about infosec bug bounty, you can search in Twitter with a hashtag and you will get lots of tweets related to this where you can collect information such as which are the companies into bug bounty. What is the new bug bounty started? Who all are participating in bug bounty, etc. Unlike other social network sites Twitter has large amount of structured information based on phrases, words, or topics.

### Google+

Google+ also known as Google+ is a social networking site by Google inc. It is also known as identity service which allows us to associate with the web-contents created by us directly by using it. It is also the second largest social networking site after Facebook with billions of registered and active users. As Google provides various services such as Gmail, Play store, YouTube, Google Wallet, etc., the Google+ account can be used as a background account for these.

Like other social networking sites we just came across, Google+ also allows us to register ourselves, but the advantage that Google+ has over other social networking sites is that most Gmail (the popular e-mail solution by Google) users will automatically be a part of it just by a click. Like other social network sites we can create profile which contains basic information like name, educational details, etc.

Unlike other social networking sites a Google+ profile is by default a public profile. It allows video conferencing via Google hangout. It allows us to customize our profile page by adding other different social media links that we own like a blog.

We can consider it as one background solution for many Google services but yet it has its own demerit. Many users has one or more Gmail accounts that they actively use but in case of Google+ they might have the same number of accounts but they can use only one as active account. So in this way there is a chance that the total number of registered accounts and active user ratio might be very less as compared to other social networking sites.

Like its competitors Google+ also allows to create, join communities, follow or add friends, share photos, videos, or locations but one feature that makes Google+ a better social networking site is its +1 button. It's quite similar to like button in Facebook but the added advantage is that when the +1 count is higher for a topic or a link it increases its PageRank in Google also.

Now the OSINT aspect of Google+, like other social networking sites Google+ also have a huge amount of structured data of billion users. Other feature that makes Google+ a better source of information gathering is that the profiles are public. So no authentication required to get information. One another advantage of Google+ over other social sources is that it's a one stop solution; here we can get information about all the Google content a user is contributing or at least the other Google services details a user is using. This can be pandora of treasure.

## ADVANCED SEARCH TECHNIQUES FOR SOME SPECIFIC SOCIAL MEDIA

Most of the social media sites provide some kind of search functionality to allow us to generally search for things or people we are interested in. These functionalities, if used in a bit smarter way, can be used to collect hidden or indirect but important information due to structural storage of user data in these social media.

### FACEBOOK

We already discussed how Facebook can be a treasure box for information gathering. One functionality that helps us to get very precious information is Facebook graph search.

Facebook graph search is a unique feature that enhances us to search people or things that are somehow related to us. We can opt for graph search to explore location, places, photos, and search for different people. It has its unique way of suggesting what we want to search based on first letters or words. It starts searching an item from different category of Facebook itself such as people, pages, groups, and places, etc. and if sufficient results are not found it starts searching on Bing search engine and provides user with sufficient results. To provide most relevant results, Facebook also looks into our relation or at least area of interest and past experience, for example, we can get those things in higher ranking result those are either liked, commented, shared, tagged, check-in, or viewed either directly by us or by our friends. We can also filter the results based on social elements such as people, pages, places, groups, apps, events, and web results. The technology that Facebook is using in its graph search can be defined as the base of the semantic web, which we will discuss at the end of this chapter.

Now though we learned about the feature that can allow us to search different things in Facebook but still the question is how? Now let's start with some simple queries.

Just put photos in search bar and you will be suggested by Facebook with some queries such as photos of my friends, photos liked by me, my photos, photos of X, etc. and similarly we can get lots of photo-related queries or we may create our own queries. So based on photos what we can get ultimately a query such as "Photos taken in Bangalore, India commented on by my friends who graduated before 2013 in Bhubaneswar, India" so it's basically about our own imagination what exactly we want to retrieve, then based on keywords we can create complex queries to get the desired results; though Facebook will suggest some of the unexpected queries based on keywords mentioned in the search bar. Similarly we can search for persons, locations, restaurant, employee of a particular company, music, etc.

Some basic queries related to different social elements are as follows:

1. Music I may like
2. Cities my friends visited
3. Restaurants in Macao, China
4. People who follow me
5. Single females who live in the United States
6. My friends who like X-Men movies
7. People who like football

Now let's combine some of these simpler queries to create a complex one

"Single women named 'Rachel' from Los Angeles, California who like football and Game of Thrones and live in the United States." Now isn't it amazing! And yes we can create query using following filters, like based on basic information such as name, age, gender, based on work, and education such as class, college passing year, degree name, based on likes and dislikes, based on tagged in, commented on, based on living, and also based on relationships. Now it's our wild imagination that can lead us to create different queries to get desired result.

**FIGURE 2.3**

Facebook graph search result.

## LINKEDIN

As we discussed how LinkedIn has its structural data of billions of users and what can we get if we search for something in particular, let's see how to search this particular platform. LinkedIn provides a search bar in top to search for people, jobs, companies, groups, universities, articles, and many more. Unlike Facebook, LinkedIn has its advance search page where we can add filters to get efficient result. Following is the page link for advanced search in LinkedIn:

   https://www.LinkedIn.com/vsearch/p?trk=advsrch&adv=true

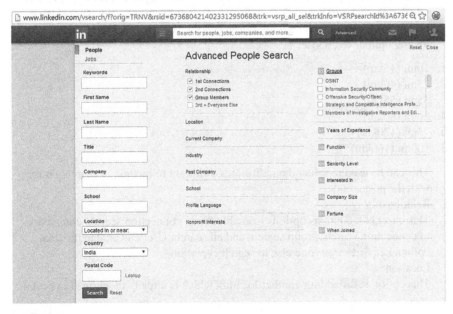

**FIGURE 2.4**

LinkedIn advanced search options.

This advanced search page allows us to search for jobs and people based on current employee, past employee, job title, zip code radius, interested in, industry type, etc. It also allows us to search based on type of connection.

Different input boxes and their uses

- Keyword

  The keyword input box allows a user to insert any type of keyword such as pentester or author, etc.
- First Name

  We can search using first name.
- Last Name

  We can search using last name.
- Title

  Title generally signifies to the work title. Using which user will be provided with a drop down menu with four options to choose like current or past, current, past, past not current to enrich the search.
- Company

  We can search using company name. It also comes with a drop down menu with the options we just discussed.
- Location

  This drop down box comes with two options, i.e, located in or near and anywhere. User can use whatever he/she wants.
- Country

  Search based on country.
- Postal Code

  Search based on postal code. There is a lookup button present for user to check whether the entered postal code is for the desired location or not. By entering postal code automatically a within drop down box enables which contains following options to choose:

1. 10mi (15km)
2. 25mi (40km)
3. 35mi (55km)
4. 50mi (80km)
5. 75mi (120km)
6. 100mi (160km)

   This can be used to select the radius area you want to include in search along with the postal code.
- Relationship

  This checkbox contains options to enable direct connection search, connection of connection search, group search, and all search. User can enable the final option, i.e., 3rd+ everyone else to search everything.
- Location

  This option is for adding another location which is already mentioned in postal code.

- Current Company
  This option allows a user to add current company details manually.
- Industry
  It provides a user with different options to choose one or more at a time.
- Past Company
  This option allows to add past company details manually.
- School
  Similar to past company we can add details manually.
- Profile Language
  It provides a user to choose different languages one or more at a time.
- Nonprofit Interests
  It provides user to choose two options either bored services or skilled volunteer or both.
  The options which are present in the right side of the advanced search page are only for premium account members. There are other added functionality also present only for premium users.
  The premium member search filter options are
- Groups
- Years of Experience
- Function
- Seniority Level
- Interested In
- Company Size
- Fortune
- When Joined
  Apart from all these LinkedIn also allows us to use Boolean operators. Below are the operators with simple examples:
- AND: It can be used for the union of two keywords such as developer AND tester.
- OR: It can be used for options. Let's say a recruiter want to recruit a guy for security industry so he/she can search something like pentester OR "security analyst" OR "consultant" OR "security consultant" OR "information security engineer."
- NOT: This can be used to exclude something from other things let's say a recruiter wants fresher level person for some job but not from training domain so he/she can use developer NOT trainer.
- (Parentheses): This is a powerful operator where a user can group something from other such as (Pentester OR "Security Analyst" OR "Consultant" OR "Security Consultant" OR "Information Security Engineer") NOT Manager.
- "Quotation": It can be used to make more than one words as a single keyword such as "Information Security Engineer." Now if we use the same word without quotation. LinkedIn will treat it as three different keywords.

Unlike search engines which can hold a limited keyword in search box, LinkedIn allows unlimited keywords that is a major plus for the recruiters to search for skill sets and other job requirement keywords in LinkedIn. So it provides the user freedom to use any number of keywords he/she wants with the use of operators wisely to create a complex query to get desired result.

Example of a complex query to look for information security professionals but who are not manager:

((Pentester OR "Security Analyst" OR "Consultant" OR "Security Consultant" OR "Information Security Engineer") AND (Analyst OR "Security Engineer" OR "Network Security Engineer")) NOT Manager.

**FIGURE 2.5**

LinkedIn advanced search result.

## TWITTER

So as we discussed earlier Twitter is basically about microblogging in the form of tweets and hence it allows us to search for tweets. Now simply inputting a keyword will get us the tweets related to that keyword but in case we need more specific results we need to use some advanced search operators. Let's get familiar with some of them.

In case we want to search tweets for specific phrases we can use the "", for example, to search for the phrase *pretty cool* the query would be "pretty cool." To look hashtag we can simply type the hashtag itself (e.g., #hashtag). In case we want to search for a term but want to exclude another specific term, we can use the - operator. Say, for example, we want to search for hack but don't want the term security, then we can use the query *hack -security*. If we want the results to contain either one or both of the terms, then we can use the *OR* operator, such as *Hack OR Security*. To look for the results related to a specific Twitter account, we simply search by its Twitter handle (@Sudhanshu_C). The *filter* operator can be used to get specific type of tweet results, for example, to get tweets containing links we can use *filter:links*. *From* and *To* operators can be used to filter the results based upon the sender and receiver respectively, e.g., *From:sudhanshu_c, To:paterva*. Similarly *Since* and *Until* can be used to specify the timeline of the tweet, e.g., *hack since:2014-01-27, hack until:2014-01-27*. All these mentioned operators can be combined to get better and much precise results. To checkout other features we can use the Twitter advanced search page at https://Twitter.com/search-advanced, which has some other exiting features such as location-based filter.

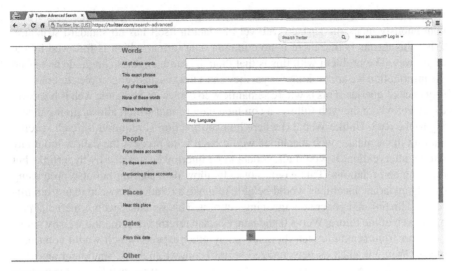

**FIGURE 2.6**

Twitter advanced search options.

## SEARCHING ANY OPEN SOCIAL MEDIA WEBSITE

So we learned about social networks and how to search some of them, but what about the platforms that we need to search, but don't support any of the advanced search features we discussed about. Don't worry we have got you covered, there is a simple Google search trick which will help us out, it is the *site* operator. A Google search operator is simply a way to restrict the search results provided by Google within a specific constraint. So what the site operator does is that it restricts the search results to a specific website only, for example, if we want to search for the word "hack," but we only want results from the Japanese Wikipedia website, the query we will input in Google would be *site:ja.wikipedia.org hack*. This will give results for the word hack in the site we specified, i.e., ja.wikipedia.org. Now if we want to search in multiple platforms at once there is another Google operator which comes in handy, it is the *OR* operator. It allows us to get results for either of the keywords mentioned before and after it. When we combine it with the site operator it allows us search results from those specific platforms. For example, if we want to search the word "hack" in Facebook as well as LinkedIn the Google query would be *site:Facebook.com OR site:LinkedIn.com hack*. As we can see these operators are simple yet very effective, we will learn more about such operators for Google as well as some of the lesser known yet efficient search engines in the coming chapters.

## WEB 3.0

So we discussed about Web 2.0 its relevance and how it affects us and also how to navigate through some of the popular social networks, now let's move forward and see what we are heading toward. Until now most of the data available on the web are unstructured, though there are various search engines like Google, Yahoo, etc., which continuously index the surface web yet the data in itself has no standard structure. What this means is that there is no common data format which is followed by the entire web. The problem with this is that though search engines can guide us to find the information we are looking for yet they can't help us answer complex queries or a sequence of queries. This is where semantic web comes in. Semantic web is basically a concept where the web follows a common data format which allows giving meaning to the data. Unlike Web 2.0 where human direction is required to fetch specific data, in the semantic web machines would be able to process the data without any human intervention. It would allow data to be interlinked not just by hyperlinks but meaning and relations. This would not only allow data sharing but also processing over boundaries, machines would be able to make a relation between data from different domains and generate a meaning out of it. This semantic web is a crucial part of the web of the future, Web 3.0 and hence is also referred as semantic web by many.

Apart from semantic web there are many other aspects which would contribute toward Web 3.0, such as personalized search, context analysis, sentiment analysis, and much more. Some of these features are already becoming visible in some parts of the web, they might not be mature enough yet the evolution is rapid and quite vivid.

# Understanding Browsers and Beyond

## 3

## INFORMATION IN THIS CHAPTER

- Browser's basics
- Browser architecture
- Custom browsers
- Addons

## INTRODUCTION

In first chapter we discussed a little about web browsers in general, then we moved on to put some light on different popular browsers such as Chrome and Firefox and also tried to simplify the process behind browsing. Now it's time to understand what exactly happens in background. You might think that why is this required. As we have gone through some of the details earlier in this book the reason to focus on browsers and discuss different aspects of it in details is because the majority of tools we will use in the course of this book are mainly web based and to communicate with those web-based tools we will use browsers a lot. That's why it is very important to understand the working of a browser and what exactly is going on in background when we do something in it. Learning the internal process of how browser operates will help us choosing and using it efficiently. Later we will also learn about ways to improve the functionalities of our daily browsers. Now without wasting much time on definitions and descriptions which we already covered, let's get to the point directly and that is "The secrets of browser operation."

## BROWSER OPERATIONS

When we open a browser, we will generally find an address bar where we can insert the web address that we want to browse; a bookmark button to save the link for future use; a Show bookmark button, where we can see what all bookmark links we already have in the browser; back and forward button to browse pages accordingly; a home button to redirect from any page to the home page which has been already set in the browser and an options button to set all the browser settings such as to set home page, download location, proxy settings, and lots of other settings. The location of these buttons might change with the versions to provide better user experience but somewhere in the interface of the browser you will find all these buttons for sure.

As all the browsers have quite similar user interfaces, with most of the functionalities common as discussed above but still there are some facilities and functionalities that make each browser unique. There are different popular browsers such as Chrome, Firefox, IE, Opera, and Safari but as discussed earlier in Chapter 1, we will focus mostly on two browsers which are also present in open source versions and they are Chrome and Firefox.

## HISTORY OF BROWSERS

The first browser was written by Tim Berners-Lee in 1991 which only displayed text-based results. The first user-friendly commercial graphical browser was Mosaic. To standardize the web technology an organization was found named World Wide Web Consortium, also known as W3C in 1994. Almost all of the browsers came into the market in mid-1990s. Today browsers are much more powerful than they were in early 1990s. The technology has evolved rapidly from text only to multimedia and is still moving on, today browsers display different type of web resources such as video, images, documents along with HTML and CSS. How a browser will display these resources are specified by W3C.

## BROWSER ARCHITECTURE

Browser architecture differs from browser to browser, so based on common components if we derive an architecture it will be something as follows.

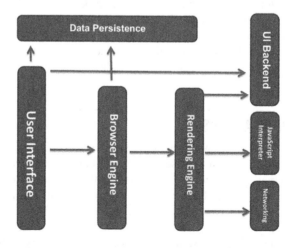

**FIGURE 3.1**

Browser architecture.

## USER INTERFACE

The user interface here is what we have already discussed above. It's all about the buttons and bars to access the general features easily.

## BROWSER ENGINE

It's the intermediate or combination of layout engine with render engine. Layout engine is nothing but the user interface.

## RENDERING ENGINE

It's responsible for displaying the requested web resources by parsing the contents. By default it can parse html, xml, and images. It uses different plugins and/or extensions to display other type of data such as flash, PDF, etc.

There are different rendering engines such as Gecko, WebKit, and Trident. Most widely used rendering engine is WebKit or its variant version. Gecko and WebKit are open source rendering engines while Trident is not. Firefox uses Gecko, Safari uses WebKit, Internet Explorer uses Trident, Chrome and Opera uses Blink, which is a variant of WebKit. Different rendering engines use different algorithms and also have their different approaches to parse a particular request. The best example to support this statement is that you might have encountered some website which work with a particular browser because that website is designed compatible to that browser's rendering engine so in other browsers they don't work well.

## NETWORKING

This is a major component of a browser. If it fails to work, all other activities will fail with it. The networking component can be described as socket manager which takes care of the resource fetching. It's a whole package which consists of application programming interfaces, optimization criteria, services, etc.

## UI BACKEND

It provides user interface widgets, drawing different boxes, fonts, etc.

## JAVASCRIPT INTERPRETER

Used to interpret and execute java script code.

## DATA PERSISTENCE

It is a subsystem that stores all the data required to save in a browser such as session data. It includes bookmarks, cookies, caches, etc. As browsers store cookies which contain user's browsing details that are often used by marketing sites to push advertisement. Let's say we wanted to buy a headphone from some e-commerce site so we visited that site but never bought that. Then from our browsing data marketing sites will get this information and will start pushing advertisements at us of the same product may be from that same e-commerce site or others. This component definitely has its own importance.

## ERROR TOLERANCE

All the browsers have traditional error tolerance to support well-known mistakes to avoid invalid syntax errors. Browsers have this unique feature to fix the invalid syntax that's why we never get any invalid syntax error on result. Though different browsers fix these errors in different way but anyhow all the browsers do it on or other way.

## THREADS

Almost every process is single threaded in all the browsers, however, network operations are multithreaded. It's done using 2–6 numbers of parallel threads. In Chrome the tab process is the main thread, while in other browsers like Firefox and Safari rendering process is the main thread.

## BROWSER FEATURES

Web browsing is a very simple and generic term that we all are aware of, but are we aware of its importance. A web browser opens a window for us to browse all the information available on the web. Browsers can be used for both the purposes, online browsing as well as offline browsing. Online browsing is that we do regularly with an internet connection. Offline browsing means opening local html contents in a browser. Modern browser also provides features to save html pages for offline browsing. These features allow a user to read or go through something later without any internet connection; we all have used this feature sometime during our browsing experience. When we save a page for offline view, sometime we might find that certain contents in a page are missing during offline browsing. The reason being that when we save a page it only saves direct media available for the page, but if a page contains resources from some other sites then those things will be found missing in offline view. Let's discuss some of the added functionalities provided by browsers.

## PRIVATE BROWSING

Incognito is the term associated with Chrome for private browsing, whereas Firefox uses private browsing only as the term. It allows us to browse the internet without saving details of what we browse for that particular browsing session. We can use private browsing for online transactions, online shopping, opening official mails on public devices, and much more.

In Firefox and Chrome we can find this option near new window option. The shortcut key to open secure browsing in Firefox is Ctrl+Shift+P and for Chrome is Ctrl+Shift+N. The difference between normal browsing window and a private browsing window is that we get some kind of extra icon present in the title bar of the window. In Firefox it's a mask icon whereas in Chrome it's a detective icon. For the fancy features, browsers use these kinds of fancy icons.

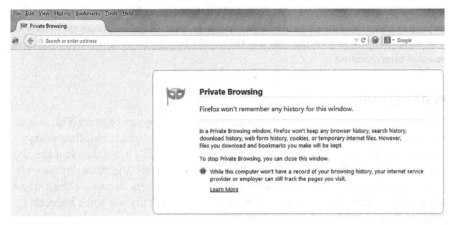

**FIGURE 3.2**

Firefox private browsing.

Private browsing will not save any visited pages details, form fill entries, search bar entries, passwords, download lists, cached files, temp files or cookies. Though the data downloaded or bookmarked during secure browsing will be saved in local system.

### What private browsing does not provide?

It only helps user to be anonymous for local system while the internet service provider, network admin, or the web admin can keep track of the browsing details and it will also not protect a user from keyloggers or spywares.

There is always an option available to delete the data stored by a browser manually. We can simply click on clear recent history button and select what needs to be deleted and it's done.

## AUTOCOMPLETE

Almost all browsers have this feature to configure it to save certain information such as form details and passwords. This feature has different names in different browsers or it is specific with different rendering engines. Some of the names are Password Autocomplete, Form Pre-filing, Form Autocomplete, Roboform, Remember password, etc.

Browsers provide user freedom to configure whether to save these information or not, if yes then whether to get some kind of prompt or not, what to be saved and in what type it should be saved.

In Firefox to avoid password storage, go to Menu → Options → Security → Uncheck "Remember passwords for sites," though we can store password in encrypted format using browser configuration.

In Chrome, go to Menu → Settings → Show advanced settings → Under Passwords and forms uncheck "Enable Auto-fill to fill out web forms in single click" and "Offer to save your web password."

Some web application treat this as a vulnerability or possible security risk so they used to add an attribute "autocomplete=off" in their form of the input box value that they do not want a browser to save, but nowadays most of the browsers either ignore it or have stopped supporting this attribute and save all the data or some based on browser configuration.

## PROXY SETUP

Proxy setup feature is also an important feature provided by any browser. This feature allows a user to forward the requests made by a browser to an intermediate proxy.

Most of the companies use some sort of proxy device to avoid data leakage and those settings can be done in browser to limit or monitor the browsing process. Proxy options are also popularly used by penetration testers to capture the request and responses sent and received by a browser. They generally use some interception proxy tool and configure the settings in browser.

In day-to-day life also proxy setup can be used for anonymous browsing or browsing or visiting some pages that are country restricted. In that case a user just has to collect one proxy IP address and the port number of some other country where that site or content is available then setting up the same in a browser to visit those pages.

### Proxy setup in Firefox

Go to Menu → Options → Advanced → Network → Connection Settings → Manual proxy configuration and add the proxy here.

### Proxy setup in Chrome

Go to Menu → Settings → Show advanced settings → Under Network click on Change proxy settings → Click on LAN Settings → Check Use a proxy server for your LAN (These settings will not apply to dial-up or VPN connections.) and add your settings.

## RAW BROWSERS

There are specific browsers available by default with specific operating systems, such as Internet Explorer for Windows and Safari for Mac. Almost all the browsers have their versions available for different operating system. But the widely used and popular browsers are not the one which comes preinstalled with operating system but the one which are open source and easily available for different operating systems, i.e., Mozilla Firefox and Google Chrome. Though Google Chrome was mostly used by Windows operating system, one of its open source version was generally found preinstalled in many Linux operating systems and is called Chromium. As the name itself has similarities with the Google Chrome browser, their features also do match with each other with a little difference.

As earlier we came across that there are different types of browser rendering engine like Gecko, WebKit, etc. and Chrome uses Blink the variant of WebKit so does Chromium. This project initially started in 2008 and now there are more than 35 updated versions. This is one of the popular browsers among the open source community. It is the concept behind Google Chrome window being used as the main process because Chromium project was made to make lightweight, fast, and efficient browser which can also be known as shell of the web by making its tab to be the main process. There are different other browsers released based on the Chromium project source code. Opera, Rockmelt, and Comodo Dragon are some of the well-known browsers based on Chromium.

Now one thing is clear from above paragraph that if a browser will be open source, then community will use that code to create different other browsers by adding some extra functionality as Comodo Group added some security and privacy feature in the Chromium and released it as Comodo Dragon. Similarly Firefox also has different custom versions. So let's consider the base version browser as Raw browser and other browsers as customized browser.

## WHY CUSTOM VERSIONS?

The custom versions are being used for different purposes, to use the true power of functionalities of the Raw browser to the fullest or in simple words to make better use of the features available by the Raw browsers. The custom browsers can help us to serve our custom requirements. Let's say we want a browser which can help us being online 24/7 in social networking sites. We can either add different social network addons on the browser of our choice to make it happen or we can start from scratch and build a version of browser which contains the required functionalities. Similarly for other cases like if we are penetration testers or security analysts, we might want a browser to perform different application security tests so we can customize a browser for the same. A normal user might need a browser to be anonymous while browsing so that no one can keep track of what he/she is browsing, this can also be done by customizing a browser. There are already a number of customized browsers available in the market to serve these purposes and similarly we can also create such customized browser according to our desire. As the process is a bit complex to be included in this chapter and would require some technical background to understand we will not be discussing it, still knowing that it is possible to do so opens a new window, for people who would like this just take it as a self-learning project.

The Chromium project has its official website, http://www.chromium.org where we can find different documentations and help materials to customize the browser for different operating systems. Apart from Chromium it is maintained at sourceforge, http://www.sourceforge.net/projects/chromium. From here we can download the browser, download browser source code, subscribe to the mailing list to get updated news about the project, and submit bugs and feature requests.

If you are interested to customize Chromium, it will be a great kick start if you subscribe the mailing list as well as explore the documentation available in source-forge. The first step to customize any browser is to get its source code. So how to get the source code of Chromium? It's quite easy, we just need to download the latest tar or zip version of the browser. Later by performing untar or unzip we will be able to get the source code along with the documentation details inside.

Now let's move on to discuss some already customized browsers and their functionalities.

## SOME OF THE WELL-KNOWN CUSTOM BROWSERS
### EPIC (https://www.epicbrowser.com/)

Epic is a privacy browser as its tagline describes itself with the line "We believe what you browse and search should always be private." It is made to extend the online privacy of a user. This browser is based on the Chromium project and developed by the Hidden Reflex group and is available for both for Windows and OSX.

On visiting their official website, we will get one paragraph with heading "Why privacy is important?", this paragraph contains some of the unique and effective reasons for it, one such is that when we browse the data collected from that can decide whether we are eligible to get a job, credit, or insurance. Epic was first developed based on Mozilla Firefox but later it was changed to the Chromium-based browser. It works quite similar to the secure browsing feature by Firefox and Chrome. It deletes every session data such as cookies, caches, and any other temporary data after exiting the browser. It removes the services provided by Chrome to send any kind of information to any particular server and it adds a no tracking header to avoid tracking by data collection companies. It also prefers SSL connection over browsing and also contains a proxy to hide user IP address. To avoid leak of the search preferences, Epic routes all the search details through a proxy.

Here we saw a customizing Chromium project, Epic which was developed as a privacy centric browser.

### HconSTF (http://www.hcon.in/downloads.html)

HconSTF stands for Hcon security testing framework. It is a browser-based testing framework. With the package of different addons added in the browser, it allows a user to perform web application penetration testing, web exploit development, web malware analysis along with OSINT in a semiautomated fashion.

HconSTF has two variants; one is based on Firefox that is known as Fire base and the other based on Chromium that is known as Aqua base. The rendering engines are also different as per the base Raw browser. Fire base uses Gecko and Aqua base uses WebKit. Both the versions are loaded with tons of addons.

The core idea or inspiration of this project is taken from hackerfox but it's not quite similar to that. Hackerfox http://sourceforge.net/projects/hackfox/ is portable

Firefox with tons of addons loaded by Yangon Ethical Hacker Group. Hackerfox only contains addons, whereas HconSTF is a bit advanced than hackerfox and contains better toolset. This is available for Windows and all popular Linux versions for both 32 and 64 bit architecture operating systems. The installation process is very easy, just download the package and run it, no need to install anything. It has different code names for different versions. The first public version or V0.3 was known as "Hfox." The next one known as "freedom" and the V0.5 is called "Prime."

The user interface is very user-friendly and everything is perfectly organized. The author also provides a well-documented manual which contains all the details about the project including the release history, architecture, tools details, and settings with screenshots. The HconSTF contains addons, scripts, and search aggregator plugins. It also allows a user to update the addons and scripts by selecting update in respective places (Hmenu → settings → addons) but it does not allow a user to upgrade the framework. To upgrade the framework user need to check the official site of the project manually.

HconSTF covers tools in groups. The specified groups are
- Recon/mapping
- Editors/debuggers
- Exploitation/audit
- Request manipulation
- Anonymity
- Cryptography
- Database
- Scripting/automation
- Network utilities
- Reporting

The version 0.5 or "Prime" comes with some surprising package for the user such as integrated database (IDB). An IDB is used for different popular web attack payloads such as for cross-site scripting (XSS) and SQL Injection. Apart from this it facilitates a user by providing quick search links to get lots of search data and a large collection of bookmark to use for reference and research.

## MANTRA (http://www.getmantra.com/)

Mantra is an Open Web Application Security Project (OWASP) project. It is a project quite similar to HconSTF but unlike HconSTF, it is fully dedicated to web application security testing. Simply stated it is a web application security testing framework based on top of browser. The earlier version came with the Firefox base but later its Chromium version also released which is also well known as MOC or Mantra on Chromium. Like other customized security framework browsers it also supports 32 and 64 bit operating system architecture of Windows, Linux as well as Macintosh. Mantra has an added feature that most other browser-based framework does not, i.e., it is available in nine different languages such as English, Portuguese, Russian,

Arabic, Spanish, Turkish, French, Chinese simplified, and also in Chinese traditional. As it is very popular in the security community it comes by default installed in popular security operating systems such as Backtrack and Matriux.

It has security addons preinstalled and configured and with its simple yet user-friendly user interface, Mantra is an integral part of every web application pen tester's arsenal. The tools available in Mantra not only focus on web application testing but also on web services and network application penetration testing. It contains tools to switch user agent, manipulate cookie, manipulate parameters and their values, add proxy, and many more. FireCAT is also included in Mantra and that makes it more powerful tool (we will cover FireCAT in next topic separately).

Some of the popular tools groups are mentioned below:
- Information gathering
- Flagfox
- Passiverecon
- Wappalyzer
- Application audit
- Rest client
- Hackbar
- Dom inspector
- Editors
- Firebug
- Proxy
- Foxyproxy
- Network utilities
- Fireftp
- FireSSH
- Misc
- Event spy
- Session manager

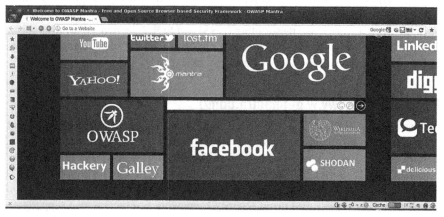

**FIGURE 3.3**

Mantra browser interface.

Apart from tools it also contains bookmarks. The bookmark is divided into two sections. First section is known as Hackery. It is a collection of different penetration testing links which will help a user in understanding and referring a particular attack. The other section contains gallery. It contains all the tools links that can be used for penetration testing.

We can download both the versions of Mantra from the following URL, http://www.getmantra.com/download.html or the individual download links are below. Where Mantra based on Firefox is available for different operating systems like Windows, Linux, and Macintosh whereas MOC is only available for Windows.

Mantra based on Firefox can be downloaded from http://www.getmantra.com/download.html.

Mantra based on Chromium can be downloaded from http://www.getmantra.com/mantra-on-chromium.html.

## FireCAT (http://firecat.toolswatch.org/download.html)

FireCAT or Firefox Catalog for Auditing exTensions is a mind map collection of different security addons in a categorized manner. Now it's collaborated with OWASP Mantra project to provide one stop solutions to security addons based on browser customization. FireCAT contains seven different categories and more than 15 subcategories.

The categories and subcategories:
- Information gathering
  - Whois
  - Location info
  - Enumeration and fingerprint
  - Data mining
  - Googling and spidering
- Proxies and web utilities
- Editors
- Network utilities
  - Intrusion detection system
  - Sniffers
  - Wireless
  - Passwords
  - Protocols and applications
- Misc
  - Tweaks and hacks
  - Encryption/hashing
  - Antivirus and malware scanner
  - Antispoof
  - Antiphishing/pharming/jacking
- Automation
  - Logs and history
  - Backup/synchronization
  - Protection
- IT security related
- Application auditing

There is a category present "IT security related." This one is an interesting category because it provides you plugins to collect information about the common vulnerabilities and exposures (CVEs) and exploits from various sources such as Open Sourced Vulnerability Database (OSDV), Packet storm, SecurityFocus, Exploit-DB, etc.

## ORYON C (http://sourceforge.net/projects/oryon/)

Oryon C portable is an open source intelligence framework based on Chromium browser meant for open source intelligence analysts and researchers. Like other customized browsers it also comes with lots of preinstalled tools and addons to support the OSINT investigation. It also contains links to different online tools for better reference and research. It is a project by "osintinsight" so some of the functions a user can only use after subscribing some package of OsintInsight.

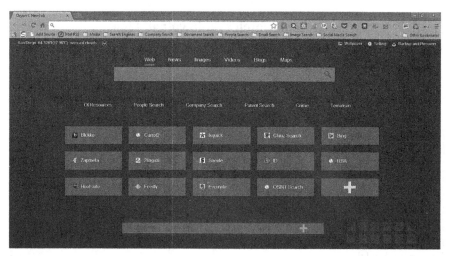

**FIGURE 3.4**

Oryon C browser interface.

It's a straightaway use tool so no need to install Oryon C, just download and run it. It only supports Windows operating system 32 and 64 bit. The huge list of useful addons and categorized bookmarks makes it a must-have for any online investigator.

## WhiteHat Aviator (https://www.whitehatsec.com/aviator/)

Though WhiteHat Aviator is not the one of its kind available but definitely it is a product of a reliable big brand security organization. WhiteHat Aviator is a private browsing browser. It's quite similar to the Epic browser we discussed earlier in this chapter. It removes ads, eliminates online tracking to ensure a user to surf anonymously.

Like Epic browser Aviator is also based on Chromium. By default it runs in incognito or private browsing mode to allow a user to surf without storing any history, cookie, temporary file, or browsing preferences. It also disables autoplay of different media types, user has to allow a media such as flash in any page if he/she wants to see it. It also uses a private search engine duckduckgo to avoid string search preferences of the user.

Unlike Epic browser it is not open source, so open security community cannot audit the code or contribute much. Aviator is available for Windows as well as Macintosh operating system.

## TOR BUNDLE (https//www.torproject.org/projects/torbrowser.html.en)

TOR or the onion routing project is very popular project. Most of us definitely have used, heard, or read about it somewhere some time. Though we will discuss about it in detail in a later chapter but for the time being let's discuss the basics about the tor browser bundle. Like Epic browser and Whitehat Aviator, tor browser is also a privacy centric browser. But the way it works is quite different from the other two. Through the tor application it uses the volunteer distributed relay network and bounces around before sending or receiving connection. It makes it difficult to backtrack the location of the user and provides privacy and anonymity to the user. Due to its proxy chaining type of concept it can be used to view the contents that are blocked for a particular location such as a country. The tor browser is available for different operating systems such as Windows, Linux, and Macintosh and can be used straightaway without installation. Tor browser or previously known as TBB or tor browser bundle is a customized browser based on Firefox. It contains tor button, tor launcher, tor proxy, HTTPS everywhere, NoScript, and lots of other addons. Like OWASP Mantra it is also available in 15 different languages.

## CUSTOM BROWSER CATEGORY

As we came across different custom browsers, their base build, what rendering engine they use etc. Let's categorize them to understand their usability.

For easy understanding let's make three categories.

1. Penetration testing
2. OSINT
3. Privacy and anonymity

Under the first category we can find HconSTF, Mantra, FireCAT, whereas under OSINT category we can add HconSTF and Oryon C, likewise we can put Epic browser, Whitehat Aviator and tor browser under privacy and anonymity category. If we look at the core, what puts all these different browsers in different category, the answer will be the addons or the extensions. So by adding some similar functional addons we can create a customized browser for a specific purpose. If we want to create our own browser for some specific purposes we must keep this in mind.

## PROS AND CONS OF EACH OF THESE BROWSERS

Let's start with the first browser we discussed and that is Epic browser. The advantage of using this browser is that it fully focuses on user privacy and anonymity. Apart from that it's open source and it can be used by all kind of users, technical as well as nontechnical. The only disadvantage is that the reliability factor. Is this browser does what it intends to do or does it do something else. As trust on the source is the key here. So either trust the source and use the product or use it then trust the product.

The advantage of using HconSTF is that it's a one stop solution for information security researchers. The only disadvantage it has is that it does not allow a user to upgrade it to the next level.

The advantage of OWASP Mantra is that it is available in different languages to support security community from the different parts of the world. It has only one disadvantage is that the light version or the MOC is only available for Windows, not for other operating systems like Linux or Macintosh.

The advantage of Oryon C is that it is very helpful in OSINT exercises, but there are different disadvantages like to use some of the modules a user need to subscribe and also it is only available for Windows.

The disadvantage of the Whitehat Aviator is that it is not open source and it does not have a version for Linux operating system.

TBB has the advantage is that it provides anonymity with a disadvantage like it only comes with one rendering engine Gecko.

As we already discussed these custom browser categories; based on category, user can choose which browser to use, but definitely the browsers for anonymity and privacy have larger scope as they do not belong to any single category of users. Any user who is concern about his/her online privacy can use these browsers. Like for e-shopping, netbanking, social networking as well as e-mailing, these browser can be helpful to all.

## ADDONS

Browser addon, or in other terms browser extension or plugins are the same things but known differently in terms of different browsers. As in Firefox it's known as addon and in Chrome as extension. Though plugin is a different component from addons but still some use it as synonym for addon. In reality plugin can be a part of addon.

Browser addons are typically used to enhance the functionality of a browser. These are nothing but applications designed using web technology such as HTML, CSS, and JavaScript. Though due to difference in rendering engines the structure and code are different for different browser addons, but nowadays there are different tools and frameworks available to design a cross browser addon.

Addons are so popular that every web user might have used it already at some point or another. Some of the popular addons are YouTube downloader, Google translate in common and SOA client, Rest client, and hackbar in case of penetration testers.

We can install addon quite easily in both the browsers, Firefox as well as Chrome by simply clicking on install button. Addons are not always safe so choose them wisely so download from trusted sources and also after going through reviews. Sometimes we need to restart the browser to run a particular addon. Like other softwares, addons also keep on looking for their updates and update themselves automatically. Sometimes we might see that the addon is not compatible with the browser version that means there are two possibilities, (1) browser version is outdated, (2) addon is not updated to match with the require-ments of latest browser installed. Sometime it's also possible that an addon might affect the performance of a browser and can even make the browser slow. So choose your addons wisely.

Let's discuss some common addons and extensions that are available for both Firefox as well as Chrome to serve in day-to-day life. Let's see what kind of addons are available and to serve what purpose.

We all use YouTube to watch video and share. Sometimes we also want to download some YouTube videos so for that a number of addons are available by installing which we do not need to install any other additional downloading software. Another major issue we feel while watching videos in YouTube is that the ads. Sometime we are allowed to skip the ads after 5 s and sometime we have to watch the full 20 s ad. That is pretty annoying so there are addons available to block ads on YouTube. Most of the people are addicted to social networking sites, we generally open one or all of these at least once every day. Social networks like Facebook, LinkedIn, Twitter are like part of our life now. Sometime we need to see the pictures of our friends or someone else in social networking sites and we need to click on the picture to zoom that. It wastes lots of valuable time, so if we want an addon to zoom all those for us when we point your mouse on the picture then there is addons available known as hoverzoom both in Firefox as well as Chrome.

There are different addons also available for chat notification, e-mail notification, news, weather. It looks like think there are addons available for almost everything, we just need to explore and definitely we will get one that will simplify our life. This is just for brainstorm, now let's discuss about some of the popular addons which will help us in various different important tasks.

## SHODAN

It is a plugin available for Chrome. A user just has to install and forget about it. While we browse an application, it will collect information available about the particular site from its database and provide details such as what is the IP address of the website, who owns that IP, where is it hosted, along with open ports with popular services and some of the popular security vulnerability such as HeartBleed. This is definitely very helpful for penetration testers, if you haven't tried it yet, you must. The only limitation of this addon is that it will only show the results for the sites, for which information is already available in shodan sources. It generally won't show results for new sites and staging sites as its database might not contain information on them.

## WAPPALYZER

It is also a popular addon available for both the browsers Firefox and Chrome. It uncovers the technology used by the web application. Similar to shodan, for wappalyzer also we simply need to install and forget, wappalyzer will show details about technology used while we browse a page. The way exactly wappalyzer works is that it collects information related to the technology and versions from the response header, source code, and other sources based on the signatures.

It identifies various different technologies such as CMS or content management systems, e-commerce platforms, web servers details, operating system details, JavaScript framework details, and many other things.

Some of the types of technologies identified by wappalyzer are:
- Advertising networks
- Analytics platforms
- Content management system
- Databases
- E-commerce
- Issue trackers
- JavaScript frameworks
- Operating systems
- Programming languages
- Search engines
- Video players
- Wikis

## BUILDWITH

Buildwith is similar to wappalyzer. It also identifies technologies used by a web applications based on signatures, using page source code, banner, cookie names, etc. While wappalyzer is open source, buildwith is not. The paid version of buildwith has way more features from its free version like contact information detection and subdomain detection, etc. which can be very helpful at times.

**FIGURE 3.5**

Buildwith identifying technologies on Twitter.

## FOLLOW

Follow.net is a competitive intelligence tool which helps us to stay updated by the online movement of our competitors and can be accessed using the browser addon provided by it. The major difficulty faced to keep track of the competitor is that we have to waste lots of time visiting their websites, blogs, tweets, YouTube channel, etc. After visiting lots of website we don't have a structured data from that we can understand the trend being followed. So here is follow.net that do most of these and much more for us and provides us report on how our competitor is trending on the web. It collects information from various sources such as alexa, Twitter, keyword-spy, etc. It will also send us a notification related to our competitors, if something new comes up. The simple addon of follow provides a complete interface to browse through all this information in an efficient manner.

So if we are starting a business want to learn the success mantra of your competitor then it is a must-have. The follow.net addon is available for both Firefox as well as Chrome browser.

## RIFFLE

Riffle by CrowdRiff is a social analytics addon. It's focused on the popular micro-blogging site Twitter. It provides us with a smart Twitter dashboard which displays useful analytical data about a Twitter user of our choice.

It provides us the helpful information to create a popular account by giving reference to some influential tweets and accounts who posted them. It also provides quick insight about a Twitter user so that it will help us to understand and reply to that particular user in a particular way.

**FIGURE 3.6**

Riffle interface integrated into the browser.

Some of the key feature provided by this extension is that it helps in tweet source tracking, activity breakdown, engagement assessments, etc. with a clean user interface. It's a must-have for power users of Twitter.

## WhoWorks.at

Similar to Riffle a Twitter focused addon, we have whoworks.at a LinkedIn specific addon. Let's take a scenario where we are salespersons and we need to gather information about the key influential persons of a company, so how do we proceed. We will go to LinkedIn, search for that particular company and then find the 1st degree, 2nd degree, or 3rd degree connections. Based on their title we might want to add them to discuss business. This is the old fashion way. Now there is another way to do the same in a more automated manner. Now let's install whoworks.at extension on Chrome, visit the company website that we are interested in and let the extension show us the 1st degree, 2nd degree, and 3rd degree connections from that company along with details such as recent hires, promotions, or title changes.

This is the power of whoworks.at, it finds the connections for us when we visit a website and saves us a lot of time.

## ONETAB

Onetab is an addon or extension available for both the browsers Firefox as well as Chrome. It provides us solution for tab management. It helps us to make a list of tabs that are open in our browser and aggregate them under a single tab, especially in Google Chrome as we already learned that it is a tab centric browser. The tab is the main thread in Chrome so by using onetab we can save lot of memory because it converts tabs into a list, which we can later restore one by one or all at a time as per our wish.

## SALESLOFT

Most of the sales people must have used it, if not they need to. It's simply a dream addon for salespersons. It allows to create a prospecting list from browsing profiles from different social networks for leads focusing on a particular segment of market. It allows a user to run specific search based on title, organization, or industry name. Some of the popular features are it allows to gather contact information from a prospect from LinkedIn. Contact information contains name, e-mail id, and phone number. We are allowed to add any result as a prospector by single click. Import prospects from LinkedIn and export it to excel or Google spreadsheets. It also allows to synchronize the data directly with salesforce.com

It is a one stop free and lightweight solution for every sales person. Use it and enhance your lead generation with its semiautomated approach.

## PROJECT NAPTHA

We all know how it's nearly impossible to copy the text present in any image, one method is that we type it manually but that is definitely a bizarre experience. So here is the solution, Project Naptha. It is an awesome addon which provides us freedom to copy, highlight, edit, and also translate available text on any image present on the web using its advanced OCR technology. It's available for Google Chrome.

## TINEYE

Tineye is a reverse image search engine, so its addon is also used for same. As we enter keywords in search engines to get the required result, Tineye can be used to search for a particular picture in the Tineye database. It has a large amount of images indexed in its database. The myth behind the image identification technology is that it creates a unique signature for each and every image it indexes in its database. When user search for a picture it starts comparing that signature, and most of the time it gives exact result. Apart from exact result it also gives similar results. Another great feature of Tineye is that it can search for cropped, resized, and edited images and give almost exact result. Tineye is available for both the browsers Firefox as well as Chrome.

## REVEYE

Reveye is quite similar to Tineye. This addon is only available for Chrome. It works very simple. It gives a user result of reverse image search based on results provided by Google reverse image search as well as Tineye reverse image search.

## CONTACTMONKEY

Contactmonkey is a very useful addon for all professionals, especially sales. It helps us to track our e-mails. Using this simple addon we can identify if the person we have sent an e-mail has opened it or not and at what time. This can help us to identify whether our mails are being read or are simply filling up the spam folder and also what is the best time to contact a person. Though the free version has some limitations yet it is very useful.

If you want to improve your user experience of Google Chrome browser this list by digital inspiration is a must to look at. The list contains some of the Chrome extensions and apps list which will enhance Chrome features and also enhance user experience. Following is the URL where you can get the list, http://digitalinspiration.com/google-Chrome.

## BOOKMARK

Bookmark is a common feature of every browser. It allows us to save a website's URL under a name for later use. Most of the time while browsing we get different interesting pages but due to lack of time we cannot go through all those pages at that time. There bookmark help us to save those links for future use.

There are popularly two ways to save the bookmark:

1. By clicking on bookmark button when we are on the page that needs to bookmark.
2. By clicking on ctrl+d when we are in the page that needs to bookmark.

We can even import and as well as export bookmarks from one browser to another. We can also create a new folder for a list of bookmarks. In Firefox we need to go to show all bookmark link or click on ctrl+shift+B where we will get all those options directly or by right clicking on that page. Similarly for Chrome we need to go to bookmark manager. There also we will find all the options on the page itself or otherwise we need to right click on that page to get those options.

## THREATS POSED BY BROWSERS

As we discussed browsers are a great tool which allows us to access the web and the availability of various addons simply enhances its functionalities. This wide usage of browsers also present a huge threat. Browsers being one of the most widely used softwares are the favorite attack vector of many cyber attackers. Attackers try to exploit most of the client side vulnerabilities using browser only, starting from phishing, cookie theft, session hijacking, cross-site scripting, and lots of others. Similarly browsers are one of the biggest actors which play a role in identity leakage. So use your browser wisely. In later chapters we will discuss about some methods to stay secure and anonymous online. For now let's move to our next chapter where we will learn about various types of unconventional but useful search engines.

# Search the Web—Beyond Convention

## 4

## INFORMATION IN THIS CHAPTER

- Search engines
- Unconventional search engines
- Unconventional search engine categories
- Examples and usage

## INTRODUCTION

So in the second chapter we learned how to utilize advanced search of some of the social network platforms to get precise results, then in the third chapter we moved on to see how to better utilize our common browsers in uncommon ways and now this chapter is about search engines.

We all are familiar with search engines and use them for our day to day research. So as discussed in previous chapters, what search engines basically do is crawl through the web using web spiders and index the web pages based on a wide range of parameters, such as keywords, backlinks, etc. and based on this indexing we get our results for the keywords we supply. Some of the most popular search engines are Google, Yahoo, and Bing.

Different search engines use different methods to rate different links and based upon their algorithm, assign different websites and different ranks. When we search for a term(s), the search engines provide results based upon these ranks. These ranks keep on changing based upon various different factors and this is why we might get different results for same query on different dates.

So now it is safe to say that as an average user we are familiar with search engines and their usage. As stated earlier this chapter is about search engines; but not the conventional ones we use daily. The search engines we will be dealing with in this chapter are specialized, some of these perform their search operations in a different manner and some of them provide search facility for specific domain. But are they really required when we have search engines like Google which are very advanced and keep on updating with new features? The short answer is yes. Though search engines like Google are very good at what they do, they provide generic results in the form of website links which according to them are relevant for the query keywords, but sometimes we need specific answers related to specific domain, this is when we need specific types of search engines. Let's go ahead and get familiar with these and find out how useful they are.

## META SEARCH

When we send a request to a regular search engine, it looks up into its own database for the relevant results and presents them, but what if we want to get results from multiple search engines. This is where meta search engines comes in. What meta search engines do is that they send the user's query to multiple data sources, such as search engines, databases, etc. at once and aggregates the results into a single interface. This makes the search results more comprehensive and relevant and also saves the time of searching multiple sources one at a time. Meta search engines do not create a database of their own, but rely on various other databases for collecting the results.

### Polymeta (http://www.polymeta.com/)

Polymeta is a great meta search engine which sends the search query to a wide range of sources and then takes the top result from each one of them and further ranks them. The search results of Polymeta not only contain the URLs but also its social network likability through number of Facebook likes for that URL. We can further drill down into the results through the search within feature which allows us to search for keywords inside the already aggregated results.

**FIGURE 4.1**

Meta search engine—Polymeta.

Polymeta categorizes the results into topics, which are displayed inside a panel on the left; results for news, images, videos, blogs are displayed in separate panels on the right. It also allows us to select the sources from a list for different categories.

### Ixquick (https://www.ixquick.com)

Ixquick is another meta search engine and in its own words is "the world's most private search engine." Apart from its great capability to search and present results from various sources it also provides a feature to use Ixquick proxy to access the results. In the search results itself, below every result there is an option named as "proxy," clicking on which will take us to the result URL but through the proxy (https://ixquick-proxy.com), which allows us as a user to maintain our anonymity.

Apart from the regular web, images, and video search, Ixquick provides a unique search capability, i.e., phone search. We can not only search for the phone number of people but can also do a reverse phone search. It means that we need to provide the phone number and choose the country code and it will fetch the information of the owner. Not only this, this phone search functionality also allows us to search for phone numbers of businesses, we simply need to provide the business name and location details. Ixquick also provides advanced search, which can be accessed by the following URL https://www.ixquick.com/eng/advanced-search.html.

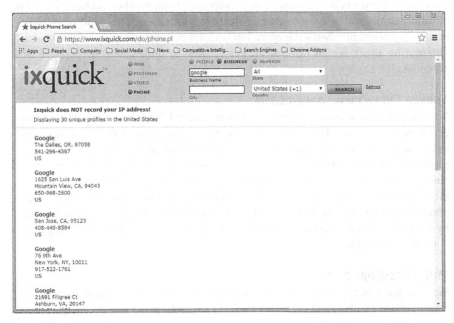

**FIGURE 4.2**

Ixquick phone search.

### Mamma (http://mamma.com/)

Mamma is yet another meta search engine. Similar to any meta search engine it also aggregates its results from various sources, but that is not all what makes it stand out. The clean and simple interface provided by Mamma makes it very easy to use even for a first time user. The result page is clean and very elegant. We can access various categories such as news, images, video, etc. through simple tabs which are integrated into the interface itself once used. Clicking on the Local button allows us to get the region specific results.

The tabulation feature we discussed not only creates different tabs for categories but also for different queries which allows us to access results from previous search easily.

## PEOPLE SEARCH

Now we have a fair understanding of how meta search works, let's move on to learn how to lookout for people online. There are many popular social media platforms like Facebook (facebook.com), LinkedIn (linkedin.com), etc. where we can find out a lot about people, here we will discuss about search engines which index results from platforms like these. In this section we will learn how to search for people online and find related information. The information we expect from this kind of engagements is full name, e-mail address, phone number, address, etc.; this all information can be used to extract further information. This kind of information is very relevant when we require information about person to perform a social engineering attack for an InfoSec project or need to understand the persona of a potential client.

### Spokeo (http://www.spokeo.com)

When it comes to searching people, especially in the US no one comes close to this people search engine. Though most of the information provided by it is now paid as opposed to its previous versions, but speaking from past experience it is a great platform which provides a variety of information related to a person ranging from basic information such as name, e-mail, address to information like neighborhood, income, social profiles, and much more. It allows to search people by name, e-mail, phone, username, and even address. The price package of the information provided by it seems reasonable and is recommended for anyone who deals with digging information about people.

### Pipl (https://pipl.com/)

Pipl is a great place to start looking for people. It allows us to search using name, e-mail, phone number, and even username. The search results can be further refined by providing a location. Unlike most search engines which crawl through the surface web only, Pipl digs the deep web to extract information for us (concept of deep web will be discussed in detail in a later chapter), this unique ability allows it to provide results which other search engines won't be able to. The results provided are pretty comprehensive and are also categorized into sections such as Background, Profiles, Public Records, etc. The results can be filtered based upon age also. All in all it is one of the few places which provide relevant people search results without much effort and hence must be tried.

**FIGURE 4.3**

Searching people using Pipl.

## PeekYou (http://www.peekyou.com/)

PeekYou is yet another people search engine which not only allows to search using the usual keywords types such as name, e-mail, username, phone, etc. but also using terms of the type interests, city, work, and school. These unique types make it very useful when we are searching for alumni or coworkers or even people from past with whom we lived in the same city. The sources of information it uses are quite wide and hence the results and the best part is it's all free.

## Yasni (http://www.yasni.com/)

Yasni is a tool for people who want to find people with specific skill sets. It not only allows us to search people by their name but also by the domain they specialize in or profession. The wide range of categories of results provided by Yasni makes it easy to find the person of interest. Some of the categories are images, telephone and address, interests, business profile, interests, documents, and much more. This platform provides a one stop shop for multiple requirements related to searching people online.

## LittleSis (http://littlesis.org/)

LittleSis is exactly not a general people search, but is more focused on people at the top of the business and political food chain, so searching for common people here would be a waste of time. Although it is good at what it does and can reveal interesting and useful information about business tycoons and political czars. Apart from the basic information such as introduction, DoB, sex, family, friends, education, etc., it also shows information like relationships, which lists down the positions and memberships that the person holds or ever held; interlocks, which lists people with position in the same organizations, etc. It is a good place to research about people with power and who they are associated with.

### MarketVisual (http://www.marketvisual.com/)

MarketVisual is also a specialized search engine which allows us to search for professionals. We can search for professionals by their name, title, or company name. Once the search is complete it presents a list of entities with associated information such as number of relationships, title, and company. The best part about MarketVisual is the visualization it creates of the relationships of the entity once we click on it. These data can further be downloaded in various forms for later analysis. It is a great tool for market research.

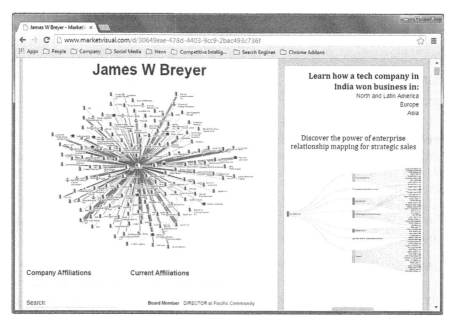

**FIGURE 4.4**

MarketVisual displaying connection graph.

### TheyRule (http://theyrule.net/)

Similar to MarketVisual, TheyRule also provides the medium to search professionals across top global corporates. First look at the interface, it makes us doubt if there is actually any information, as there is a small list of links on the top left corner, that too in smaller than average font size; but once we start to explore these links we can find an ocean of interesting information. Clicking on the companies link provides a huge list of companies, once we click on a company it will present a visual representation of it. Hovering over this icon provides option to show directors and research further. The directors are further represented through the visualization. If any director is on more than one boards, then hovering over his/her icon provides the option to show that as well. It also provides an option to find connections between two companies, Apart from this it also lists interesting maps created by other such as Too Big To Fail Banks and also lets us save ours.

## BUSINESS/COMPANY SEARCH

Today almost every company has an online presence in the form of a website, one or more social media profile, etc. These mediums provide a great deal of information about the organization they belong to, but sometimes we need more. Be it researching a competitive business, potential client, potential partner, or simply the organization where we applied for an opening, there are platforms which can help us to understand them better. Let's learn about some of them.

### LinkedIn (https://www.linkedin.com/vsearch/c)

LinkedIn is one of the most popular professional social media website. We have already discussed about LinkedIn search in a previous chapter, but when it comes to searching about companies we simply can't ignore it. Most of the tech savvy corporates do have LinkedIn profiles. These profiles list some interesting information which is usually not found on corporate websites, such as company size, their type, and specific industry. It also shows the number of employees of the company who have a profile on the platform. We can simply see the list of these employees and check their profiles, depending upon who/what we are looking for. Apart from this we can also see regular updates from the company on their profile page and understand what they are onto. It also allows us to follow companies using a registered account so that we can receive regular updates from them.

### Glassdoor (http://www.glassdoor.com/Reviews/index.htm)

Glassdoor is a great platform for job seekers but it also provides a huge amount of relevant information on companies. Apart from the usual information such as company location, revenue, competitors, etc. we can also find information such as employee review, salary, current opportunities as well as interview experiences. The best part is that the information is provided not just by the organization itself but also its employees, hence it provides a much clear view of the internal structure and working. Similar to LinkedIn, Glassdoor also provides an option to follow company profiles to receive updates.

**FIGURE 4.5**

Glassdoor company search interface.

### Zoominfo (http://www.zoominfo.com/)

Zoominfo is a business-to-business platform which is mainly used by sales and marketing representatives to find details about companies as well as people working in them, such as e-mail, phone number, address, relationships, etc. Though the free account has various limitations yet it's a great tool to find information about organizations and their employees.

## REVERSE USERNAME/E-MAIL SEARCH

Now as we learned how to extract information related to people and companies, let's take this a step further and see what other information we can extract using the username of a person, which in most cases is the e-mail address of the person.

### EmailSherlock (http://www.emailsherlock.com/)

EmailSherlock is a reverse e-mail search engine. What it does is that once we provide an e-mail address to it, it looks up if that e-mail has been used to register an account on a wide range of websites, mostly social media and gets us the results in form of any information it can extract from these platforms. This kind of information can be very helpful in case we just have the e-mail address of the person of interest. Once we know the platform on which this particular person is registered, we can go ahead and create an account on it and might be able to extract information which we were not allowed to access otherwise. Similar to EmailSherlock there is another service called as UserSherlock (http://www.usersherlock.com/) which does the same thing for usernames.

Though the results provided by these services are not 100% accurate, yet they provide a good place to start.

**FIGURE 4.6**

EmailSherlock interface.

### CheckUsernames (http://checkusernames.com/)
Similar to UserSherlock, CheckUsernames also runs the username provided to it through a huge list of social media websites and check if that username is available on them or not.

### Namechk (http://namechk.com/)
Like CheckUsernames and UserSherlock, Namechk also checks the availability of the provided username on a huge list of social media sites.

### KnowEm (http://knowem.com/)
The website discussed above (checkusernames.com) is powered by KnowEm and similarly it can be used to check for usernames, but it additionally checks for domain names as well as trademark.

### Facebook (https://www.facebook.com/)
Unlike most of the social network sites, Facebook allows us to search people using e-mail addresses and being one of the largest social networks it can be very helpful when searching people online.

## SEMANTIC SEARCH

In chapter 2, we discussed about semantic web and how it will be an integral part of the web of the future. Let's get familiar with some of the semantic search engines and see how mature they are.

### *DuckDuckGo (https://duckduckgo.com)*

Though the name DuckDuckGo may sound a bit odd for a search engine but the search results provided by it are quite amazing. This new kid on the block is slowly challenging the search giant Google based on its unique selling proposition (USP), i.e., it does not track its users. The search results provided by it are very relevant minus the clutter. There are not many ads and sidebars to fill up the space. It provides meaning for the query which help the user to select the one of his/her intention and get the results accordingly. Similar to Google it also provides the answers to mathematical queries and even provides answers for queries like weather with the weather for our location. The definition tab simply provides the dictionary meaning of the keyword supplied. The bar under the query box is very relevant and provides the categories for topics. It is populated depending upon the search query, such as searching for a music band populates it with related videos, whereas searching for Thailand beaches will display images of the beaches, it also responds to queries like what rhymes with you with relevant results. The rapid growth and incredible features make it a real competition for major search engines like Google, Bing, and Yahoo and is slowly gaining the recognition it deserves. It is a must try for anyone who is enthusiastic about new ways of exploring the web.

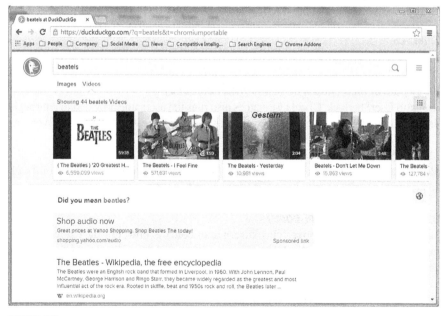

**FIGURE 4.7**

DuckDuckGo results.

### Kngine (http://kngine.com/)

Kngine is a great search engine with semantic capabilities. Unlike conventional search engines it allows us to ask questions and tries to answer it. We can input queries like "who was the president of Russia between 1990 and 2010" and it presents us with a list containing the names, images, term years, and other details related to Russia. Similarly searching for "GDP of Italy" gives a great amount of relevant information in form of data and graphs minus the website links. So next time a questions pops up in our mind we can surely give it a try.

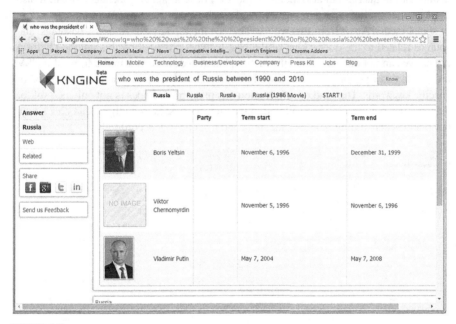

**FIGURE 4.8**

Kngine result for semantic query.

## SOCIAL MEDIA SEARCH

Social media is a vast platform and its impact is also similar, be it on personal level or corporate level. Previously we discussed about social media and also how to search through some specific social network platforms, now let's check out some of the social media search engines and their capabilities.

### SocialMention (http://socialmention.com/)

So what SocialMention provides is basically real-time social media search and analysis, but what does it mean. Let's break it up into two parts search and analysis. As for the search part, SocialMention searches various social media platforms like blogs, microblogs, social networks, events, etc. and even through the comments. The results provided can be sorted by date and source and can be filtered for timelines like last hour, day, week, etc., apart from this, SocialMention also provides advanced search option, using which we can craft queries to get more precise results. Unlike conventional search engines, searching through social media specifically has a huge advantage, which is to be able to understand the reach and intensity of terms we are searching in the content created by people. Through this we can have a better understanding how people relate to these terms and upto what level.

Now let's move on to the analysis part, SocialMention not only provides the search results for our queries but also indicates the level of sentiments associated with it. It also displays the level of strength, passion, and reach of our query terms in the vast ocean of social media. Apart from this we can also see the top keywords, users, hashtags, and sources related to the query. One of the best features provided by this unique platform is that we can not only see this information, but also download it in the form of a CSV files. If all this was not sufficient, SocialMention also allows us to setup e-mail alerts for specific keywords. The kind of information this platform provides is not only helpful for personal use but can also have a huge impact for businesses as well; we can check how our brand is performing in the social arena and respond to it accordingly.

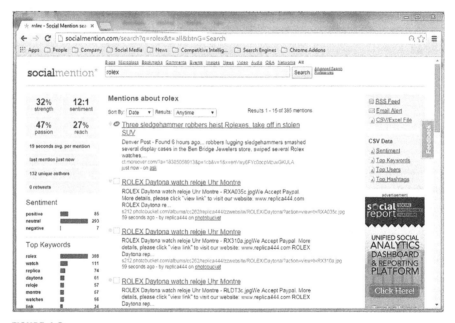

**FIGURE 4.9**

SocialMention displaying results and associated statistics.

### *Social Searcher (http://www.social-searcher.com/)*

Social Searcher is yet another social media search engine. It uses Facebook, Twitter and Google+ as its sources. The interface provided by this search engine is simple. Under the search tab the search results are distributed into three tabs based on the source, under these tabs the posts are listed with a preview, which is very helpful in identifying the ones relevant for us. Similar to SocialMention we can setup e-mail alerts also.

Under the analytics tab we can get the sentiment analysis, users, keywords, domains, and much more. One of the interesting of these is the popular tab which lists the results with more interaction such as likes, retweets, etc.

## TWITTER

Twitter is one of the most popular social networking sites with huge impact. Apart from its usual functionality to microblog, it also allows to understand the reach and user base of any entity which makes it a powerful tool for reconnaissance. Today it is widely used for market promotion as well as analyze the social landscape.

### Topsy (http://topsy.com/)

Topsy is a tool which allows us to search and monitor Twitter. Using it we can check out the trend of any keyword over Twitter and analyze its reach. The interface is pretty simple and looks like a conventional search engine, just the results are only based on Twitter. The results presented by it can be narrowed down to various timeframes such as 1 day, 30 days, etc. We can also filter out the results to only see the images, tweets, links, videos, or influencers. There is another filter which allows us to see only results containing results from specific languages. All in all Topsy is a great tool for market monitoring for specific keywords.

**FIGURE 4.10**

Topsy search.

### Trendsmap (http://trendsmap.com/)

Trendsmap is a great visual platform which shows trending topics in the form of keywords, hashtags, and Twitter handles from the Twitter platform over the world map. It is great platform which utilizes visual representation of the trends to understand what's hot in a specific region of the world. Apart for showing this visual form of information it also allows us to search through this information in the form of a topic or a location which makes it easier for us to see only what we want.

### Tweetbeep (http://tweetbeep.com/)

In its own words, Tweetbeep is like Google alerts for Twitter. It is a great service which allows us to monitor topics of interest on Twitter such as a brand name, product, or updates related to companies and even links. From market monitoring purpose it's a great tool which can help us to quickly respond to topics of interest.

### Twiangulate (http://twiangulate.com/search)

Twiangulate is a great tool which allows us to perform Twitter triangulations. Using it we can find who are the common people who are followers of and are followed by two different twitter users. Similarly it also provides the feature to compare the reach of two users. It is great tool to understand and compare the influence of different Twitter users.

## SOURCE CODE SEARCH

Most of the search engines we have used only look for the text visible on the web page, but there are some search engines which index the source code present on the internet. These kind of search engines can be very helpful when we are looking for specific technology used over the internet, such as a content management system like WordPress. Utilities of such search engines are for search engine optimization, competitive analysis, keyword research for marketing and are only limited by the creativity of the user.

Due to the storage and scalability issues earlier there were no service providers in this domain, but with technological advancements some options are opening up now, let checkout some of these.

### NerdyData (http://nerdydata.com)

NerdyData is one of the first of its kind and unique search engine which allows us to search the code of the web page. Using the platform is pretty simple, go to the URL https://search.nerdydata.com/, enter the keyword like WordPress 3.7 and NerdyData will list down the websites which contain that keyword in their source code. The results not only provide the URL of the website but also shows the section of the code with the keyword highlighted under the section Source Code Snippet. Apart from this there are various features such as contact author, fetch backlink, and others which can be very helpful but most of these are paid, yet the limited free usage of NerdyData is very useful and is worth a try.

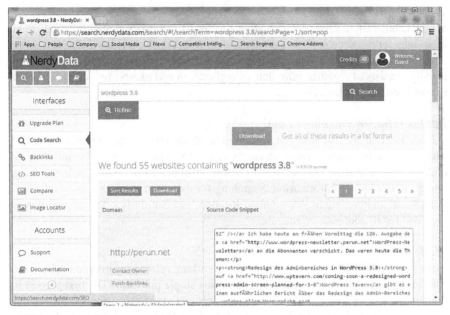

**FIGURE 4.11**

NerdyData code search results.

### *Ohloh code (https://code.ohloh.net)*

Ohloh code is another great search engine for source code searching, but it's a bit different in terms that it searches for open source code. What this means is that its source of information is the code residing in open space, such as Git repositories.

It provides great options to filter out the results based on definitions, languages (programming), extensions, etc. through a bar on the left-hand side titled "Filter Code Results."

### *Searchcode (https://searchcode.com)*

Similar to Ohloh, Searchcode also uses open source code repositories as its information source. The search filters provided by Searchcode are very helpful, some of them are repository, source, and language.

## TECHNOLOGY INFORMATION

In this special section of search engines we will be working on some unique search engines which will help us to gather information related to various different technologies and much more. In this segment we will be heavily dealing with IP addresses and related terms, so it is advised to go through the section "Defining the basic terms" in the first chapter.

### Whois (http://whois.net/)

Whois is basically a service which allows us to get information about the registrant of an internet resource such as a domain name. Whois.net provides a platform using which we can perform a Whois search for a domain or IP address. A whois record usually consists of registrar info; date of registration and expiry; registrant info such as name, e-mail address, etc.

### Robtex (http://www.robtex.com)

Robtex is great tool to find out information about internet resources such as IP address, Domain name, Autonomous System (AS) number, etc. The interface is pretty simple and straightforward. At the top left-hand corner is a search bar using which we can lookup information. Searching for a domain gives us related information like IP address, route, AS number, location, etc. Similarly other information is provided for IP addresses, route, etc.

### W3dt (https://w3dt.net/)

W3dt is great online resource to find out networking related information. There are various section which we can explore using this single platform. The first section is domain name system (DNS) tools which allows us to perform various DNS-related queries such as DNS lookup, reverse DNS lookup, DNS server fingerprinting, etc. Second section provides tools related to network/internet such as port scan, traceroute, MX record retriever, etc. The next section is web/HTTP which consists of tools such as SSL certificate info, URL encode/decode, HTTP header retrieval, etc., then comes the database lookups section under which comes MAC address lookup, Whois lookup, etc., in the end there are some general and ping-related tools. All in all it is great set of tools which allows to perform a huge list of different useful functions under single interface.

### Shodan (http://www.shodanhq.com/)

So far we have used various types of search engines which help us to explore the web in all different ways. What we haven't encountered till now is an internet search engine (remember the difference between web and internet explained in chapter 1) or simply said a computer search engine. Shodan is a computer search engine which scans the internet and grabs the service banner based on IP address and port. It allows us to search this information using IP addresses, country filters, and much more. Using it we can find out simple information such as websites using a specific type of web server such as Internet Information Services (IIS) or Apache and also information which can be quite sensitive such as IP cameras without authentication or SCADA systems over internet.

Though the free version without registration provides very limited information, which can be mitigated a bit using a registered account, yet it is sufficient enough to understand the power of this unique search engine. We can utilize the power of this tool through browser add-on or through its application programming interface also. Shodan has a very active development history and comes up with new features all the time, so we can expect much more from it in the future.

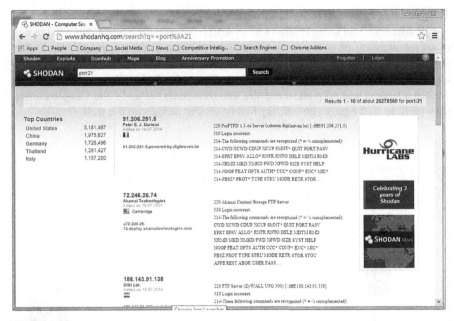

**FIGURE 4.12**

Shodan results for port 21.

## WayBack Machine (http://archive.org/web/web.php)

Internet Archive WayBack Machine is great resource to lookup how a website looked in past. Simply type the website address into the search bar and it will return back a timeline with the available snapshot highlighted on the calendar. Simply hovering over these highlighted dates over calendar will present a link to the snapshot. This is great tool to analyze how a website has evolved and thus monitor its past growth. It can also be helpful to retrieve information from a website which was available in the past but is not now.

## REVERSE IMAGE SEARCH

We all are familiar with the phrase "A picture is worth a thousand words" and its veracity and are also aware of platforms like Google Images (http://images.google.com), Flickr (https://www.flickr.com/), Deviantart (http://www.deviantart.com/), which provides us images for keywords provided. Usually when we need to lookup some information, we have a keyword or a set of them in the form of text, following the same lead the search engines we have dealt with till now take text as an input and get us the results, but in case we have an image and we want to see where it appears on the web, where do we go? This is where reverse image search engines come in, which take image as an input and looks up to find its web appearance. Let's get familiar with some of these.

### Google Images (http://images.google.com/)

We all are aware that Google allows us to search the web for images, but what many of us are unaware of is that it also allows to perform a reverse image search. We simply need to go to the URL http://images.google.com and click on the camera icon and provide the URL of the image on the web or upload a locally stored image file, we can also drag and drop an image file into the search bar and voila Google comes up with links to the pages containing that or similar images on the web.

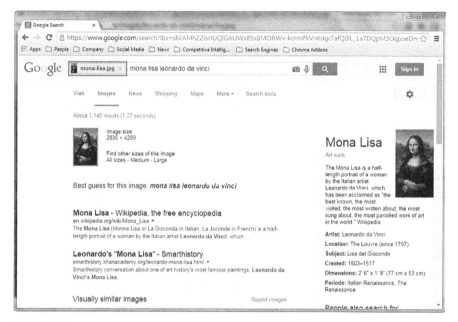

**FIGURE 4.13**

Google reverse image search.

### TinEye (https://www.tineye.com/)

TinEye is another reverse image search engine and has a huge database of images. Similar to Google images, searching on TinEye is very simple, we can provide the URL to the image, upload it, or perform a drag and drop. TinEye also provides browser plugin for major browsers, which makes the task much easier. Though the results of TinEye are not as comprehensive as Google images, yet it provides a great platform for the task and must be tried.

### ImageRaider (http://www.ImageRaider.com/)

Last but not the least in this list is ImageRaider. ImageRaider simply lists the results domain wise. If a domain contains more than one occurrence of the image then it also tells that and the links to those images are listed under the domain name.

Reverse image search can be very helpful to find out more about someone when we are hitting dead-ends using conventional methods. As many people use same profile picture for various different platforms, making a reverse image search can lead us to other platforms where the use has created a profile and also has previously undiscovered information.

## MISCELLANEOUS

We dealt with a huge list of search engines which are specialize in their domain and are popular among a community. In this section we will be dealing with some different types of search platforms which are lesser known but serve unique purposes and are very helpful in special cases.

### DataMarket (http://datamarket.com/)

DataMarket is an open portal which consists of large data sets and provides the data in a great manner through visualizations. The simple search feature provides results for global topics with list of different visualizations related to the topic, for example, searching for the keyword gold would provide results such as gold statistics, import/export of gold, and much more. The results page consists of a bar on the left which provides a list of filters using which the listed results can be narrowed down. It also allows us to upload our own data and create visualization from it. Refer to the link http://datamarket.com/topic/list/ for a huge list of topics on which DataMarket provides information.

### WolframAlpha (http://www.wolframalpha.com/)

In this chapter we learned about various search engines which take some value as input and provide us with the links which might contain the answer to the questions we are actually looking for, but what we are going to learn about now is not a search engine but a computational knowledge engine. What this means is that it takes our queries as input but does not provides with the URLs to the websites containing the information, instead it tries to understand our natural language queries and based upon an organized data set, provides a factual answer to them in form of text and sometimes apposite visualization also.

Say, for example, we want to know the purpose of .mil domain, so we can simply type in the query "what is the purpose of the .mil internet domain?" and get the results, to get the words starting with a and ending with e, a query like "words starting with a and ending with e" would give us the results, we can even check the net worth of Warren Buffett by a query like "Warren Buffett net worth." For more examples of the queries of various domains that WolframAlpha is able to answer, checkout the page http://www.wolframalpha.com/examples/.

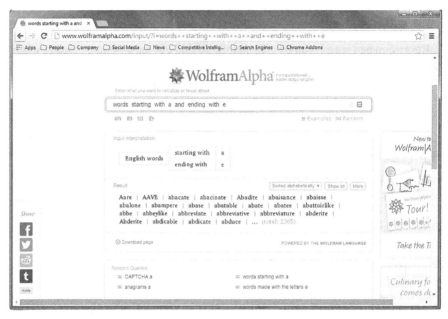

**FIGURE 4.14**

WolframAlpha result.

### Addictomatic (http://addictomatic.com)

Usually we visit various different platforms to search information related to a topic, but addictomatic aggregate various news and media sources to create a single dashboard for any topic of our interest. The content aggregated is displayed in various sections depending upon the source. It also allows us to move these sections depending upon our preference for better readability.

### Carrot2 (http://search.carrot2.org/stable/search)

Carrot2 is a search results clustering engine, what this means is that it takes search results from other search engines and organizes these results into topics using its search results clustering algorithms. Its unique capability to cluster the results into topics allows to get a better understanding of it and associated terms. These clusters are also represented in different interesting forms such as folders, circles, and FoamTree. Carrot2 can be used through its web interface which can be accessed using the URL http://search.carrot2.org/ and also through a software application which can be downloaded from http://project.carrot2.org/download.html.

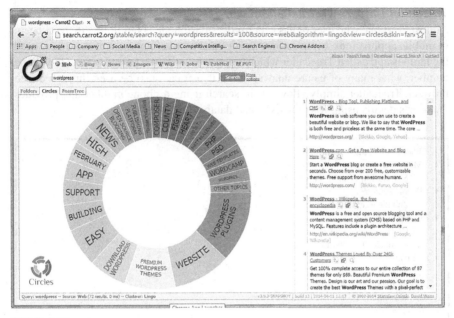

**FIGURE 4.15**

Carrot2 search result cluster.

### Boardreader (http://boardreader.com/)

Boards and forums are rich source of information as a lot of interaction and Q&A goes on in places like this. Members of such platforms range from newbies to experts in the domain to which the forum is related to. In places like this we can get answers to questions which are difficult to find elsewhere as they purely comprise of user-generated content, but how do we search them? Here is the answer Boardreader. It allows us to search forums to get results which contains content with human interaction. It also displays a trend graph of the search query keyword to show the amount of activity related to it. The advance search features provided by it such as sort by relevance, occurrence between specific dates, domain-specific search, etc. adds to its already incredible features.

### Omgili (http://omgili.com/)

Similar to Boardreader, Omgili is also a forum and boards search engine. It displays the results in the form of broad bars and these bars contain information such as date, number of posts, author, etc. which can be helpful in estimating the relevance of the result. One such information is Thread Info, which provides further information about a thread such as forum name, number of authors, and replies to the thread, without actually visiting the original thread forum page. It also allows us to filter the results based upon the timeline of their occurrence such as past month, week, day, etc.

### Truecaller (http://www.truecaller.com)

Almost everyone who uses or has ever used a smartphone is familiar with the concept of mobile applications, better known as apps and many if not most of them have used the famous app called Truecaller which helps to identify the person behind the phone number, what many of us are unaware of is that it can also be used through a web browser. Truecaller simply allows us to search using a phone number and provides the user's details using it's crowdsourced database.

Other search engines worth trying:
- Meta search engine
  - Search (http://www.search.com/)
- People search
  - ZabaSearch (http://www.zabasearch.com/)
- Company search
  - Hoovers (http://www.hoovers.com/)
  - Kompass (http://kompass.com/)
- Semantic
  - Sensebot (http://www.sensebot.net/)
- Social media search
  - Whostalkin (http://www.whostalkin.com/)
- Twitter search
  - Mentionmapp (http://mentionmapp.com/)
  - SocialCollider (http://socialcollider.net/)
  - GeoChirp (http://www.geochirp.com/)
  - Twitterfall (http://beta.twitterfall.com/)
- Source code search
  - Meanpath (https://meanpath.com)
- Technology search
  - Netcraft (http://www.netcraft.com/)
  - Serversniff (http://serversniff.net)
- Reverse image search
  - NerdyData image search (https://search.nerdydata.com/images)
- Miscellaneous
  - Freebase (http://www.freebase.com/)

So we discussed a huge list of various search engines under various categories which are not conventionally used but as we have already seen these are very useful in different scenarios. We all are addicted to Google for all our searching needs and it being one of the best in its domain has also served our purpose most of the time, but sometimes we need different and specific answers to our queries, then we need these kind of search engines. This list tries to cover most of the aspects of daily searching needs, yet surely there must be other platforms which need to be find out and used commonly to solve specific problems.

In this chapter we learned about various unconventional search engines, their features, and functionalities, but what about the conventional search engines like Google, Bing, Yahoo, etc. that we use on daily basis. Oh! we already know how to use them or do we? The search engines we use on daily basis have various advanced features which many of the users are unaware of. These features allows users to filter out the results so that we can get more information and less noise. In the next chapter we will be dealing with conventional search engines and will learn how to use them effectively to perform better search and get specific results.

# Advanced Web Searching

5

## INFORMATION IN THIS CHAPTER

- Search Engines
- Conventional Search Engines
- Advanced Search Operators of various Search Engines
- Examples and Usage

## INTRODUCTION

In the last chapter we dealt with some special platforms which allowed us to perform domain-specific searches; now let's go into the depths of conventional search engines which we use on daily basis and check out how we can utilize them more efficiently. In this chapter, basically, we will understand the working and advanced search features of some of the well-known search engines and see what all functionalities and filters they provide to serve us better.

So we already have a basic idea about what search engine is, how it crawls over the web to collect information, which are further indexed to provide us with search results. Let's revise it once and understand it in more depth.

Web pages as we see them are not actually what they look like. Web pages basically contain HyperText Markup Language (HTML) code and most of the times some JavaScript and other scripting languages. So HTML is basically a markup language and uses tags to structure the information, for example the tag <h1></h1> is used to create a heading. When we receive this HTML code from the server, our browsers interpret this code and display us the web page in its rendered form. To check the client-side source code of a web page, simply press Ctrl+U in the browser with a web page open.

Once the web crawler of a search engine reaches a web page, it goes through its HTML code. Now most of the times these pages also contain links to other pages, which are used by the crawlers to move further in their quest to collect data. The content crawled by the web crawler is then stored and indexed by search engine based on variety of factors. The pages are ranked based upon their structure (as defined in HTML), the keywords used, interlinking of the pages, media present on the page, and many other details. Once a page has been crawled and indexed it is ready to be presented to the user of the search engine depending upon the query.

Once a page has been crawled, the job of the crawler does not finish for that page. The crawler is scheduled to perform the complete process again after a specific time as the content of the page might change. So this process keeps on going and as new pages are linked they are also crawled and indexed.

Search engine is a huge industry in itself which helps us in our web exploration, but there is another industry which depends directly on search engines and that is search engine optimization (SEO). SEO is basically about increasing the rank of a website/web page or in other words to bring it up to the starting result pages of a search engine. The motivation behind this is that it will increase the visibility of that page/site and hence will get more traffic which can be helpful from a commercial or personal point of view.

Now we have a good understanding of the search engines and how they operate, let's move ahead and see how we can better use some of the conventional search engines.

## GOOGLE

Google is one of the most widely used search engines and is the starting point for web exploration for most of us. Initially Google search was accessible through very simple interface and provided limited information. Apart from the search box there were some special search links, links about the company, and a subscription box where we could enter our email to get updates. There were no ads, no different language options, no login, etc.

It's not only the look and feel of the interface that has changed over the years but also the functionalities. It has evolved from providing simple web links to the pages containing relevant information to a whole bunch of related tools which not only allow us to search different media types and categories but also narrow down these results using various filters. Today there are various categories of search results such as images, news, maps, videos, and much more. These plethora of functionalities provided by Google today has certainly made our lives much easier and made the act of finding information on the web a piece of cake. Still sometimes we face difficulty in finding the exact information we are looking for and the main reason behind it is not the lack of information but to the contrary the abundance of it.

Let's move on to see how we perform Google search and how to improve it. So whenever we need to search something in Google we simply think about some of the keywords associated with it and type them into the search bar and hit Enter. Based upon the indexing Google simply provides us with the associated resources. Now if we want to get better results or filter the existing results based upon various factors, we need to use Google advanced search operators. Let's have a look at these operators and their usage.

### site:

It fetches results only for the site provided. It is very useful when to limit our search to some specific domain. It can be used with another keyword and Google will bring back related pages from the site specified. For an information security perspective it is very useful to find out different sub domains related to a particular domain.

Examples: site:gov, site:house.gov

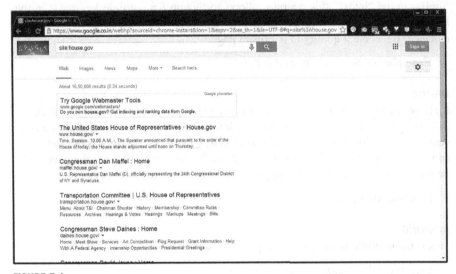

**FIGURE 5.1**

Google "site" operator usage.

### inurl:

This operator allows looking for keywords in the uniform resource locator (URL) of the site. It is useful to find out pages which follow a usual keyword for specific pages, such as contact us. Generally, as the URL contains some keywords associated with the body contents, it will help us to find out the equivalent page for the keyword we are searching for.

Example: inurl:hack

### allinurl:

Similar to "inurl" this operator allows looking for multiple keywords in the URL. So we can search for multiple keywords in the URL of a page. This also enhances the chances of getting quality content of what we are looking for.

Example: allinurl:hack security

### intext:

This operator makes sure that the keyword specified is present in the text of the page. Sometimes just for the sake of SEO, we can find some pages only contain keywords to enhance the page rank but not the associated content. In that case we can use this query parameter to get the appropriate content from a page for the keyword we are looking for.

Example: intext:hack

### *allintext:*

Similar to the "intext" this operator allows to lookup for multiple keywords in the text. As we discussed earlier the feature of searching for multiple keywords always enhances the content quality in the result page.

Example: allintext:data marketing

### *intitle:*

It allows us to restrict the results by the keywords present in the title of the pages (title tag: <title>XYZ</title>). It can be helpful to identify pages which follow a convention for the title of the pages such as directory listing by the keywords "index of" and most of the sites provide the keywords in the title for improving the page rank. So this query parameter always helps to search for a particular keyword.

Example: intitle:blueocean

### *allintitle:*

This is the multiple keyword counterpart of "intitle" operator.

Example: allintitle:blueocean market

### *filetype:*

This operator is used to find out files of a specific kind. It supports multiple file types such as pdf, swf, kml, doc, svg, txt, etc. This operator comes handy when we are only looking for specific type of files on a specific domain.

Example: filetype:pdf, site:xyz.com, filetype:doc

### *ext:*

The operator ext simply stands for extension and it works similar to the filetype operator.

Example: ext:pdf

### *define:*

This operator is used to find out the meaning of the keyword supplied. Google returns dictionary meaning and synonyms for the keyword.

Example: define:data

### *AROUND*

This operator is helpful when we are looking for the results which contain two different keywords, but in close association. It allows us to restrict the number of words as the maximum distance between two different keywords in the search results.

Example: A AROUND(6) Z

## AND

A simple Boolean operator which makes sure keywords on both the side are present in the search results.

Example: data AND market

## OR

Another Boolean operator which provides search results that contain either of the keyword present on both the sides of the operator.

Example: data OR intelligence

## NOT

Yet another Boolean operator which excludes the search results that contain the keyword followed by it.

Example: lotus NOT flower

## ""

This operator is useful when we need to search for the results which contain the provided keyword in the exact sequence. For example we can search pages which contain quotes or some lyrics.

Example: "time is precious"

## -

This operator excludes the search results which contain the keyword followed by it (no space).

Example: lotus -flower

## *

This wildcard operator is used as a generic placeholder for the unknown term. We can use this to get quotes which we partially remember or to check variants of one.

Example: "* is precious"

## ..

This special operator is used to provide a number range. It is quite useful to enforce a price range, time range (date), etc.

Example: japan volcano 1990..2000

### info:

The info operator provides information what Google has on a specific domain. Links to different types of information are present in the results, such as cache, similar websites, etc.

Example: info:elsevier.com

### related:

This operator is used to find out other web pages similar to the provided domain. It is very helpful when we are looking for websites which provide similar services to a website or to find the competitors of it.

Example: related:elsevier.com

### cache:

This operator redirects to the latest cache of the page that Google has crawled. In case we don't get a result for a website which was accessible earlier, this is a good option to try.

Example: cache:elsevier.com

Advanced Google search can also be performed using the page http://www.google.com/advanced_search, which allows us to perform restricted search without using the operators mentioned above.

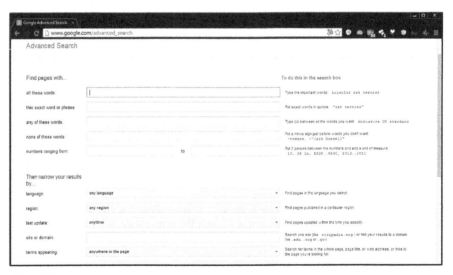

**FIGURE 5.2**

Google advanced search page.

Apart from the operators Google also provide some operations which allow us to check information about current events and also perform some other useful things. Some examples are:

### time

Simply entering this keyword displays the current time of the location we are residing in. We can also use name of region to get its current time.

Example: time france

### weather

This keyword shows the current weather condition of our current location. Similar to "time" keyword we can also use it to get the weather conditions of a different region.

Example: weather sweden

### Calculator

Google also solves mathematical equations and also provides a calculator.

Example: 39*(9823-312)+44/3

### Convertor

Google can be used to perform conversions for different types of units like measurement units, currency, time, etc.

Example: 6 feet in meters

This is not all, sometimes Google also shows relevant information related to global events as and when they happen; for example, FIFA World Cup.

Apart from searching the web, in general, Google also allows us to search specific categories such as images, news, videos, etc. All these categories, including web have some common and some specific search filters of their own. These options can simply be accessed by clicking on the "Search tools" tab just below the search bar. We can find options which allow us to restrict the results based upon the country, time of publish for web; for images there are options like the color of image, its type, usage rights, etc. and similarly other relevant filters for different categories. These options can be very helpful in finding the required information of a category as they are designed according to that specific category. For example if we are looking for an old photograph of something it is a good idea to see only the results which are black and white.

The operators we discussed are certainly very useful for anyone who needs to find out some information on the web, but the InfoSec community has certainly taken it to next level. These simple and innocent operators we just discussed are widely used in the cyber security industry to find and demonstrate how without even touching the target system, critical and compromising information can be retrieved. This technique of using Google search engine operators to find such information is termed as "Google Hacking."

When it comes to "Google Hacking" one name that jumps out in mind is Johnny Long. Johnny was an early adopter and pioneer in the field of creating such Google queries which could provide sensitive information related to the target. These queries are widely popular by the name Google Dorks.

Let's understand how this technique works. We saw a number of operators which can narrow down search results to a specific domain, filetype, title value, etc. Now in Google Hacking our motive is to find sensitive information related to the target; for this people have come up with various different signatures for different files and pages which are known to contain such information. For example, let's just say we know the name of a sensitive directory which should not be directly accessible to any user publicly, but remains public by default after the installation of the related application. So now if we want to find out the sites which have not changed the accessibility for this directory, we can simply use the query "inurl:/sensitive_directory_name/" and we will get a bunch of websites which haven't changed the setting. Now if we want to further narrow it down for a specific website, we can combine the query with the operator "site," as "site:targetdomain.com inurl://sensitive_directory_name/." Similarly we can find out sensitive files that are existing on a website by using the operators "site" and "filetype" in collaboration.

Let's take another example of Google Hacking which can help us to discover high severity vulnerability in a website. Many developers use flash to make websites more interactive and visually appealing. Small web format (SWF) is a flash file format used to create such multimedia. Now there are many SWF players known to be vulnerable to cross-site scripting (XSS), which could lead to an account compromise. Now if we want to find out if the target domain is vulnerable to such attack, then we can simply put in the query "site:targetdomain.com filetype:swf SWFPlayer_signature_keyword" and test the resulting pages using publicly available payloads to verify. There are huge number of signatures to find out various types of pages such as sensitive directories, web server identification, files containing username/password, admin login pages, and much more.

The Google Hacking Database created by Johnny Long can be found at http://www.hackersforcharity.org/ghdb/ though it is not updated, yet it is a great place to understand and learn how we can use Google to find out sensitive information. A regularly updated version can be found at http://www.exploit-db.com/google-dorks/.

**FIGURE 5.3**

Google hacking database- www.exploit-db.com/google-dorks/.

# BING

Microsoft has been providing search engine solutions from a long time and they have been known with different names. Bing is latest and most feature-rich search engine in this series. Unlike its predecessors Bing provides a more clean and simple interface. As Microsoft covers a major part of operating system market, the general perspective of a user in terms of search engine is that Bing is just another side-product from a technology giant and hence most of them do not take it seriously. But unfortunately it is wrong. Like all the search engines Bing also has some unique features that will force you to use Bing when you need those features. Definitely those features have a unique mark on how we search. We will discuss not only about the special features but also the general operators which can allow us to understand the search engine and its functionalities.

## +

This operator works quite similar in all the search engines. This allows a user to forcefully add single or multiple keywords in a search query. Bing will make sure the keywords come after + operator must present in the result pages.

Example: power +search

## -

This operator is also known as NOT operator. This is used to exclude something from a set of things, such as excluding a cuisine.

Example: Italian food -pizza

Here Bing will display all the Italian foods available but not pizza. We can write this in another form which can also fetch same result such as the below example

Example: Italian food NOT pizza

## ""

This is also same in most of the search engines. This is used to search for exact phrase used inside double quotation.

Example: "How to do Power Searching?"

## |

This is also known as OR operator, mostly used for getting result from one of the two keywords or one of the many keywords added with this operator.

Example:    ios | android
            ios OR android

*&*

This operator is also known as AND operator. This is the by-default used search operator. If we do nothing and add multiple keywords then Bing will do a AND search in the backend and give us the result.

> Example:   power AND search
>
> power & search

As this is the default search, it's very important to keep in mind that until and unless we use OR and NOT in capital, Bing won't understand it as operators.

*()*

This can be called as group operator.

Grouping of Bing operators supported in following order.
    ()
    ""
    NOT/-
    And/&
    OR/|

As parenthesis has the top priority order, we can add the lower preferred operators such as OR in that and create a group query to execute the lower priority operators first.

> Example: android phone AND (nexus OR xperia)

*site:*

This operator will help to search a particular keyword within a specific website. This operator works quite the same in most of the search engines.

> Example: site:owasp.org clickjacking

*filetype:*

This allows a user to search for data in specific type of file. Bing supports all file types but few, mostly those are supported by Google are also supported by Bing.

> Example: hack filetype:pdf

*ip:*

This unique operator provided by Bing allows us to search web pages based upon IP address. Using it we can perform a reverse IP search, which means it allows us to look for pages hosted on the specified IP).

> Example: ip:176.65.66.66

**FIGURE 5.4**

Bing "ip" search.

### *feed:*

Yet another unique operator provided by Bing is feed, which allows us to look for web feed pages containing the provided keyword.

One other feature that Bing provides is to perform social search using the page https://www.bing.com/explore/social. It allows us to connect our social network accounts with Bing and perform search within them.

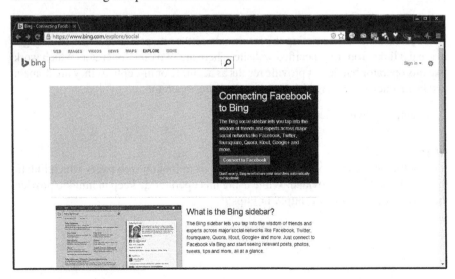

**FIGURE 5.5**

Bing social search.

## YAHOO

Yahoo is one of the oldest players in the search engine arena and has been quite popular. The search page for Yahoo also has a lot of content such as news, trending topics, weather, financial information, and much more. Earlier Yahoo has utilized third party services to power its search capabilities, later it shifted to become independent and once again has joined forces with Bing for its searching services. Though there is not too much that Yahoo offers in terms of advanced searching as compared to other search engines, the ones provided are worth trying comparing to others. Let's see some of the operators that can be useful.

### +

This operator is used to make sure the search results contain the keyword followed by it.

   Example: +data

### -

Opposite to the "+" operator, this operator is used to exclude any specific keyword from the search results.

   Example: -info

### OR

This operator allows us to get results for either of the keywords supplied.

   Example: data OR info

### site:

This operator allows restricting the result only to the site provided. We will only get to see the links from the specified website. There are two other operators which work like this operator but do not provide results as accurate or in-depth as they are domain and hostname. Their usage is similar to the "site" operator.

   Example: site:elsevier.com

### link:

It is another interesting operator which allows us to lookup web pages which link to the specific web page provided. While using this operator do keep in mind to provide the URL with the protocol (http:// or https://).

Example: link:http://www.elsevier.com/

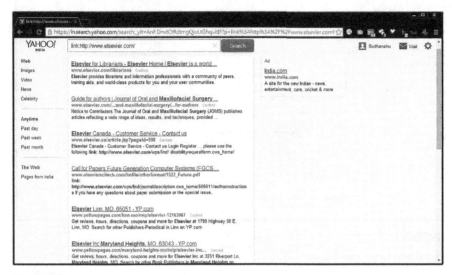

**FIGURE 5.6**

Yahoo "link" search.

## define:

We can use this operator to find out the dictionary meaning of a word.

Example: define:data

## intitle:

The "intitle" operator is used to get the results which contain the specified keyword in their title tag.

Example: intitle:data

So these are the operators which Yahoo supports. Apart from these we can access the Yahoo advanced search page at http://search.yahoo.com/search/options?fr=fp-top&p=, which allows us to achieve well-filtered search results. One other thing that Yahoo offers is advanced news search which can be performed using the page http://news.search.yahoo.com/advanced .

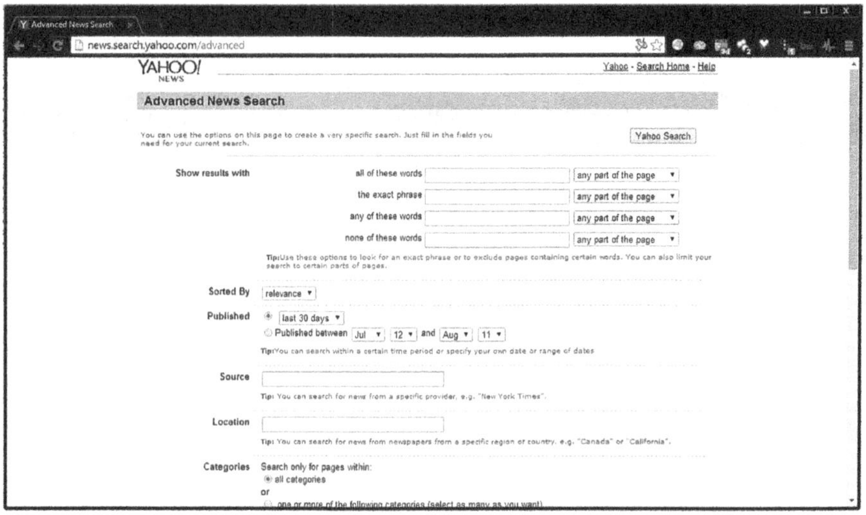

**FIGURE 5.7**

Yahoo advanced search page.

## YANDEX:

Yandex is Russian search engine and is not too much popular outside the country, but it's one of the most powerful search engines available. Like Google, Bing, Yahoo it has its own unique keywords and data indexed. Yandex is the most popular and widely used search engine in Russia. It's the fourth largest search engine in the world. Apart from Russia, it is also used in countries like Ukraine, Kazakhstan, Turkey, and Belarus. It is also most under rated search engine as its use is only limited to specific country but in security community we see it otherwise. Most of the people are either happy with their conventional search engine or they think all the internet information is available in the search engine they are using. But the fact is that search engines like Yandex also have many unique features that can provide us with way efficient result as compared to other search engines.

Here we will discuss how Yandex can be a game changer in searching data on internet and how to use it efficiently.

As discussed earlier like other search engines, Yandex has its own operators such as lang, parenthesis, Boolean, and all. Let's get familiar with these operators and their usage.

### +

This operator works quite same for all the search engines. Here also for Yandex, + operator is used to include a keyword in a search result page. The keyword added after + operator is the primary keyword in the search query. The result fetched by the search engine must contain that keyword.

Example: osint +tools

Here the result page might not contain the OSINT keyword but must contain tools keyword. So when we want to focus on a particular keyword or set of keywords in Yandex, we must use + operator.

~~

This is used as NOT operator which is used to exclude a keyword from a search result page. It can be used in excluding a particular thing from a set of the things. Let's say we want to buy mobile phone but not windows phone. Then we can craft a query accordingly to avoid windows phone from search result by using ~~ operator.

Example: mobile phone ~~ windows

~

Unlike ~~ operator ~ is used to exclude a keyword not from search result page but search result sentence. That means we might have both or all the keywords present in the query in a page but the excluded keyword must not be in any sentence with the other keywords mentioned. I understand it being little complicated so let me explain simply. Let's start with the above query

mobile phone ~~ windows

Here if a page contains both mobile phone as well as windows, Yandex will exclude that page from search result.

Example: mobile phone ~ windows

But for the example shown above, it will show all the pages that contains both mobile phone as well as windows but not if these two keywords are in same sentence.

### &&

The && operator is used to show pages that contains both the keywords in search result.

Example: power && searching

It will provide the results of all the pages that contain both these keywords.

### &

This operator is used to show only pages that contains both the keywords in a sentence. It provides more refined result for both the keywords.

Example: power & searching

### /number

It's a special operator which can be used for different purposes according to the number used after slash. It's used for defining the closeness of the keywords. It is quite similar to AROUND operator of Google and NEAR operator of Bing. The number used with slash defines the word distance between two keywords.

Example: power /4 searching

Yandex will make sure that the result page must contain these two keywords with in four words from each other irrespective of keyword position. That means the order in which we created the query with the keywords might change in result page.

What if we need to fix the order? Yes, Yandex has a solution for that also: adding a +sign with the number.

Example: power /+4 searching

By adding the + operator before the number will force Yandex to respond with the results with only pages where these two keywords are in same order and in within 4 word count.

What if we need the reverse of it, let's say we need to get results of keyword "searching" first and after that "power" within 4 word count and not vice versa. In that case negative number will come pretty handy where we can use - sign to reverse what we just did without getting the vice versa result.

Example: power /-4 searching

This will only display pages which contain searching keyword and power after that within 4 word count.

Let's say we want to setup a radius or boundary for a keyword with respect to another; in that case we have to specify that keyword in second position.

Example: power /(-3 +4) searching

Here we are setting up a radius for searching with respect to power. This means that the page is displayed in results shown only if either "searching" will be found within 3 words before or after "power" within 4 word count.

This can be helpful when we are searching for two people's names. In that case we cannot guess that which name will come first and which name will come next so it's better to create a radius for those two names, and the query will serve our purpose.

As we discussed a lot about word-based keyword search, now let's put some light on sentence-based keyword search. For sentence based keyword search we can use Yandex && operator with this number operator.

Example: power && /4 searching

In this case we can get result pages containing these two keywords with in 4 sentence difference irrespective of the position of the keyword. That means either "power" may come first and "searching" after that or vice versa.

*!*

This operator does something special. And this is one of my favorite keyword. It gives a user freedom to only search a specific keyword without similar word search or extended search and all. What exactly happens in general search is that if you search for a keyword, let's say AND, you will get some results showing only AND and then the results will extend to ANDroid or AMD and so on. If we want to get only result for AND keyword; use this operator.

Example: !and

This will restrict the search engine to provide results only showing pages which contains this particular keyword AND.

## !!

It can be used to search the dictionary form of the keyword.

Example: !!and

## ()

When we want to create a complex query with different keywords and operators we can use these brackets to group them. As we already used these brackets above, now we will see some other example to understand the true power of this.

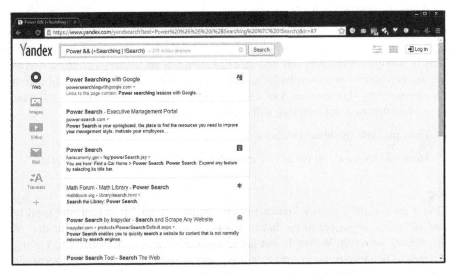

**FIGURE 5.8**

Yandex complex query.

Example: power && (+searching | !search)

Here the query will search for both sets of keywords first power searching and power search but not both in same result.

## ""

Now it's about a keyword let's say we want to search a particular string or set of keywords then what to do? Here this operator "" comes for rescue. It is quite similar as Google's "". This will allow a user to search for exact keywords or string which is put inside the double quotes.

Example: "What is OSINT?"

It will search for exact string and if available will give us the result accordingly.

**\***

This operator can be refereed as wildcard operator. The use of this operator is quite same in most of the search engines. This operator is used to fill the missing keyword or suggest relevant keywords according to the other keywords used in the search query.

Example: osint is * of technology

It will search for auto fill the space where * is used to complete the query with relevant keywords. In this case that can be ocean or treasure or anything. We can also use this operator with double quote to get more efficient and accurate result.

Example: "OSINT is * of technology"

**|**

This is also quite similar to OR operator of Google. It allows us to go for different keywords where we want results for any of them. In-real time scenario we can search for options using this operator. Let's say I want to buy a laptop and I have different options: in that case this operator will come to picture.

Example: dell | toshiba | macbook

Here we can get result for any of these three options but not all in one result.

**<<**

This is an unusual operator known as non-ranking "AND." It is basically used to add additional keywords to the list of keywords without impacting the ranking of the website on result. We might not get to know what exactly it does by just going through its definitions. So in simple words it can be used to tag additional keywords to the query list without impacting the page rankings.

Example: power searching << OSINT

It can be used to additionally search for OSINT along with the other two key-words without impacting the page ranking in the result page.

### *title:*
This is quite equivalent to the "intitle." It can be used to search the pages with the keyword (s) specified after title query parameter.

Example: title:osint

This will provide pages that contain OSINT in the title of the web page. Similarly we can use this title query parameter to search for more than one keyword.

Example: title:(power searching)

### url:

This "url" search query parameter is also an add-on. It searches for the exact URL provided by the user in Yandex database.

Example: url:http://attacker.in

Here Yandex will provide a result if and only if the URL has been crawled and indexed in its database.

### inurl:

It can be used to search for keywords present in a URL or in other words for URL fragment search. This "inurl" query parameter works quite similar in all the search engines.

Example: inurl:osint

It will search for all the URLs that contain osint keyword no matter what the position of the keyword is.

### mime:filetype

This query parameter is quite similar to "filetype" query parameter of Google. This helps a user to search for a particular file type.

Example: osint mime:pdf

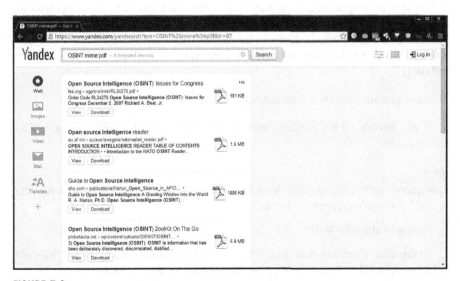

**FIGURE 5.9**

Yandex file search.

It will provide us all the PDF links that contains osint keyword. The file types supported by Yandex mime are

PDF, RTF, SWF, DOC, XLS, PPT, DOCX, PPTX, XLSX, ODT, ODS, ODP, ODG

### host:

It can be used to search all the available hosts. This can be used by the penetration testers mostly.

Example: host:owasp.org

### rhost:

It is quite similar to host but "rhost" searches for reverse hosts. This can also be used by the penetration testers to get all the reverse host details.

It can be used in two ways. One is for subdomains by using the wildcard operator * at the end or another without that.

Example:    rhost:org.owasp.*

rhost:org.owasp.www

### site:

This operator is like the best friend of a penetration tester or hacker. This is available in most of the search engines. It provides all the details of subdomains of the provided URL.

For penetration testers or hackers finding the right place to search for vulnerability is most important. As in most cases the main sites are much secured as compared to the subdomains, if any operator helps to simplify the process by providing details of the subdomains to any hacker or penetration tester then half work is done. So the importance of this operator is definitely felt in security industry.

Example: site:http://www.owasp.org

It will provide all the available subdomains of the domain owasp.com as well as all the pages.

### date:

This query can be used to either limit the search data to a specific date or to specific period by a little enhancement in the query.

Example: date:201408*

In this case, format of date used is YYYYMMDD, but in case of the DD we used wildcard operator "*" so we will get results limited to August 2014.

We can also limit the same to a particular date of the August 2014 by changing a bit in the query.

date:20140808

It will only show results belong to that date.

We can also use "=" in place of ":" and it will still work the same. So the above query can be changed to

date=201408*
date=20140808

As we discussed earlier we can also limit the search results to a particular time period. Let's say we want to search something from a particular date to till date. In that case we can use

date=>20140808

It will provide results from 8th August 2014 to till date, but what if we want to limit both the start date and the end date. In that case also Yandex provide us a provision of providing range.

date=20140808..20140810

Here we will get the results form date 8th August 2014 to 10th August 2014.

### domain:

It can be used to specify the search results based of top level domains (TLDs). Mostly this type of the domain search was done to get results from country-specific domains. Let's say we wanted to get the list of CERT-empanelled security service providing company names from different countries. In that case we can search for the country-specific domain extension let's say we want to get these details for New Zealand then its TLD is nz. So we can craft a query like

Example: "cert empanelled company" domain:nz

### lang:

It can be used to search pages written in specific languages.

Yandex supports some specific languages such as
RU: Russian
UK: Ukrainian
BE: Belorussian
EN: English
FR: French
DE: German
KK: Kazakh
TT: Tatar
TR: Turkish

Though we can always use Google translator to translate the page from any languages to English or any other languages, it's an added feature provided by Yandex to fulfill minimum requirements of the regions where Yandex is used popularly.

So to search a page we need to provide the short form of the languages.

Example: power searching lang:en

It will search for the pages in English that contains power searching.

### cat:

It is also something unique provided by Yandex. Cat stands for category. Yandex categorizes different things based on region id or topic id. Using cat we can search for a result based on region or topic assigned in Yandex database.

The details of Regional codes: http://search.yaca.yandex.ru/geo.c2n.
The details of Topic codes: http://search.yaca.yandex.ru/cat.c2n.

Though the pages contains data in Russian language, we can always use Google translate to serve this purpose.

As we discussed in the beginning that Yandex is an underrated search engine some of its cool features are definitely going to put a mark on our life once we go through this chapter. One of such feature is its advanced search GUI.

There are lazy people like me who want everything in GUI so that they just have to customize everything by providing limited details and selecting some checkbox or radio buttons. Yandex provides that in the below link

http://www.yandex.com/search/advanced?&lr=10558

Here we have to just select what we want and most importantly it covers most of the operators we discussed above. So go to the page, select what you want, and search efficiently using GUI.

Definitely after going through all these operators we can easily feel the impact of the advance search or we can also use the term power search for that. The advance search facilitates a user with faster, efficient, and reliable data in the result. It always reduces our manual efforts to get the desired data. And the content quality is also better in advance search as we limit the search to what we are actually looking for. It can be either country-specific domain search, a particular file type, or content from a specific date. These things cannot be done easily with simple keyword search.

We are in an age where information is everything. Then the reliability factor comes in to picture and if we want bulk of reliable information from the net in very less time span then we need to focus on the advance search. We can use any conventional search engine of our choice. Most of the search engines have quite similar operators to serve the purpose but there are some special features present; so look for those special features and use different search engines for different customized advance search.

So we learned about various search engines and their operators and how to utilize these operators to search better and get precise results. For some operators we say their individual operations and how they can help to narrow down the results and for some we saw how they can be used with other operators to generate a great query which directly gets us to what we want. Though there are some operators for different search engines which work more or less in the same fashion yet as the crawling and indexing techniques of different platforms are different, it is worthwhile to check which one of them provides better results depending upon our requirements. One thing that we need to keep in mind is that the search providers keep on deprecating the operators or features which are not used frequently enough and also some functionalities are not available in some regions.

We saw how easily we can get the results that we actually want with the use of some small but effective techniques. The impact of these techniques is not just limited to finding out the links to websites, but if used creatively they can be implemented in various fields. Apart from finding the information on the web, which certainly is useful for everyone, these techniques can be used to find out details which are profession specific. For example a marketing professional can scale the size of the website of competitor using the operator "site," or a sales professional can find out emails for a company using the wildcard operator "*@randomcompany.com." We also saw how search engine dorks are used by cyber security professionals to find out sensitive and compromising information just by using some simple keywords and operators. The takeaway here is not just to learn about the operators but also about how we can use them creatively in our profession.

We have covered a lot about how to perform searching using different searching platforms in this and some previous chapters. Till now we have mainly focused on browser-based applications or we can say web applications. In the next chapter we will be moving on and learn about various tools which need to be installed as applications and provide us various features for extracting data related to various fields, using various methods.

# OSINT Tools and Techniques

## 6

## INFORMATION IN THIS CHAPTER

- OSINT Tools
- Geolocation
- Information Harvesting
- Shodan
- Search Diggity
- Recon-ng
- Yahoo Pipes
- Maltego

## INTRODUCTION

In the previous chapters we learned about the basics of the internet and effective ways to search it. We went to great depths of searching social media to unconventional search engines and further learned about effective techniques to use regular search engines. In this chapter we will move a step further and will discuss about some of the automated tools and web-based services which are used frequently to perform reconnaissance by professionals of various intelligence-related domains specially information security. We will start from the installation part to understanding their interface and will further learn about their functionality and usage. Some of these tools provide a rich graphic interface (GUI) and some of them are command line based (CLI), but don't judge them by their interface but by their functionality and relevance in our field of work.

Before moving any further we must install the dependencies for these tools so that we don't have to face any issues during their installation and usage. The packages we need are

- Java latest version
- Python 2.7
- Microsoft .NET Framework v4

We simply need to download the relevant package depending upon our system configuration and we are good to go.

101

# CREEPY

Most of us are addicted to social networks, and image sharing is one of the most utilized features of these platforms. But sometimes when we share these pictures it's not just the image that we are sharing but might also the exact location where that picture was taken.

Creepy is a Python application which can extract out this information and display the geolocation on a map. Currently Creepy supports search for Twitter, Flickr, and Instagram. It extracts the geolocation based on EXIF information stored in images, geolocation information available through application programming interface (API), and some other techniques.

It can be downloaded from http://ilektrojohn.github.io/creepy/. We simply need to select the version according to our platform and install it. The next phase after installation of Creepy is to configure the plugins that are available in it, for which we simply need to click on the Plug-in Configuration button present under the edit tab. Here we can select the plugins and using their individual configuration wizard configure them accordingly. Once the configuration is done we can check whether it is working properly or not using the Test Plugin Configuration button.

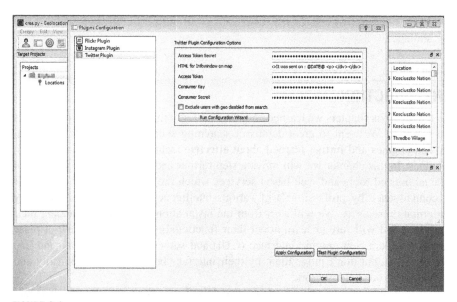

**FIGURE 6.1**

Configure Creepy.

After the configuration phase is done, we can start a new project by clicking on the person icon on the top bar. Here we can name the project and search for people on different portals. From the search results we can select the person of interest and include him/her in the target list and finish the wizard. After this our project will be displayed under the project bar at the right-hand side.

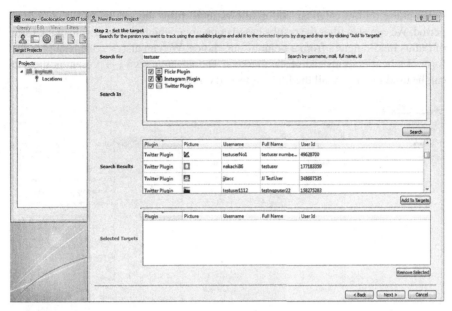

**FIGURE 6.2**

Search users.

Now we simply need to select our project and click on the target icon or right click on the project and click Analyze Current Project. After this Creepy will start the analysis, which will take some time. Once the analysis is complete, Creepy will display the results on the map.

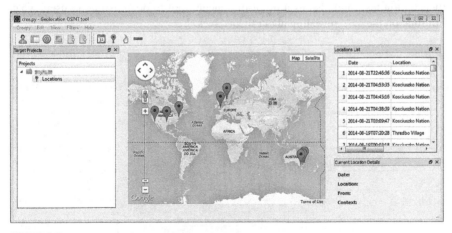

**FIGURE 6.3**

Creepy results.

Now we can see the results in which the map is populated with the markers according the identified geolocation. Now Creepy further allows us to narrow down these results based on various filters.

Clicking on the calendar button allows us to filter the results based on a time period. We can also filter the results based upon area, which we can define in the form of radius in kilometers from a point of our choice. We can also see the results in the form of a heat map instead of the markers. The negative sign (−) present at the end can be used to remove all the filters imposed on the results.

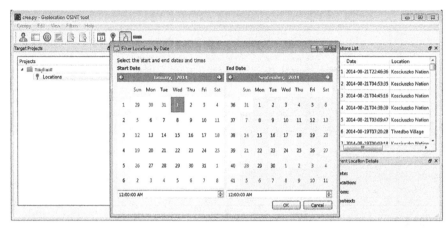

**FIGURE 6.4**

Applying filter.

The results that we get from Creepy can also be downloaded in the form of CSV file and also as KML, which can be used to display the markers in another map.

Creepy can be used for the information-gathering phase during a pentest (penetration test) and also as a proof-of-concept tool to demonstrate to users what information they are revealing about themselves.

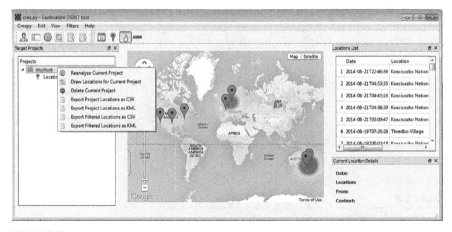

**FIGURE 6.5**

Download Creepy results.

# THEHARVESTER

TheHarvester is an open source intelligence tool (OSINT) for obtaining e-mail addresses, employee name, open ports, subdomains, hosts banners, etc. from public sources such as search engines like Google, Bing and other sites such as LinkedIn. It's a simple Python tool which is easy to use and contains different information-gathering functions. Being a Python tool it's quite understandable that to use this tool we must have Python installed in our system. This tool is created by Christian Martorella and one of the simple, popular, and widely used tools in terms of information gathering.

TheHarvester can be found here: http://www.edge-security.com/theharvester.php

Generally we need to input a domain name or company name to collect relevant information such as email addresses, subdomains, or the other details mentioned in the above paragraph. But we can use keywords also to collect related information.

We can specify our search, such as from which particular public source we want to use for the information gathering. There are lots of public source that Harvester use for information gathering but before moving to that let's understand how to use Harvester.

EX: theharvester -d example.com -l 500 -b Google

-d = Generally, domain name or company name
-l = Number of result limits to work with
-b = Specifying the data source such as in the above command its Google, but apart from that we can use LinkedIn and all (to use all the available public sources) as a source also to collect information.

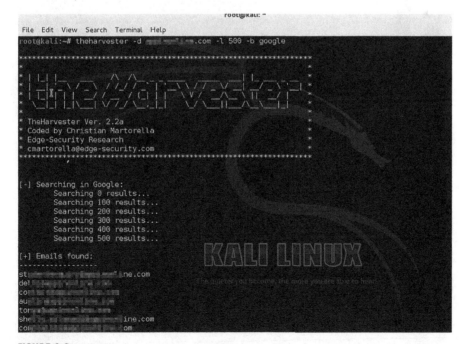

**FIGURE 6.6**

TheHarvester in action.

Apart from the above mentioned one harvester also has other options to specify, such as:

-s = to start with a particular result number (the default value is 0)
-v = to get virtual hosts by verifying hostnames via DNS resolution
-f = for saving the data. (formats available either html or xml)
-n = to perform DNS resolve query for all the discovered ranges
-c = to perform DNS bruteforce for all domain names
-t = to perform a DNS TLD expansion discovery
-e = to use a specific DNS server
-l = To limit the number of result to work with
-h = to use Shodan database to query discovered hosts.

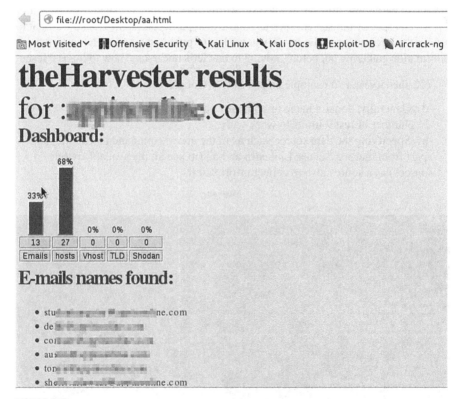

**FIGURE 6.7**

TheHarvester HTML results.

The sources it uses are Google, Google profiles, Bing, pretty good privacy (PGP) servers, LinkedIn, Jigsaw, Shodan, Yandex, name servers, people123, and

Exalead. Google, Yandex, Bing, and Exalead are search engines that are used in backend as a source, while Shodan is also a search engine but not the conventional one and we already discussed a bit about it earlier and we will discuss in detail about the same in this chapter later. PGP servers are like key servers used for data security and those are also a good source to collect e-mail details. The people123 is for searching for a particular person and Jigsaw is the cloud-based solution for lead generation and other sales stuffs. From different sources harvester collects different information such as for e-mail harvesting it uses Google, Bing, PGP servers, and sometimes Exalead and run their specific queries in the background to get the desired result. Similarly for subdomains or host names it uses again Google, Bing, Yandex, Exalead, PGP servers, and Exalead. And finally for the list for employee names it uses LinkedIn, Google profiles, people123, and Jigsaw as a main source.

This is how theHarvester harvests all the information and gives us the desired result as per our query. So craft your query wisely to harvest all the required information.

## SHODAN

We have previously discussed about Shodan briefly in Chapter 4, but this unique search engine deserves much more than a paragraph to discuss its usage and impact. As discussed earlier Shodan is a computer search engine. The internet consists of various different types of devices connected online and available publicly. Most of these devices have a banner, which they send as a response to the application request send by a client. Many if not most of these banners contains information which can be called sensitive in nature, such as server version, device type, authentication mode, etc. Shodan allows us to search such devices over internet and also provides filters to narrow down the results.

It is highly recommended to create an account to utilize this great tool, as it removes some of the restrictions imposed on the free usage. So after logging into the application we will simply go to the dashboard at http://www.shodanhq.com/home. Here we can see some the recent searches as well as popular searches made on this platform. This page also shows a quick reference to the filters that we can use. Moving on let's see more popular searches listed under the URL http://www.shodanhq.com/browse. Here we can see there are various different search queries which look quite interesting, such as webcam, default password, SCADA, etc. Clicking on one of these directly takes us to the result page and lists details of machines on the internet with that specific keyword. The page http://www.shodanhq.com/help/filters shows the list of all the filters that we can use in Shodan to perform a more focused search, such as country, hostname, port, etc., including the usual filters "+,""-," and "|."

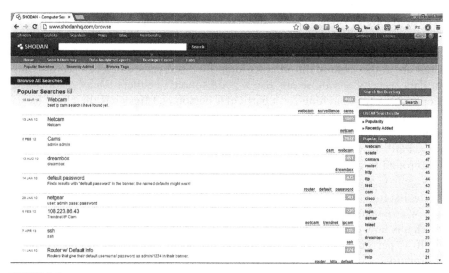

**FIGURE 6.8**

Shodan popular searches.

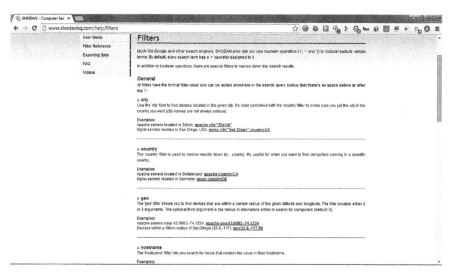

**FIGURE 6.9**

Shodan filters.

Let's perform a simple search on Shodan for the keyword "webcam." Shodan has simply found more than 15,000 results for this keyword; though we cannot view all the results under the free package, yet what we get is enough to understand its reach and availability of such devices on the internet. Some of these might be protected by some kind of authentication mechanism such as username and password, but some might be publicly accessible without any such mechanism. We can simply find out by opening their listed IP address in our browsers (Warning: It might be illegal to do so depending upon the laws of the country, etc.). We can further narrow down these results to a country by using the "country" filter. So our new query is "webcams country:us" which gives us a list of webcams in the United States of America.

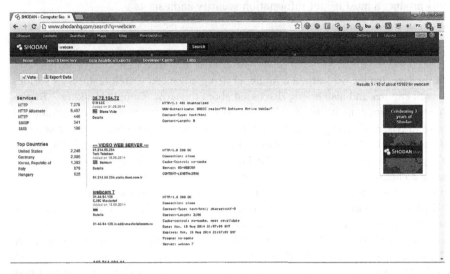

**FIGURE 6.10**

Shodan results for query "webcam"

To get a list of machines with file transfer protocol (FTP) service, residing in India, we can use the query "port:21 country:in". We can also perform search for specific IP address or range of it using the filter "net." Shodan is providing a great deal of relevant information and its application is only limited by the creativity of its users.

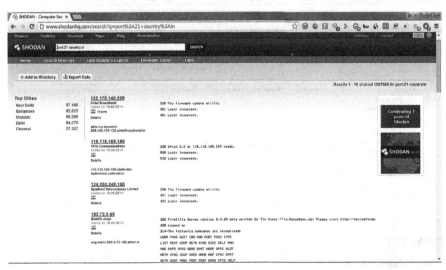

**FIGURE 6.11**

Shodan results for query "port:21 country:in."

Apart from this Shodan also offers an API to integrate its data into our own application. There are also some other services provided by it at a price and are worth a try for anyone working in the information security domain. Recently there has been a lot of development in Shodan and its associated services which makes this product a must try for information security enthusiasts.

## SEARCH DIGGITY

In the last chapter we learned a lot about using advanced search features of various search engines and also briefly discussed about the term "Google Hacking." To perform such functions we need to have the list of operations that we can use and will have to type each query to see if anything is vulnerable, but what if there was a tool which has a database of such queries and we can simply run it. Here enters the Search Diggity. Search Diggity is tool by Bishop Fox which has a huge set of options and a large database of queries for various search engines which allow us to gather compromising information related to our target. It can be downloaded from http://www.bishopfox.com/resources/tools/google-hacking-diggity/attack-tools/. The basic requirement for its installation is Microsoft .NET framework v4

Once we have downloaded and installed the application, the things we need are the search ids and API keys. These search ids/API keys are required so that we can perform more number of searcher without too many restrictions. We can find how to get and use these keys in the contents section under the Help tab and also from a some simple Google searches. Once all the keys (Google, Bing, Shodan, etc.) are at their place we can move forward with the usage of the tool.

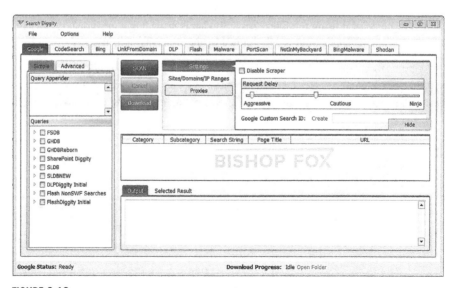

**FIGURE 6.12**

Search Diggity interface.

There are many tabs in the tool such as Google, Bing, DLP, Flash, Shodan etc. Each of these tabs provides specialized functions to perform targeted search to identify information which can be critical from an information security point of view.

To use the tool we simply need to select one of the tabs at the top and further select the type of queries that we want to use. We can also specify the domain that we want to target and simply perform the scan. Depending upon what is available online the tool will provide us the results for various different queries related to the query type we have selected. It is highly recommended to select only the query types that we are really interested into, as it will help us to narrow down the total number of queries. The queries present are categorized properly to identify and make choice accordingly.

Let's use the queries to identify SharePoint Administrative pages. For this we simply need to select the Google tab and from the left-hand menu, check the Administrative checkbox under SharePoint Diggity, and run the scan.

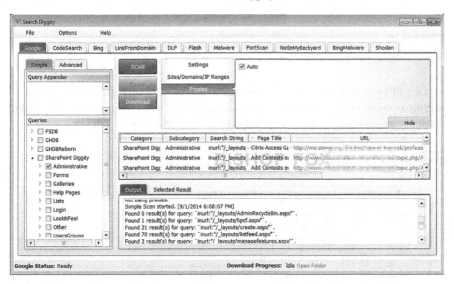

**FIGURE 6.13**

Search Diggity scan—Google tab.

To make this scan more targeted we can specify a list of targets under the option Sites/Domains/IP Ranges. As soon as we start the scan we can see the results coming up with various information like category, page title, URL, etc. Similarly we can also use the Bing scan which has its own set of search queries.

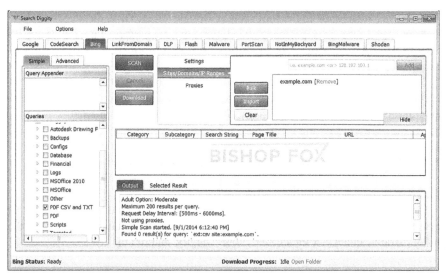

**FIGURE 6.14**

Search Diggity scan—Bing tab.

One of the interesting options is NotInMyBackyard which allows us to specify various options such as locations, filetypes, and keyword to get interesting data. Similarly we can also access information from Shodan using its API key.

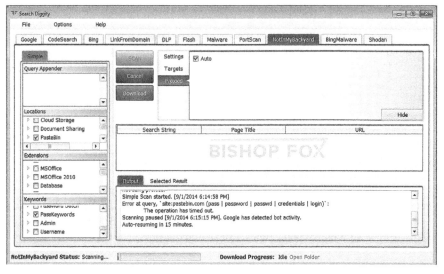

**FIGURE 6.15**

Search Diggity—NotInMyBackyard.

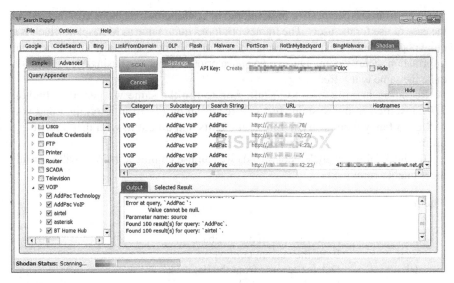

**FIGURE 6.16**

Search Diggity—Shodan scan.

# Recon-ng

There are many tools for reconnaissance but a special mention should be given to Recon-ng. This is an open source tool written in Python majorly by Tim Tomes (@Lanmaster53). There are many other researchers, coders, and developers who have contributed to this project. This project is one of its kind in terms of complete OSINT framework. The authors might have different opinion on my previous statement but still this framework helps all the OSINT enthusiast to perform various stages of reconnaissance in automated way.

It mainly focus on web-based open-source reconnaissance and provides its users with unique independent modules, elaborated and much required command based help, database interaction and command completion facility to perform reconnaissance deeply and fast paced. Apart from that it's made in a fashion that if a newbie into the field of security wants to contribute to it, he/she can easily do it with a little Python knowledge. It's just possible only because of well-structured modules, fully fledged documentation, and the uses of only-native Python functions that a new user or contributor will not face problem to download and install third party modules of Python for a specific task.

The tool can be downloaded from: https://bitbucket.org/LaNMaSteR53/recon-ng
The user guide: https://bitbucket.org/LaNMaSteR53/recon-ng/wiki/Usage_Guide
The development guide: https://bitbucket.org/LaNMaSteR53/recon-ng/wiki/Development_Guide

Apart from the perspective of developer or contributor the author also focused on the ease of use for the users. The framework looks quite same as Metasploit which is a quite popular tool for exploitation in information security community. If you are from information security community or you have prior experience of using Metasploit, it's quite the same to use Recon-ng.

Recon-ng is quite easy to install. And to run the same we just need Python 2.7.x installed in our system. Just call recon-ng.py file from a terminal and you will get a fancy banner of the toll with credits and all along with that a recon-ng prompt.

To check all the available commands we can use command help. It will show all the available commands

> help

| | |
|---|---|
| add | Adds records to the database |
| back | Exits the current context |
| del | Deletes records from the database |
| exit | Exits the framework |
| help | Displays this menu |
| keys | Manages framework API keys |
| load | Loads specified module |
| pdb | Starts a Python Debugger session |
| query | Queries the database |
| record | Records commands to a resource file |
| reload | Reloads all modules |
| resource | Executes commands from a resource file |
| search | Searches available modules |
| set | Sets module options |
| shell | Executes shell commands |
| show | Shows various framework items |
| spool | Spools output to a file |
| unset | Unsets module options |
| use | Loads specified module |
| workspaces | Manages workspaces |

Here in this framework some fine features are provided such as workspaces. It consists of different settings, database, etc., and a self-independent place for a single project.

To know more about workspaces, we can use the command

> help workspaces

This command is used to manage workspaces such as providing user freedom to list down, add, select, delete workspaces. If a user does not set a workspace externally, then he/she will be under default workspace. If we want to check in which workspace we are exactly then the command is

> show workspaces

```
+------------+
| Workspaces |
+------------+
| default    |
+------------+
```

And we will get something similar to this showing that we are under default workspace.

Let's say we want to change the workspace to something that we want, let's say osint, then the command would be

> workspaces add osint

The prompt itself shows the workspace so the default prompt we will get in fresh installation is

[recon-ng] [default] >

After the above command the prompt will change in to

[recon-ng] [osint] >

Now it's time to explore the commands and its capabilities. If you are using this tool for the first time the most needed command after "help" is "show."

[recon-ng] [osint] > show

Using this command we can see available details of banner, companies, contacts, credentials, dashboard, domains, hosts, keys, leaks, locations, modules, netblocks, options, ports, pushpins, schema, vulnerabilities, and workspaces details but here we want to explore the modules section to see what all are possibilities available.

---

Basically recon-ng consists of five different sections of modules.
1. Discovery
2. Exploitation
3. Import
4. Recon
5. Reporting

**FIGURE 6.17**

Recon-ng modules.

And by using following commands we will able to see more details as off the available options about these five sections

[recon-ng] [osint] > show modules

such as under-discovery interesting files, under-exploitation command injection, under-import CSV files, under-recon company contacts, credentials, host details, location information and many more and last but not the least under-reporting CSV, HTML, XML, etc.

Now we can use these modules based on our requirements. To use any of these modules, first, we need to load that module using following command but before that we must know that this framework has a unique capability to load a module by auto completing it or if more modules are available with a single keyword then giving all the module list. Let's say we want to check the pwnedlist and we are so lazy to type the absolute command. Nothing to worry just do as shown below

[recon-ng] [osint] > load pwnedlist

Now recon-ng will check whether this string is associated with a single module or multiple modules. If it is associated with a single module then it will load that or else it will give the user all the available modules that contain this keyword.

As in our case pwnedlist keyword is associated with multiple functions, thus it will show all. Let's say we want to use the module recon/contacts-creds/pwnedlist the command we will use is

[recon-ng] [osint] > load recon/contacts-creds/pwnedlist

Once a module get loaded, for easy understanding it gets added in the prompt so the prompt will change to

[recon-ng] [osint] [pwnedlist] >

As we wanted to use this module first we need to check the options available. To check that the command is as follows

[recon-ng] [osint] [pwnedlist] > show options

This command will show all the required details in a tabular manner such as name of the required field, its current status or value, whether it is mandatory field or not, description in a bit.

**FIGURE 6.18**

Recon-ng module options.

If we are still in confusion then this framework has other command to elaborate in more detailed fashion about a module:

[recon-ng] [osint] [pwnedlist] > show info

**FIGURE 6.19**

Recon-ng module detailed information.

This command provides detailed information, name of the module, path, author name, and description in details.

As we can see from the above figure that we need to add a SOURCE as an input to run this module, and what kind of input needed is also mentioned in the bottom part of the same figure. We can craft a command such as

[recon-ng] [osint] [pwnedlist] > set SOURCE google@gmail.com

This command is taken as we provided a proper and valued input. Now the command to run this module to check whether the above e-mail id is pwned somewhere or not is

[recon-ng] [osint] [pwnedlist] > run

```
 File  Edit  View  Search  Terminal  Help
[recon-ng][osint][pwnedlist] > set SOURCE google@gmail.com
SOURCE => google@gmail.com
[recon-ng][osint][pwnedlist] > run
[*] google@gmail.com => Pwned! Seen at least 27 times, as recent as 2014-08-28.

-------
SUMMARY
-------
[*] 1 total (0 new) items found.
```

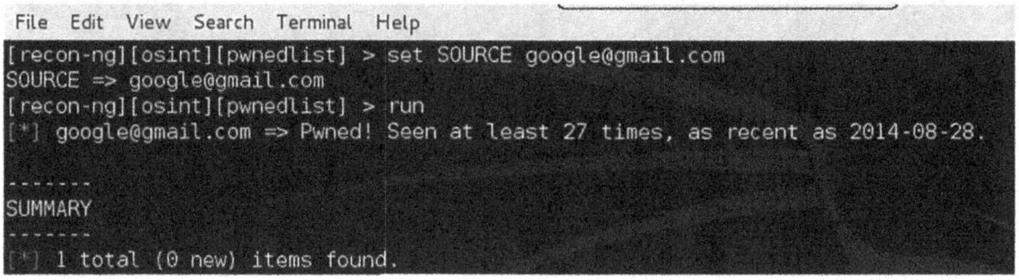

**FIGURE 6.20**

Recon-ng results.

Voilà! The above e-mail id has been pwned somewhere. If we want to use some other modules we can simply use the "load" command along with the module name to load and use the same.

This is how we can easily use this recon-ng. The commands and approaches will remain quite same. First look for the modules. Choose the required module, load it, check for its options, provide values to the required fields, and then run. If required repeat the same process to extend the reconnaissance.

Now let's discuss some of the scenarios and the modules that can be handy for the same.

## CASE 1

If we are into sales and desperately wanted to collect database to gather prospective clients then there are certain modules available here that will be pretty helpful. If we want to gather these information from social networking sites, LinkedIn is the only place where we can get exact names and other details as compared to other sites which generally consists of fancy aliases. And if we are in to core sales then we might have heard of portals like Sales Force or Jigsaw, where we can get certain details either by free or by paying reasonable amount of money. And mostly nowadays in IT sector sales teams focus less on cold calling and more on spreading details on e-mail. So getting valid e-mails from a target organization is always like half work done for sales team. So here we will discuss the sources available to get these information and its associated modules in recon-ng.

Available modules:

recon/companies-contacts/facebook
recon/companies-contacts/jigsaw
recon/companies-contacts/linkedin_auth

These are some of the modules but not all that can be helpful to gather information such as name, position, address, etc.

But e-mail addresses are the key to contact. So let's look into some options to collect e-mail addresses. We can collect some e-mail id details from Whois database. Search engines also sometimes play a vital role in collecting e-mail address, using PGP servers.

Available modules:

recon/domains-contacts/pgp_search
recon/domains-contacts/whois_pocs

## CASE 2

Physical tracking. The use of smart phones intentionally or unintentionally allowed users to add their geolocation with data that they upload to different public sites such as YouTube, Picasa, etc. In that case we can collect information by the help of geotagged media. This can be used for behavioral analysis, understanding a person's likes and dislikes, etc.

Available modules:

recon/locations-pushpins/flickr
recon/locations-pushpins/picasa
recon/locations-pushpins/shodan
recon/locations-pushpins/twitter
recon/locations-pushpins/youtube

## CASE 3

If some organization or person wants to check whether he/she or any of a company's e-mail id has been hacked, then there are certain modules that can be helpful. Similar to what we already discussed above, i.e., pwnedlist, there are other modules that can give similar results:

recon/contacts-creds/pwnedlist
recon/contacts-creds/haveibeenpwned
recon/contacts-creds/should_change_password

## CASE 4

For penetration testers it is also like hidden treasure because they can perform penetration testing without sending a single packet from their environment. The first approach to do any penetration testing is information gathering. Let's say we want to perform a web application penetration testing then the first thing we want to enumerate is what technology or server the site is running on. So that we can manually search later for the publicly available exploits to exploit the same. In this case reconng has a module to find the technology details for us.

Available module:

recon/domains-contacts/builtwith

Now after getting these details, generally, we look into the vulnerabilities available in the net associated with that technology. But we can also look at the vulnerabilities associated with that domain. And it is possible by the use of punkspider module. Punkspider uses a web scanner to scan the entire web and collect detailed vulnerabilities and store it in its database, which can be used to directly search for the available exposed vulnerabilities in a site.

Available modules:

recon/domains-vulnerabilities/punkspider
recon/domains-vulnerabilities/xssed

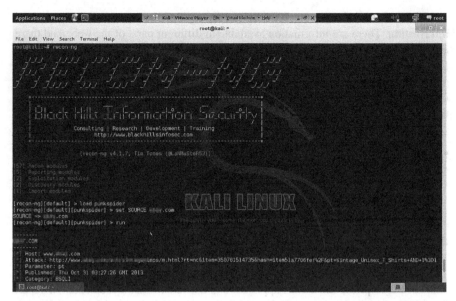

**FIGURE 6.21**

Recon-ng PunkSpider in progress.

Now for a network penetration-testing perspective port scanning is also an important thing. And this framework has modules to perform port scanning.
Available module:

recon/netblocks-ports/census_2012

Apart from these there are direct exploitation modules available such as

exploitation/injection/command_injector
exploitation/injection/xpath_bruter

There are different modules for different functions; one major function among them is the credential harvest. Still researchers are contributing in this project and authors expanding the features. The ease of use and structural modules makes this framework one of the popular tools for OSINT.

# YAHOO PIPES

Yahoo Pipes is a unique piece of application from Yahoo which provides user the freedom to select different information sources and enable some customized rules according to own requirements to get filtered output. The best thing about the tool is the cool GUI where a normal internet user can also create his/her own pipes to get desired filtered information from different sources.

As we all are OSINT enthusiasts, the only thing that matters to us is valid required information. There are information available in different parts of the web. And there are different sources to get information regularly. The problem is that how to differentiate the information we want from the numerous information provided by a particular source. If we need to filter the required information manually from a set of information then it requires a lot of manual effort. So to ease the process this application will help us a lot.

Requirements:

- A web browser
- Internet connectivity
- Yahoo Id

As it's a web application we can access it from anywhere, and the lesser dependency make it more usable along with its user friendly GUI. We can access the application from below mentioned URL.

https://pipes.yahoo.com/

Visit this URL, login with your yahoo id and we are all set to use this application. Another major plus point of this application is its well-formed documentation. Apart from that we can find links to different tutorials (text as well as video) in the application site itself describing how to start and other advance stuffs. Along with that for reference purpose there are also links to popular pipes available. Let's create our own pipe.

To create an own pipe we need to click on Create pipe button on the application. It will redirect to http://pipes.yahoo.com/pipes/pipe.edit

In the right top corner we can find tabs like new, save, and properties. By default there is no necessity to do anything with these tabs. As we are about to start creating a new pipe, the things to be noted are that in the left side of the application we will find different tabs and subtabs such as sources, user inputs, operators, URL, etc.

These are the tabs from where we can drag the modules to design the pipe. Basically a pipe starts with a source or multiple sources. Then we need to create some filters as per our requirements using operators, date, location, etc., and then finally need to add an output to get the desired filtered information.

So to start with lets drag a source from the source sub tab, there are different options available such as Fetch CSV, Fetch data, Fetch feed, etc. Let's fetch from feeds as it's a very good source of information. Drag the Fetch Feed sub tab to the center of the application. When we drag anything to the center it will generate an output box for us, where it will ask us to add the feed URL. Add any feed URL in my case I am using http://feeads.bbci.co.uk/news/rss.xml?edition=int.

For the demo purpose I'll show only single source example but we can also add multiple sources for one pipe. Now it's very important to create a proper filter, which will give us the proper output. Now drag filter sub tab from Operators tab. By default we will see "block," "all," "contains" keywords there and some blank spaces to fill. Change that to "Permit," keep the "all" as it is and add item description in first blank space following with "contains" following with US. So our filter will provide us data which contains only keyword "US" in its item description.

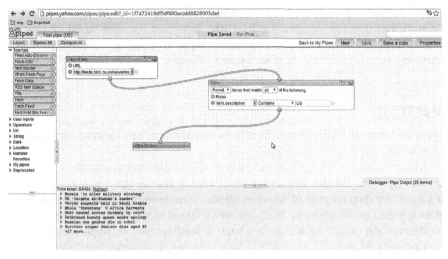

**FIGURE 6.22**

Creating a Yahoo Pipe.

Now connect all the pipe points from sources box (Fetch Feed) to Filters box and from Filter box to Pipe Output box. First save the pipes and then run the pipes to get the output in a new tab.

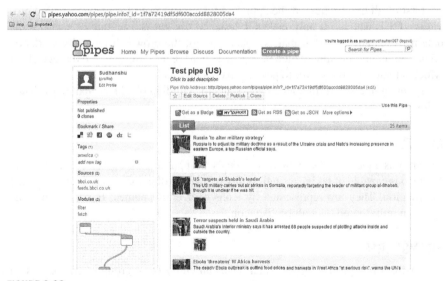

**FIGURE 6.23**

Yahoo Pipe result.

We can use it in many other scenarios like collecting images of a specific person from flicker, filtering information by URL, date- and location-based and many others. Explore this to create as customized pipes as possible. This tool provides freedom to create pipes way beyond our imagination.

## MALTEGO

There are many OSINT tools available in the market, but one tool stands out because of its unique capabilities, Maltego.

Maltego is an OSINT application which provides a platform to not only extract data but also represent that data in a format which is easy to understand as well as analyze. It's a one stop shop for most of the recon requirements during a pentest, what adds to its already great functionalities is the feature which allows users to create custom add-ons for the platform (which we will discuss later) depending upon the requirement.

Currently Maltego is available in two versions: commercial and community. Commercial version is paid and we need a license key for it. The community version however is free and we only need to register at the site of Pateva (creator of Maltego) at this page: https://www.paterva.com/web6/community/maltego/index.php. Though community version has some limitations in comparison to commercial version, like limited amount of data extraction, no user support, etc., still it is good enough to feel the power of this great tool. During this chapter we will be using the community version for the demo purpose.

Let's see how this tool works and what we can utilize it for.

First of all unlike most of the application software used for recon, Maltego provides a GUI, which not only makes it easier to use but is a feature in itself, as the data representation is what makes it stand out of the crowd. It basically works on client–server architecture, which means that what we as a user get is a Maltego client which interacts with a server to perform its operations.

Before going any further let's understand the building blocks of Maltego as listed below.

### ENTITY

An entity is a piece of data which is taken as an input to extract further information. Maltego is capable of taking a single entity or a group of entities as an input to extract information. They are represented by icons over entity names. E.g. domain name xyz.com represented by a globe-like icon

### TRANSFORM

A transform is a piece of code which takes an entity (or a group of entities) as an input and extracts data in the form of entity (or entities) based upon the relationship. E.g. DomainToDNSNameSchema: this transform will try to test various name schemas against a domain (entity).

## MACHINE

A machine is basically a set of transforms linked programmatically. A machine is very useful in cases where the starting data (in form of an entity) and the desired output data are not directly linked through a single transform but can be reached through a series of transforms in a custom fashion. E.g. Footprint L1: a transform which takes a domain as an input and generates various types of information related to the organization such as e-mails, Autonomous System AS number, etc.

First of all as mentioned above, we need to create an account for the community version. Once we have an account we need to download it from https://www.pater va.com/web6/products/download3.php. The installation of the application is pretty straightforward and the only requirement is Java. Once the installation is complete we simply need to open the application and login using the credentials created during the registration process.

Now as the installation and login processes are complete, let's move on to the interface of Maltego and understand how it works. Once we are logged into the application it will provide us with some options to start with; we will be starting with a blank graph so that we can understand the application from scratch. Now Maltego will present a blank page with different options on top bar and a palette bar on the left. This is the final interface we will be working on.

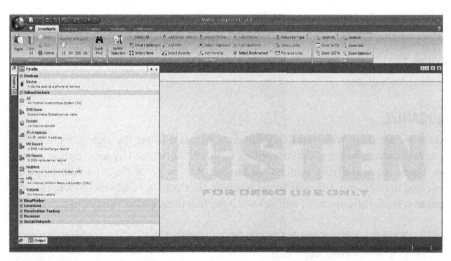

**FIGURE 6.24**

Maltego interface.

On the top left corner of the interface is the Maltego logo, clicking on which will list down the options to create a new graph, save the graph, import/export configurations/entities, etc. The top bar in the interface presents five options, let's discuss them in detail:

## INVESTIGATE

This is the first option in the top bar which provides basic functions such as cut, copy, paste, search, link/entity selection, as well as addition. One important option provided is Select by Type, this options comes in handy when there is a huge amount of data present in the graph after running a different set of transforms or machines and we are seeking a specific data type.

## MANAGE

The Manage option basically deals with entity and transform management with some other minor functions such as notes and different panel arrangements. Under the Entities tab we get the options to create new entities, manage existing ones, and their import/export; similarly the Transforms tab presents the options to discover new transforms, manage existing ones, and create new local transforms (we will discuss creating local transforms in later chapter.

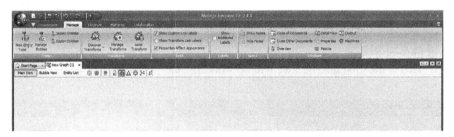

**FIGURE 6.25**

Maltego Manage tab.

## ORGANIZE

Once we are done with extracting the data, we need to set the arrangement of the graph to make a better understanding of it, this is where the Organize option comes in. Using the underlying options we can set the layout of the complete graph or selected entities into different forms, such as Hierarchical, Circular, Block, etc. We can also set the alignment of entities using the functions under "Align Selection" tab.

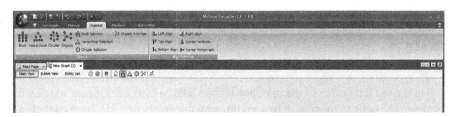

**FIGURE 6.26**

Maltego Organize tab.

## MACHINES

As described before machines are an integral part of the application. Machines tab provides the options to run a machine, stop all machines at once, create new machines (which we will discuss in later chapter) and to manage existing ones.

## COLLABORATION

This tab is used to utilize the feature introduced in late version of Maltego which allows different users to work as a team. Using the underlying options users can share their graphs with other users in real time as well as communicate through the chat feature. This feature can be very helpful in Red Team environments.

The palette bar on the left is used to list all the different types of entities present in Maltego. The listed entities are categorized according to their domain. Currently Maltego provides 20+ entities by default.

Now as we are familiar with the interface we can move on to the working of Maltego.

First of all to start with Maltego we need a base entity. To bring an entity into the graph we simply need to drag and drop the entity type we need to start with, from the palette bar on the left. Once we have the entity in the graph, we can either double click on the name of the entity to change its value to the value of our desire or double click on the entity icon which pops up the details window where we can change data, create note about that entity, attach an image, etc. One thing that we need to keep in mind before going any further is to provide the entity value correctly depending upon the entity type e.g. don't provide a URL for an entity type "domain."

Once we have set the value of an entity we need to right click on that entity and check the transforms listed for that specific entity type. Under the "Run Transform" tab we can see the "All Transforms" tab at the top, which will list all the transforms available for the specific entity type; below that tab we can see different tabs which contains the same transforms classified under different categories. The last tab is again "All Transforms," but use this one carefully as it will execute all the listed transforms at once. This will take up a lot of time and resources and might result into a huge amount of data that we don't desire.

Now let's take up the example of a domain and run some transforms. To do this simply drag and drop the domain entity under infrastructure from the palette bar to the graph screen. Now double click on the label of the entity and change it to let's say google.com. Now right click on it and go to "All Transforms" and select the "To DNS Name - NS (name server)." This transforms will find the name server records of a domain. Once we select the transform we can see that results start to populate on the graph screen. The progress bar at the bottom of the interface shows if the transform is complete or is still running. Now we can see that Maltego has found some name server (NS) records for the domain. We can further select all the listed NS records and run a single transform on them. To do this simply, select the region containing all the records and right click to select a transform. Let's run the transform "To Netblock [Blocks delegated to this NS]," this transform will check if the NS record have any (reverse) DNS netblocks delegated to them. In the graph window itself we can see at the top that there are some options to try like Bubble View, which shows the graph as a social network diagram with the entity size depending upon the number of inbound and outbound edges; the Entity List as the name suggests lists down all the entities in the graph and some others like freeze view, change layout to Block, Hierarchical, Circular, etc.

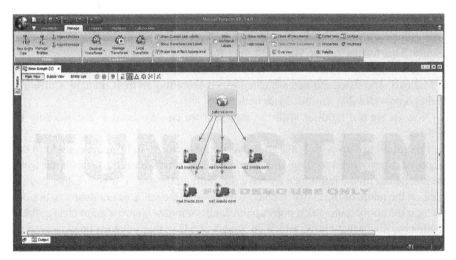

**FIGURE 6.27**

Maltego Transform result (Domain to DNS Name - NS (name server)).

Similar to running a transform on an entity we can also run a machine. Let's stick to our example and take a domain entity with value google.com. Now we simply need to right click on the entity, go to "Run Machines" tab and select a machine. For this example let's simply run the machine "Footprint L1." This machine will perform a basic footprint of the domain provided. Once this machine is executed completely we can see that it displays a graph with different entities such as name servers, IP addresses, websites, AS number, etc. Let's move forward and see some specific scenarios for data extraction.

## DOMAIN TO WEBSITE IP ADDRESSES

Simply take a domain entity. Run the transform "To Website DNS [using Search Engine]." It queries a search engine for websites and returns the response as website entities. Now select all the website entities we got after running the transform and run the transform "To IP Address [DNS]." This will simply run a DNS query and get us the IP addresses for the websites. This sequence of transforms can help us to get a fair understanding of the IP range owned by the organization (owning the domain). We can also see which websites have multiple IP addresses allocated to them. Simply changing the layout of the graph, to say circular, can be helpful in getting a better understanding of this particular infrastructure. Information like this is crucial for an in-depth pentest and can play a game changing role.

E.g.: Domain = google.com

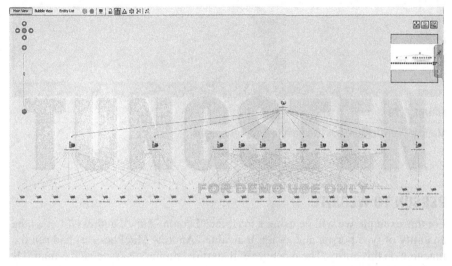

**FIGURE 6.28**

Maltego Transform result (Domain to Website IP).

## DOMAIN TO E-MAIL ADDRESS

There is a set of transforms for extracting e-mail address directly from a domain, but for this example we will be following a different approach using metadata. Let's again take a domain entity and run all the transforms in the set "Files and Documents from Domain." As the name itself says, it will look for files listed in search engine for the domain. Once we get a bunch of files, we can select them and run the transform "Parse meta information." It will extract the metadata from the listed files. Now let's run all the transforms in the set "Email addresses from person" on the entities of type entity and provide the appropriate domain (domain we are looking for in the e-mail address) and a blank for additional terms. We can see the result from this final transform and compare it with the result of running the transform set for e-mail extraction running directly on the domain and see how the results are different.

E.g.: Domain = paterva.com

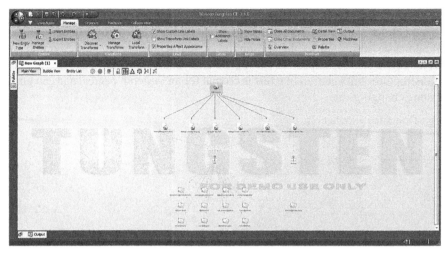

**FIGURE 6.29**

Maltego Transform result (Domain to Email address).

## PERSON TO WEBSITE

For this example we will be using a machine "Person - Email address." Let's take an entity of type person and assign it a value "Andrew MacPherson" and run the machine on this entity. The machine will start to enumerate associated e-mail IDs using different transforms. Once it has completed running one set of transforms it will provide us the option to move forward with selected entities, enumerated till now. From the above example we know "andrew@punks.co.za" is a valid e-mail address so we will go ahead with this specific entity only. What we get as an end result is websites where this specific e-mail address occurs, by running the transform "To Website [using Search Engine]" (as a part of the machine).

The examples shown clearly demonstrate the power of this sophisticated tool. Running a series of transforms or a machine can enumerate a lot of data which can be very helpful during a pentest or a threat-modeling exercise. Extracting a specific type of data from another data type can be done in different ways (using different series of transforms). The best way to achieve what we want is to run a series of transforms, eliminate the data we don't need, then parallely run another sequence of transforms to verify the data we have got. This exercise not only helps to verify the credibility of the data we have got but sometimes also produce unique revelation.

Maltego even allows to save the graph we have generated into a single file in "mtgx" format for later usage or sharing. We can even import and export entities as well as configuration. This feature allows us to carry our custom environment with us and use it even on different machines.

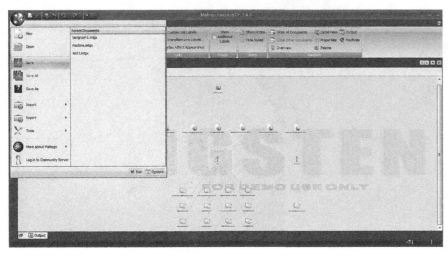

**FIGURE 6.30**

Saving Maltego results.

Apart from the prebuilt transforms Maltego allows us to create our own transforms. This feature allows us to customize the tool to extract data from various other sources that we find useful for specific purpose, for example an API which allows to get the company name from its phone number.

For custom transforms we have got two options:

Local transforms: These transforms are stored locally in the machine on which the client is running. These type of transforms are very useful when we don't need/want others to run the transform or execute a task locally. They are simple to create and deploy. Major drawback is that if we need to run it on multiple machines we need install them separately on each one of them, and same is the case for updates.
TDS transforms: TDS stands for transform distribution server. It is a web application which allows the distribution as well as management of transforms. The client simply probes the TDS, which calls the transform scripts and presents the data back to the client. Compared to local transforms they are easy to setup and update.

We will learn how to create transforms in later chapter.

So these are some of the tools which can play a very crucial part in an information-gathering exercise. Some of these are more focused on information security and some are generic. The main takeaway here is that there are a bunch of tools out there which can help us to extract relevant information within minutes and if used in a proper and efficient manner these tools can play a game changing role in our data extraction process. There is something for everyone, it's just a matter of knowing how data is interconnected and hence how one tiny bit of information may lead to the box of Pandora. In the next chapter we will move forward and learn about the exciting world of metadata. We will deal with topics like what is metadata, how is it useful, how to extract it, etc. We will also deal with topics like how it can be used against us and how to prevent that from happening.

# Metadata

## 7

## INFORMATION IN THIS CHAPTER

- Metadata
- Impact
- Metadata Extraction
- Data Leakage Protection (DLP)

## INTRODUCTION

In the last few chapters we have learned extensively about how to find information online. We learned about different platforms, different techniques to better utilize these platforms, and also tools which can automate the process of data extraction. In this chapter we will deal with a special kind of data, which is quite interesting but usually gets ignored, the metadata.

Earlier metadata was a term mostly talked about in the field of information science domain only, but with the recent news circulation stating that National Security Agency has been snooping metadata related to phone records of its citizens, it is becoming a household name. Though still many people don't understand exactly what metadata is and how it can be used against them, let alone how to safeguard themselves from an information security point of view.

The very basic definition of metadata is that it's "data about data," but sometimes it's a bit confusing. So for the understanding purpose we can say that metadata is something which describes the content somehow but is not the part of the content itself. For example in a video file the length of the video can be its metadata as it describes how long the video will play, but it is not the part of the video itself. Similarly for an image file, the make of the camera used to click that picture can be its metadata or the date when the picture is taken as it tells us something related to the picture, but is not actually the content of the picture. We all have encountered this kind of data related to different files at some point of time. Metadata can be anything, the name of the creator of the content, time of creation, reason of creation, copyright information, etc.

The creation of metadata actually started long ago in libraries, when people had information in the form of scrolls but no way to categorize them and find them quickly when needed. Today in the digital age we still use metadata to categorize files, search them, interconnect them, and much more. Most of the files that reside in our computer systems have some kind of metadata. It is also one of the key components needed for the creation of the semantic web.

Metadata is very helpful in managing and organizing files and hence is used extensively nowadays. Most of the times we don't even make a distinction between the actual content and its metadata. It is usually added to the file by the underlying software which is used to create the file. For a picture it can be the camera that was used to click it, for a doc file it can be the operating system used, for an audio file it can be the recording device. Usually it is harmless as it does not reveal any data which can be sensitive from information security perspective, or is it? We will see soon in the following portion of this chapter.

There are huge number of places where metadata is used, from the files in our systems to the websites on the internet. In this chapter we will mainly focus on extracting metadata from places which are critical from information security view point.

## METADATA EXTRACTION TOOLS

Let's discuss about some of the tool which can be used for the metadata extraction.

### JEFFREY'S EXIF VIEWER

Exif (exchangeable image file format) is basically a standard used by devices which handle images and audio files, such as video recorder, smartphone cameras etc., It contains data like the image resolution, the camera used, color type, compression etc. Most of the smartphones today contain a camera, a GPS (global positioning system) device, and internet connectivity. In many of the smartphones when we click a picture it automatically tracks our geolocation using the GPS device and embeds that information into the picture just clicked. We being active on social networks share these pictures with the whole world.

Jeffrey's Exif Viewer is an online application (http://regex.info/exif.cgi) which allows us to see this Exif data present in any image file. We can simply upload it from our machine or provide the URL for the file. If an image contains the geolocations, it will be presented in the form of coordinates. Exif Viewer is based on the Exif Tool by Phil Harvey, which can be downloaded from http://www.sno.phy.queensu.ca/~phil/exiftool/. It not only allows to read the Exif data but also write it to the files. Exif Tool supports a huge list of different formats like XMP, GFIF, ID3, etc., which are also listed on the page.

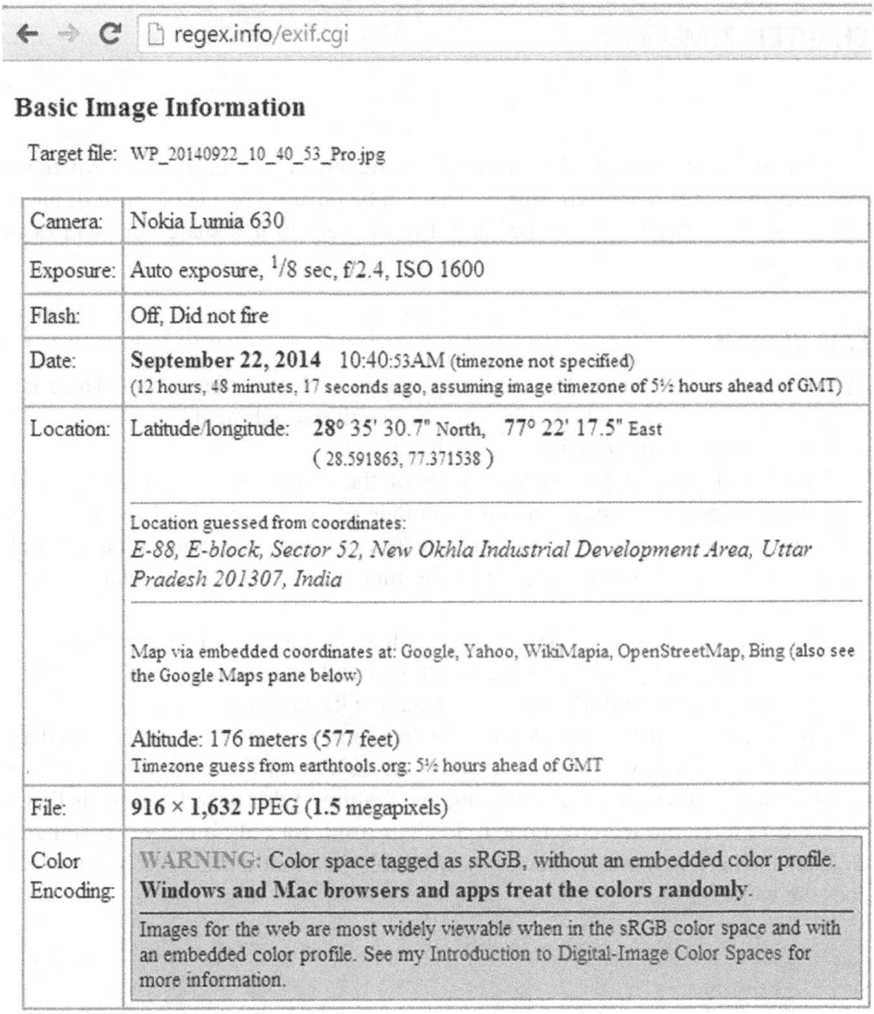
regex.info/exif.cgi
Basic Image Information
Target file: WP_20140922_10_40_53_Pro.jpg
Camera: Nokia Lumia 630
Exposure: Auto exposure, 1/8 sec, f/2.4, ISO 1600
Flash: Off, Did not fire
Date: September 22, 2014 10:40:53AM (timezone not specified)
(12 hours, 48 minutes, 17 seconds ago, assuming image timezone of 5½ hours ahead of GMT)
Location: Latitude/longitude: 28° 35' 30.7" North, 77° 22' 17.5" East
( 28.591863, 77.371538 )
Location guessed from coordinates:
E-88, E-block, Sector 52, New Okhla Industrial Development Area, Uttar Pradesh 201307, India
Map via embedded coordinates at: Google, Yahoo, WikiMapia, OpenStreetMap, Bing (also see the Google Maps pane below)
Altitude: 176 meters (577 feet)
Timezone guess from earthtools.org: 5½ hours ahead of GMT
File: 916 × 1,632 JPEG (1.5 megapixels)
Color Encoding: WARNING: Color space tagged as sRGB, without an embedded color profile. Windows and Mac browsers and apps treat the colors randomly.
Images for the web are most widely viewable when in the sRGB color space and with an embedded color profile. See my Introduction to Digital-Image Color Spaces for more information.

**FIGURE 7.1**

Jeffrey's Exif Viewer.

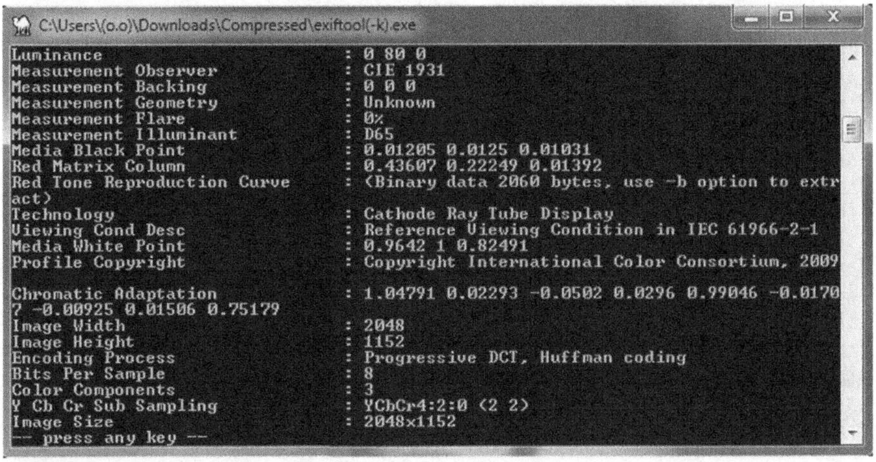
C:\Users\(o.o)\Downloads\Compressed\exiftool(-k).exe
Luminance : 0 80 0
Measurement Observer : CIE 1931
Measurement Backing : 0 0 0
Measurement Geometry : Unknown
Measurement Flare : 0%
Measurement Illuminant : D65
Media Black Point : 0.01205 0.0125 0.01031
Red Matrix Column : 0.43607 0.22249 0.01392
Red Tone Reproduction Curve : (Binary data 2060 bytes, use -b option to extract)
Technology : Cathode Ray Tube Display
Viewing Cond Desc : Reference Viewing Condition in IEC 61966-2-1
Media White Point : 0.9642 1 0.82491
Profile Copyright : Copyright International Color Consortium, 2009
Chromatic Adaptation : 1.04791 0.02293 -0.0502 0.0296 0.99046 -0.01707 -0.00925 0.01506 0.75179
Image Width : 2048
Image Height : 1152
Encoding Process : Progressive DCT, Huffman coding
Bits Per Sample : 8
Color Components : 3
Y Cb Cr Sub Sampling : YCbCr4:2:0 (2 2)
Image Size : 2048x1152
-- press any key --

**FIGURE 7.2**

Exif Tool interface.

Using the geolocation in the images we share, anyone can easily track where we were exactly at the time of clicking it. This can be misused by people with ill intentions or stalkers. So we should be careful if we want to just share our pictures or locations too.

## EXIF SEARCH

We just discussed about the Exif and its power to geolocate the content. There is a dedicated search engine which allows us to search through geotagged images, it's called Exif Search (http://www.exif-search.com/).

This search engine provides data about the images and pictures from all over the internet. It contains a huge number of searchable Exif images from different mobile devices. Being totally different from traditional image search engines, which tend to just provide us the image as a result, Exif also provides the metadata.

When we search in Exif Search, it searches the image and its information in its own database and provides us the result. Currently it has more than 100 million images with metadata and it's constantly updating its database.

This search engine provides user the freedom to search an image based on location, date, and device type. It also allows us to sort the data based on these date location or device type. Another unique feature of this search engine is that it allows us to force the search engine to fetch us result for only images that contains GPS data. There is a small check box available just below the search bar which does the work for us.

**FIGURE 7.3**

Exif-search.com interface.

It also supports a huge number of devices. The list can be found http://www.exif-search.com/devices.php, some of them are Canon, Nikon, Apple and Fujifilm etc.

**FIGURE 7.4**

Exif-search.com sample search result.

## ivMeta

Similar to images, video files can also contain GPS coordinates in their metadata. ivMeta is a tool created by Robin Wood (http://digi.ninja/projects/ivmeta.php) which allows us to extract data such as software version, date, GPS coordinates, model number from iPhone videos. iPhone is one of the most popular smartphone available and has a huge fan base. With more than a million users, their activity to show the uniqueness of the iPhone standard makes them more vulnerable to metadata extraction. No doubt on the camera quality of the devices and the unique apps to make the pictures and videos look more trendy, iPhone users upload lots of such data content everyday in different social networking sites. Though there is an option available on the device to deactivate geotagging, the by-default setting and the use of GPS allows to create metadata about any image or video taken. In this case this tool comes handy to gather all the such information from iPhone videos. This tool is a Python script, so running it requires Python installed (2.7+). It can be very helpful in forensic examination of iPhone videos.

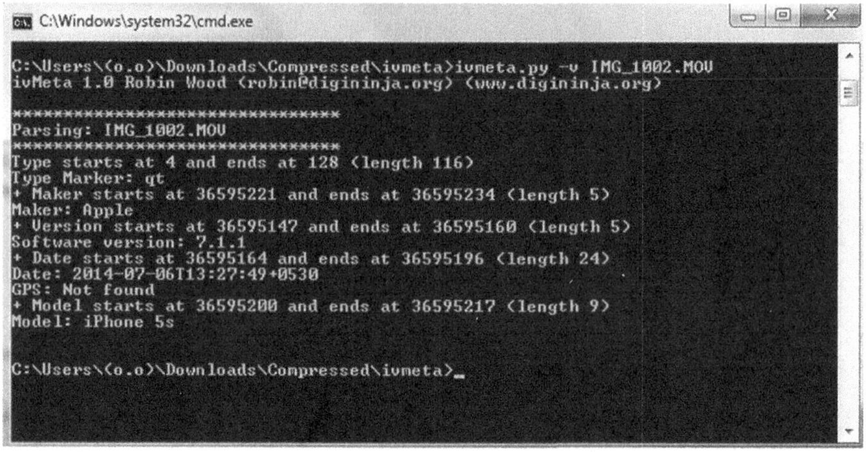

**FIGURE 7.5**

ivMeta in action.

## HACHOIR-METADATA

Hachoir-metadata is based on hachoir Python library. This is one of the hachoir project used for metadata extraction. As its base library is Python, this tool is also a Python tool which can be used to extract metadata from not only image, audio and video but also archives. This supports more than 30 different formats to extract metadata that is also a unique feature on its own.

Some other features that make this tool stand apart from other similar tools are that it supports invalid and truncated files and its ability to avoid duplicate data. Apart from these, it also provides freedom to the users to filter the metadata by setting priorities to the values. This tool is generally available for different Linux versions and can be downloaded from the URL: https://bitbucket.org/haypo/hachoir/wiki/Install.

Some of the popular formats supported by this tool are bzip2, gzip, tar, zip, etc., in archive files; bmp, ico, gif, jpeg, png etc., in images. There is also a popular format supported by this tool, PhotoShop Document (PSD). As Adobe PhotoShop is very popular software for image editing in the multimedia industry, supporting this format is definitely a plus for the users who want to extract metadata. In audio it supports mpeg and real audio, where real audio is the default audio format used in Apple devices. In video it supports flv format. This is again definitely a plus because it is widely used in YouTube, one of the largest video sharing site and it also supports mov, the Apple QuickTime movie support that can be well used in Apple device video forensics. The other popular supported formats are exe, which expands the metadata extraction to another level by allowing all the Microsoft portable executables. It also supports torrent files, which are the easy solution to most of the data sharing requirements. So torrent metadata extraction is definitely one of its unique feature. Who even would thought of extracting metadata from ttf or true type fonts, but yes this tool also supports ttf format. There are many other formats it supports. we can get the details from the following url: https://bitbucket.org/haypo/hachoir/wiki/hachoir-metadata.

This hachoir-metadata is basically a command-line tool, and by default it's very verbose. That means running the same without any switches, it provides lots of information.

# hachoir-metadata xyz.png

We can also run this tool with multiple and different file formats at a time to get the desired result.

# hachoir-metadata xyz.png abc.mp3 ppp.flv

When we need only mime details we can use

# hachoir-metadata --mime xyz.png abc.mp3 ppp.flv

When we need little more information other than mime we can use -type switch

# hachoir-metadata --type xyz.png abc.mp3 ppp.flv

for exploring the tool for other options we can use

# hachoir-metadata --help

## FOCA

On a daily basis we work with a huge number of files such as DOC, PPT, PDF, etc. Sometimes we create them, sometimes edit, and sometimes just read through. Apart from the data we type into these files, metadata is also added to them. To a normal user this data might seem harmless, but actually it can reveal a lot of sensitive information about the system used to create it.

Most of the organizations today have online presence in the form of websites and social profiles. Apart from the web pages, organizations also use different files to share information with general public and these files may contain this metadata. In Chapter 5 we discussed how we can utilize search engines to find the files that are listed on a websites (E.g. In Google: "site:xyzorg.com filetype:pdf"). So once we have listed all these files, we simply need to download them and use a tool which can extract metadata from them.

FOCA is a tool which does this complete process for us. Though FOCA means seal in Spanish, the tool stands for 'Fingerprinting Organizations with Collected Archives'. It can be downloaded from https://www.elevenpaths.com/labstools/foca/index.html. After downloading the zip file, simply extract it and execute the application file inside the bin folder.

To use FOCA we simply need to create a new project, provide it with a name and the domain to scan. Once this is saved as a project file, FOCA allows us to choose the search engines and the file extensions that we need to search for. After that we can simply start by clicking on the button "Search All." Once we click on this button FOCA will start a search for the ticked file types on the mentioned domain, using different search engines. Once this search is complete it will display the list of all the documents found, their type, URL, size, etc.

Now we have the list of the documents present on the domain. Next thing we need to do is download the file(s) by right clicking on any one and choosing the option Download/Download All. Once the download is complete the file(s) is/are ready for inspection. So now we need to right click on the file(s) and click on the Extract Metadata option. Once this is complete we can see that under the option Metadata at the right-hand side bar FOCA has listed all the information extracted from the document(s).

This information might contain the username of the system used to create the file, the exact version of the software application used to create it, system path, and much more which can be very helpful for an attacker. Though metadata extraction is not the only functionality provided by FOCA, we can also use to it to identify vulnerabilities, perform network analysis, backups search and much more information gathering, the most prevalent functionality.

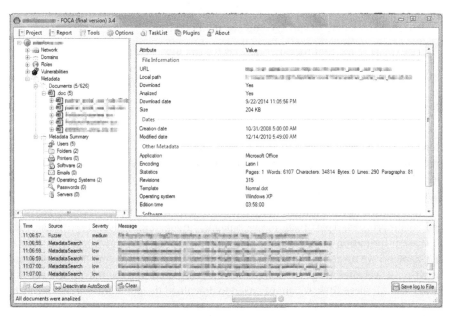

**FIGURE 7.6**

FOCA result.

## METAGOOFIL

Similar to FOCA, Metagoofil is yet another tool to extract metadata from documents which are available online. Metagoofil is basically a Python based command line too.

The tool can be downloaded from https://code.google.com/p/metagoofil/downloads/list. Using this tool is fairly easy; there are a few simple switches that can be used to perform the task.

The list of the options is as following:

Metagoofil options
-d: domain to search
-t: filetype to download (pdf, doc, xls, ppt, odp, ods, docx, xlsx, pptx)
-l: limit of results to search (default 200)
-h: work with documents in directory (use "yes" for local analysis)
-n: limit of files to download
-o: working directory (location to save downloaded files)
-f: output file

We can provide the queries such as the one mentioned below to run a scan on target domain and get the result in the form of a HTML file, which can be easily read in any browser:

metagoofil -d example.com -t doc,pdf -l 100 -n 7 -o /root/Desktop/meta -f /root/Desktop/meta/result.html

**FIGURE 7.7**

Metagoofil interface.

Similar to FOCA, Metagoofil also performs search for documents using search engine and downloads them locally to perform metadata extraction using various

Python libraries. Once the extraction process is complete the results are simply displayed in the console. As mentioned above these results can also be saved as a HTML file for future reference using the -f switch.

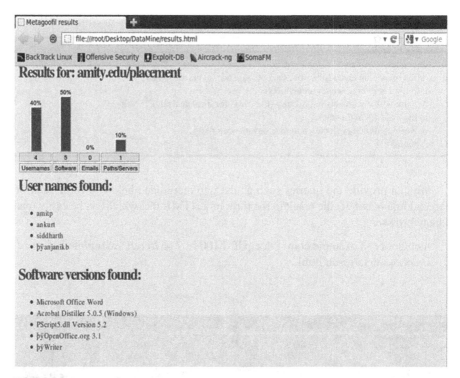

**FIGURE 7.8**

Metagoofil result.

---

Similarly there are other tools which can be used for metadata extraction from various different files, some of these are listed below:
- MediaInfo—audio and video files (http://mediaarea.net/en/MediaInfo)
- Gspot—video files (http://gspot.headbands.com/)
- VideoInspector—video files (http://www.kcsoftwares.com/?vtb#help)
- SWF Investigator—SWF/flash files http://labs.adobe.com/downloads/swfinvestigator.html)
- Audacity—audio files (http://audacity.sourceforge.net/)

---

## IMPACT

The information collected using metadata extraction can be handy and used to craft many different attacks on the victim by stalkers, people with wrong motivations and even government organizations. The real-life scenario can be worse than what we can expect. As information collected from the above process provide victims' device details, area of interest, and sometime geolocation also, the information such as username, software used, operating system etc. is also very critical for an attacker. This information can be used against the victim using simple methods such as social engineering or to exploit any device-specific vulnerability that harms the victim personally in real life as it also provides exact location where the victim generally spends time.

And all those things are possible just because of some data that mostly nobody cares or some might not even realize its existence, even if they do, then also most of them are not aware where this data can lead to and how it makes their real as well as virtual life vulnerable.

As we have seen that how much critical information is revealed through the documents and files uploaded without us realizing it and what are possibilities of turning this data as critical information against a victim and use them as an attack vector. Now there must be a way to stop this, and it's called as data leakage protection (DLP).

## SEARCH DIGGITY

In the last chapter we learned a about advanced search features of this interesting tool. For a quick review Search Diggity is tool by Bishop Fox which has a huge set of options and a large database of queries for various search engines which allow us to gather compromising information related to our target. But in this chapter we are most interested on one of the specific tab of this tool and that is DLP.

There are wide numbers of options to choose from side bar of DLP tab in search Diggity. Some of the options are credit card, bank account number, passwords, sensitive files, etc.

This DLP tab generally is a dependent one. We cannot directly use this. First we have to run some search queries on a domain of our interest then select and download all the files those are found after completion of that search query than provide the path in DLP tab to check whether any sensitive data is exposed to public for that particular domain or not. To do so we can choose either Google tab or Bing tab which means either Google search engine or Bing and in that have to select "DLPDiggity initial" option to start searching for backup, config files, financial details, database details, logs and other files such as text or word document, and many more from that domain of our interest. Though there is a option to only choose some specific suboptions from "DLPDiggity initial" option, from demo prospective let's search for all the suboptions. After completion of the query we will get all the available files in tabular format in a result section of this tool. Select all the files that we got and download the same. It will save all the files in default path and in a folder called DiggityDownloads.

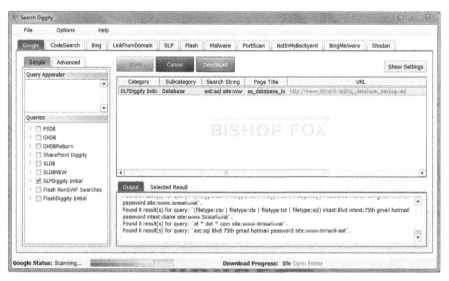

**FIGURE 7.9**

DLPDiggity Initial scanning.

Now switch the tab to DLP. In the top we can see the default DiggityDownloads path will be present in scan result path. So just select one or more options available in DLP tab. For demo we will select quick Checks option and click on Search to get the result.

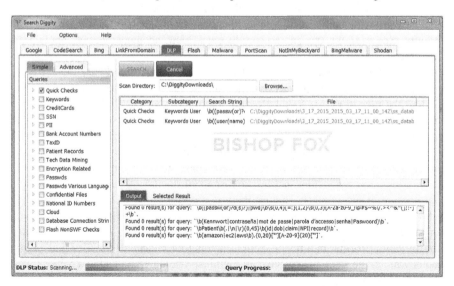

**FIGURE 7.10**

DLP Quick Checks.

The result sometimes might show scary results such as credit card numbers, bunch of passwords, etc. That is the power of this tool. But our main focus is not about discovery of sensitive files but DLP. So get all the details from the tool's final result. The result shows in an easy and understandable manner, in what page or document what data is available. So that the domain owner can remove or encrypt the same to avoid data loss.

## METADATA REMOVAL/DLP TOOLS

As DLP is an important method to avoid data loss. The above example is quite generic to get us some idea about how DLP works. Now as per our topic we are more interested on metadata removal. So there are also different tools available to remove metadata or we can also say them as metadata DLP tools. Some of those are mentioned below.

### METASHIELD PROTECTOR

MetaShield Protector is a solution which helps to prevent data loss through office documents published on the website. It is installed and integrated at web server level of the website. The only limitation of this is that, it is only available for IIS web server. Other than that It supports a wide range of office documents. Some of the popular file types are ppt, doc, xls, pptx, docx, xlsx, jpeg, pdf, etc. On a request for any of these document types, it cleans it on the fly and then delivers it. MetaShield Protector can be found at https://www.elevenpaths.com/services/html_en/metashield.html. The tool is available at https://www.elevenpaths.com/labstools/emetrules/index.html.

### MAT

MAT or metadata anonymization toolkit is a graphical user interface tool which also helps to remove metadata from different types of files. It is developed in Python and utilizes hachoir library for the purpose. As earlier we discussed a bit about hachoir Python library and one of its project in hachoir-metadata portion, this is another project based on the same library. The details regarding the same can be found here https://mat.boum.org/.

The best thing about MAT is that it is open source and supports a wide range of file extensions such as png, jpeg, docx, pptx, xlsx, pdf, tar, mp3, torrent etc.

### MyDLP

It is a product by Comodo which also provides wide range of security product and services. MyDLP is an one stop solution for different potential data leak areas. In an organization not only documents but also emails, USB devices, and other similar devices are potential source of data leak. And in this case it allows an organization to easily deploy and configure this solution to monitor, inspect, and prevent all the outgoing critical data. The details of MyDLP can be found here. http://www.mydlp.com.

## OpenDLP

OpenDLP is an open source centrally managed data loss prevention tool released under the GPL. From a centralized web application it can identify sensitive data in different types of systems such as Windows and Unix as well as different types of databases such as MySQL and MSSQL. The project can be found here. https://code.google.com/p/opendlp/.

## DOC SCRUBBER

A freeware to scrub off hidden data from word documents (.doc). Some of its popular features are it allows to scrub multiple doc files at a time. Doc Scrubber can be downloaded from http://www.javacoolsoftware.com/dsdownload.html.

## REMOVING GEO-TAGS

As we discussed earlier that how geotags can be dangerous for a user in an attacker point of view, as it reveals exact location about a user, here some settings in Picasa can help us to remove these geotags. Picasa, the image organizing and editing application by Google can help to remove geotags from images. The link to the help and support page is http://support.google.com/picasa/bin/answer.py?hl=en&answer=70822.

We can also use Exif Tool discussed earlier to remove such data.

Though mainly metadata is used for the organization and linking of data it can also be critical during cyber investigations as well as pentest exercises. As discussed earlier, most of them are harmless but sometimes it can reveal some sensitive data. As many individuals as well as organizations are unaware of its existence, they don't pay much attention to it. The solutions discussed above must be tried to make it easier to mitigate any risk arising from such information.

# Online Anonymity

# 8

## INFORMATION IN THIS CHAPTER

- Anonymity
- Online anonymity
- Proxy
- Virtual private network
- Anonymous network

## ANONYMITY

Anonymity, the basic definition of this term is "being without a name." Simply understood someone is anonymous if his/her identity is not known. Psychologically speaking, being anonymous may be perceived as a reduction in the accountability for the actions performed by the person. Anonymity is also associated with privacy as sometimes it is desirable not to have a direct link with a specific entity, though sometimes it is required by law to present an identity before and/or during an action is performed. In the physical world we have different forms of identification, such as Social Security Number (SSN), driving license, passport etc., which are widely acceptable.

## ONLINE ANONYMITY

In the virtual space we do not have any concrete form of ID verification system. We usually use pseudonyms to make a statement. These pseudonyms are usually are not related to our actual identity and hence provide a sense of anonymity. But the anonymity present on the internet is not complete. Online we may not be identified by our name, SSN, or passport number, but we do reveal our external IP address. This IP address can be used to track back to the computer used. Also on some platforms like social network websites we create a virtual identification as they relate to our relationships in physical world. Some websites have also started to ask users to present some form of identification or information which can be related directly to a person, in the name of security. So basically we are not completely anonymous in the cyber space. Usually we do reveal some information which might be used to trace the machine and/or the person.

## WHY DO WE NEED TO BE ANONYMOUS

There are many reasons to be anonymous. Different people have different reasons for that some may want to be anonymous due to their work demands such as those who are into cyber investigation, journalism, and some might want to be anonymous because of their concern of their privacy etc. There are times when we want to protest on something good but doing that openly might create some problems so we want to be anonymous. As we say in physical life, people who do bad things like a criminal after doing a crime want to go underground the same way in virtual life or in the internet. Cyber-criminals and hackers wanted to be anonymous.

Being anonymous is just a choice. It does not always need a reason. It's just a state to be in virtual life. It's a virtual lifestyle and while some want to enjoy the same and others might be forced to be. Similar to the physical world we do have a need or desire to stay anonymous on the internet. It may just be that we are concerned about our privacy, we want to make a statement but won't do it with our true identity, we need to report something to someone without getting directly involved, communicate sensitive information, or simply want to be a stranger to strangers (anonymous forums, chat rooms etc.). Apart from the mentioned reason, we may simply want to bypass a restriction put up by the authority (e.g., college Wi-Fi) to visit certain portions of the web. The motivation behind it can be anything, but a requirement is surely there.

People might get confused of being anonymous that means just hiding the identity. It can also about hiding what you are doing and what you want to be. A simple example can help us to understand this. Let's say we wanted to buy something and we visited an e-commerce site to buy it. We liked the product but due to some reasons we did not buy that. But as we were surfing normally, we may found advertisement of the same product all over the internet. It's just a marketing policy for the e-commerce giants by tracking a user's cookies to understand his/her likes and dislikes and post the advertisement according to that.

Some might like this and some might not. It's not just about somebody is monitoring on what are you doing in the internet but also about flooding adds about similar things to lure us to buy. To avoid such scenarios also people might prefer to browse anonymous. For a quick revision, there are private browsing options available in most of the browsers and there are specific anonymous browsers available that do this work for us.

In this chapter we will deal with different ways to stay anonymous online. 100% anonymity cannot be guaranteed on the internet, still with the tools and techniques that will be mentioned in this chapter, we can hide our identity up to a reasonable level.

## WAYS TO BE ANONYMOUS

There are many ways to be anonymous and there are many aspects of being anonymous. Some might focus on the personal details to be hidden such as in social networking sites by using aliases, generic information or fake information, generic e-mail id, and other details. Some might want to be anonymous while browsing so that nobody can track what resource they are looking into. Some might want to hide their virtual identity address such as IP address etc.

There are different ways to achieve the above conditions. But the major and popular solutions available are either proxy or virtual private network (VPN). Though there are other methods to be anonymous but still these two are widely used and we will focus on these majorly in this chapter.

## PROXY

Proxy is a word generally used for doing stuffs on behalf of someone or something. Similarly in technology, proxy can be treated as an intermediate solution that forwards the request sent by the source to the destination and collects response from the destination and sends it to the source again.

It is one of the widely used solutions used for anonymity. The only reason to use proxy is to hide the IP address. There are different proxy solutions available such as web proxy, proxy software etc. Basically all the solutions work on a basic principle to redirect traffic to the destination from some other IP address. The process might differ from solution to solution but the bottom line remains the same.

Though proxy can be used for many other purposes just apart from being anonymous, we will focus only the anonymity as the chapter demands the same.

Before focusing into the very deep technical aspects of proxy let's look into some work around to be anonymous. As in earlier chapters we learned how to use search engines efficiently and power searching. Now it's time to look into how a search engine can be used as a proxy to provide anonymity.

As Google is a popular search engine it can also be used as proxy with its feature called as Google Translate. Google provides its services in many countries apart from the English speaking ones and it also supports multiple languages. The Google Translate option allows a user to read web content in any other language a user wants. For a generic example, a non-English content can be translated to English and vice versa. So this feature allows a user to use Google server to forward the request and collect the response on his/her behalf, which is the basic fundamental of a proxy.

Now for testing the same, first we will look into our own IP address using a site called http://whatismyipaddress.com/ and later use Google translator to check the same site. The work of this site is to tell the IP address used to send the request to the site. If for the normal browsing and browsing through Google Translate the IP address differs, it means we achieved anonymity using Google Translate.

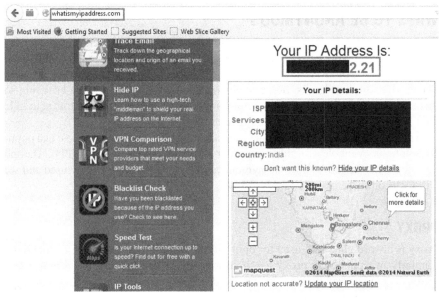

**FIGURE 8.1**

whatismyipaddress.com.

Now visit translate.google.com. Select any language in source and any other language in destination to translate this web page as shown in below image.

**FIGURE 8.2**

Google Translate.

Now click on Translate to check the whether the IP address matches with the IP address disclosed in above image for direct browsing or not.

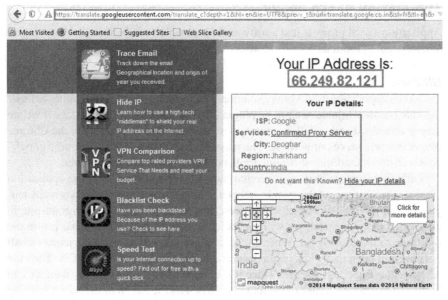

**FIGURE 8.3**

Page opened inside Google Translate.

We can see from the above image that the IP addresses of direct browsing and of browsing using Google Translate are different. Thus it is proved that we can use Google Translate as proxy server to serve our purpose. In many cases it will work fine. Though it's just a work around it's very simple and effective. In terms of full anonymity it might not be helpful but still we may use this method where we need a quick anonymity solution.

## PROXY IN TERMS OF ANONYMITY

As we came across one example where we can use search engine feature as proxy. But the point to be considered is anonymity. There are different levels of anonymity based on different proxy solutions. Some proxies just hide our details but keeping the same in their logs, and sometime some proxies can be detected as proxy by the server and some might not. That's not the best solution if you want full anonymity. There are some solutions available which cannot be detected as proxy by the destination server and also delete all the user details the time user ends the session. Those are the best solutions for full anonymity. It all depends on our requirement to choose what service or what kind of proxy we want to use because fully anonymous proxy might charge the user some amount to use the solution.

## TYPES OF PROXY SOLUTIONS

Now there are different types of proxy solutions available some are based on anonymity and also based on its type such as whether application-based or web-based. So let's start exploring some of the available options in application-based proxy.

## APPLICATION-BASED PROXY

Application-based proxy is just a software or tool which can be installed in our operating system to use it as proxy solution.

### Ultrasurf

It is an application-based proxy solution which can be found at http://ultrasurf.us/.

This is now available as Chrome plugin also. Though this is in beta stage if we are lazy to download and install it in our system and then use, we might use the Chrome plugin that will serve our purpose. The plugin can be found at https://chrome.google.com/webstore/detail/ultrasurf/mjnbclmflcpookeapghfhapeffmpodij?hl=en.

Let's first explore its plugin version then we will go deep in to the application version. The best part of this plugin is that it's simple to use and it supports many languages such as English, French, Portuguese, and Roman etc. Once the chrome plugin gets added in the browser, we will see its icon on the right top addon bar just in the right side of the address bar. When we have to use that just click on the icon, a small window will open then click on the switch available in that window to ON. Then the addon will connect to its server. Once it is connected to the server only then we can browse anonymous. In case of we forgot to switch on the addon or the addon is trying to connect to the server or the addon is unable to connect the server then all the thing we browse will be as normal browsing. So put it in mind to switch on and let it connect to the server before browsing or else all the anonymity process will go to vain.

The application version can be downloaded quite easily from the link http://ultrasurf.us/download/u.zip.

It's just a compressed file, extracting the file we can get the application. The best part of this process is that we need not to install the application. We can simply double click on that and that will configure the required settings in our system and let us browse anonymously. The default settings allow to open the Internet Explorer by double clicking the application. We can change the application settings using its options tab.

Though the tool was earlier developed for anticensorship protest in china, now it's used widely as a proxy solution. It not only just helps user to hide the details but also allows a user to communicate using encryption mechanism. This can be used in many different areas but the most general use can be while browsing using free Wi-Fi hotspot. Because in that case, there is a chance of rogue access point collecting all the information about us.

The main advantage of using this tool is connection speed. Generally when we use any kind of proxy solution as it redirects the traffic through that server the connection speed reduces drastically and user can feel that; but in this case it's very fast as compared to other proxy solutions. Apart from that we can see the connection speed in the tool itself and it provides three connection options, user can switch to any one of them any moment to avoid speed drop. To distinguish between normal browsing and browsing using Ultrasurf, this tool provides a cool lock symbol in the right corner of the browser to make sure that user is browsing anonymously.

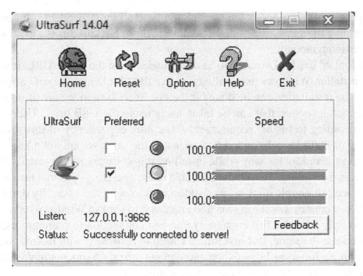

**FIGURE 8.4**

UltraSurf interface.

A small drawback about this tool is that this tool supports only Windows. And another drawback is that the IP-checking solutions detect it as proxy server. But as we discussed earlier, this can be used in different other conditions based on our requirements and it's easy to use. Just download, run, and browse anonymously.

### JonDo

JonDo previously known as JAP is a proxy tool available at https://anonymous-proxy-servers.net/en/jondo.html.

It is available for wide range of operating systems such as Windows, Mac, for different flavors of Linux, and also for Android mobile. The full-fledged documentation of how to install and use makes it very essential as a proxy solution. Different proxy solutions come up with different types. It also provides one of its type for Firefox anonymous browsing known as JonDoFox.

Before exploring JonDo let's first look into the Firefox anonymous browsing solution i.e., JonDoFox. It can be found at https://anonymous-proxy-servers.net/en/jondofox.html.

As JonDo, JonDoFox is also available for different operating systems such as Windows, Mac, and Linux. User can download as per his/her operating system from the above URL. The documentation of how to install is also available just next to the download link. But let's download and install while we discuss more about the same.

Windows users will get JonDoFox.paf after downloading. After installing the same it will create a Firefox profile in name of JonDoFox. If user selects the same, the profile consists of many Firefox addons such as cookie manager, adblocker, etc., which will come to act. But to use it for full anonymity user needs to install certain dependent softwares such as Tor etc.

It's good to use JonDoFox but user has to install all the dependent softwares once after installing the same. Some might not love to do so but still this is a great solution to browse anonymously.

Like JonDoFox, JonDo can also be downloaded from the above URL. It will give you the installer. Windows user will get an exe file "JonDoSetuup.paf" after downloading. The installation can be done for the operating system we are using and also for the portable version that can be taken away using the USB drive. User needs to choose according to his/her requirements. The only dependency of this software is JAVA. But as earlier we discussed how to install the same we are not going to touch that here again and by the way while installing this software it also installs JAVA, if it won't find the compatible version available in the operating system. Once JonDo is installed, we can double click on its desktop icon to open the same. By default after installation it creates a desktop icon and enables it to start in Windows startup.

JonDo only provides full anonymity and fast connection to premium users. But we still can use the same. But first time we need to activate it with its free code. Test coupon can be found at https://shop.anonymous-proxy-servers.net/bin/testcoupon? lang=en but we need to provide our e-mail address to get it.

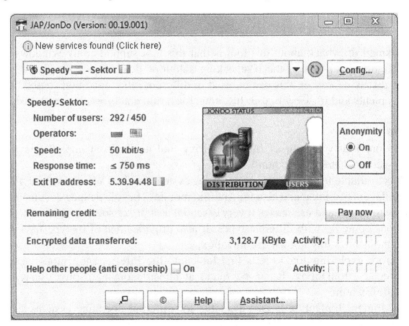

**FIGURE 8.5**

JonDo interface.

After providing the e-mail address we will get a link in our e-mail id. Visit the link to get the free code. Once we get the free code, put it in the software to complete the installation process.

**FIGURE 8.6**

JonDO test.

If you want to use JonDo you need to install JonDoFox also; as we already covered JonDoFox, we can assume that it is already present in the system. When both the softwares are installed in a system, if we want to use just JonDoFox then we can simply use that by opening Firefox with JonDoFox profile. To test whether we are browsing anonymously, we just need to check the IP address using whatismyipaddress.com.

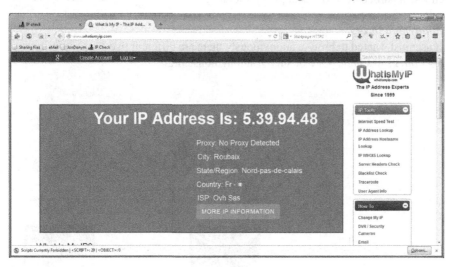

**FIGURE 8.7**

JonDo running.

If we want to use JonDo then we need to configure the same in the browser. In case of Mozilla go to Tools → Options → Advanced → Network → Connection Settings → select Manual proxy configuration and use 127.0.0.1:4001 as the default port used by JonDo is 4001.

Once it's done, open Firefox with JonDoFox profile, we will see a JonDo icon in the top left corner. Click there and it will open a tab. Select "Test Anonymity" to check the IP address.

JonDo provides us with a set of proxy servers that can be changed quite easily from the dropdown box. So it is also known as JonDo the IP changer proxy solution.

As we already discussed about how to use JonDo and its paid solution for full anonymity. This tool has variety of features but the major one is its compatibility with different operating systems. This makes JonDo unique in proxy solutions.

## WEB-BASED PROXY

Web-based proxy solutions are the simple and efficient way of getting anonymity. The best thing is that we can use them anywhere. No setup needed. No dependencies. Best to use when using a shared computer or in public computers for browsing and sometime when using open Wi-Fi connections. The simple user interface makes it very popular to use. Just open the browser and open the proxy, and you are good to go.

There are many web-based proxy solutions. Some are just used for browsing and other may have more features like sending e-mails anonymously or reading news feeds. It's just depending upon our requirement and the anonymity level provided to choose a particular web-based proxy solution.

### anonymouse.org

If user just wanted to browse anonymously there are different live anonymous browsing options available. One of such is anonymouse.org.

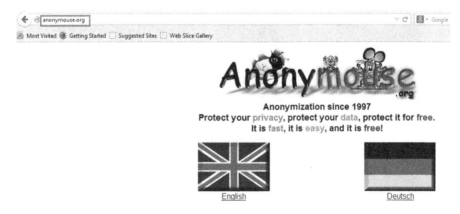

**FIGURE 8.8**

Anonymouse homepage.

It is a free site which provides its users to browse anonymously with two different languages, English and Dutch. Visit the site, choose the language in which you want to browse then type the site name in the Surf anonymously field and click on Surf anonymously to browse the site.

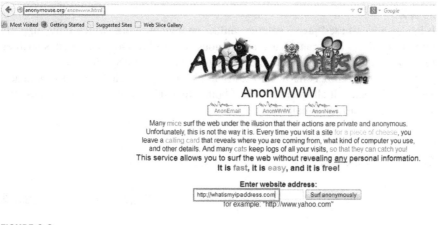

**FIGURE 8.9**

Enter website address: Anonymouse.

The only disadvantage of this site is it only supports http protocol not https. But apart from that it provides better anonymity as we can see from the below image, it's not detected as proxy server. And the IP address is also from a different location.

**FIGURE 8.10**

Anonymouse test.

As we discussed the pros and cons of this service still it's very good proxy solution for anonymous browsing and there are some other features like send e-mail and check e-news available. But as we are more focused on hiding our details on browsing, right now we will conclude this here itself.

### Zend2

It is also a web-based proxy solution unlike anonymouse.org, which only supports http protocol. So user cannot use anonymouse.org to browse popular sites such as Facebook and YouTube as these sites force to use https connection.

https://www.zend2.com/ has no restrictions on https-enabled sites or technically SSL-enabled sites. It allows user to surf both http and https sites. So user can use the same to check his/her e-mails also.

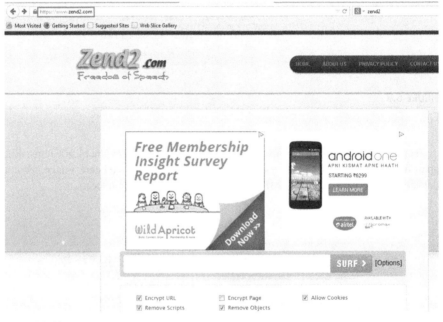

**FIGURE 8.11**

Zend2 homepage.

Apart from that for two popular web resources such as Facebook and YouTube, it also provides special GUI to use. For Facebook: https://zend2.com/facebook-proxy/. For YouTube: https://zend2.com/youtube-proxy/. The YouTube proxy page contains instructions how to unblock YouTube if it's blocked in your school, college, office, or by the ISP while the Facebook proxy page contains general information how this web proxy works.

Though we can use all these three user interfaces to visit any site, as the bottom line of all, we want it to work as intermediary between user and the server. Apart from just surfing it also provides user some options to choose such as:

- Encrypt URL
- Encrypt Page
- Allow Cookies
- Remove Scripts
- Remove Objects
- User can check whatever he/she wants as per the requirement.

### FilterBypass.me
Similar to zend2 it also allows users to surf anonymously with some more options such as Encrypt URL, Allow cookie etc. The only drawback of the proxy solution is that it fails to resolve some of the e-mail-providing sites but apart from that its user interface contains some popular site links that can be visited directly using this such as Facebook, YouTube, DailyMotion, Twitter etc.

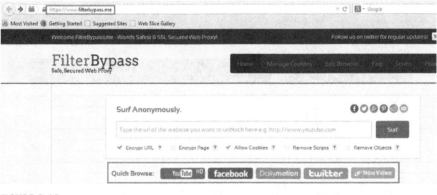

**FIGURE 8.12**

FilterBypass homepage.

### Boomproxy.com
It is quite similar to anonymouse.org as it only supports http sites to browse but the only extra feature available here is that it contains options such as Encrypt URL, Remove Objects etc.

Some more proxy solutions:
- http://www.internetcloak.com/
- http://www.crownproxy.com/
- http://www.hidesurf.us/
- http://www.webevade.com/
- http://www.proxyemails.com/
- http://www.proxytopsite.us/

*Continued*

**—cont'd**

- http://www.proxysites.net/
- http://www.everyproxy.com/
- http://www.ip-hide.com/
- http://www.greatproxies.com/
- http://proxy.org/
- http://www.proxyservers.info/
- http://thehiddenguide.com

## HOW TO SET UP PROXY MANUALLY IN A BROWSER

There are many sites that provide proxy addresses in terms of IP and port but it's not that easy to get the genuine site. It's because the list might not be updated for sometime and in the meanwhile the proxy server might not be working anymore. Though we can get still a good amount of sites, a good one is http://proxylist.hidemyass.com/.

The major benefit that user will get using this is it provides user a updated list with latest proxy IP addresses and port number along with that the expected speed, anonymity level, and country name where that IP belongs.

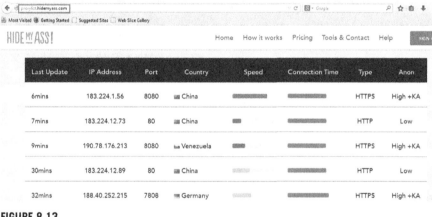

| Last Update | IP Address | Port | Country | Speed | Connection Time | Type | Anon |
|---|---|---|---|---|---|---|---|
| 6mins | 183.224.1.56 | 8080 | China | | | HTTPS | High +KA |
| 7mins | 183.224.12.73 | 80 | China | | | HTTP | Low |
| 9mins | 190.78.176.213 | 8080 | Venezuela | | | HTTPS | High +KA |
| 30mins | 183.224.12.89 | 80 | China | | | HTTP | Low |
| 32mins | 188.40.252.215 | 7808 | Germany | | | HTTPS | High +KA |

**FIGURE 8.13**

HideMyAss proxy list.

Apart from that it also allows user to filter the requirements based on country, protocol supported, connection speed, anonymity level, and many more. So this is one of the finest sources in terms of using the proxy IP and port.

Though most of the case the IP and port will work but before using it, it's better to test whether the IP is alive or not.

So simply choose an IP address and associated port based upon the requirement such as based on speed, protocol, anonymity level, and country. Try to choose the latest one which is updated in the list recently. Then open command prompt in case of Windows and terminal in case of Mac and Linux. In case of

Windows, type "ipconfig" and the chosen IP address to check whether the IP is alive or not and in case of Mac and Linux the command is "ifconfig" with the chosen IP address.

Once we see the IP is alive, configure the same in browser. In case of Mozilla Firefox we did it earlier but let's revise the process.

Go to Tools → Options → Advanced → Network → Connection Settings → select Manual proxy configuration and use the chosen IP address and port number in respective fields.

In case of Chrome go to Settings → Show advanced settings → under Network tab click on Change proxy settings → click on LAN settings → check Use a proxy server for LAN then use the chosen IP address and port number in respective fields.

This is how proxy can be configured manually.

## VIRTUAL PRIVATE NETWORK

Simply stated it allows us to create a private network across a public network. Most of the organizations use an internal private network for their day to day operations, but sometimes people need to access this network from outside, where there is no direct connection to this network. This is when VPN comes into play; it allows users to access the private network from the internet securely.

VPN basically creates a virtual point to point connection between two machines. The VPN server is installed at one point and the user accesses it using a VPN client. VPN uses different mechanisms and technologies, such as authentication, authorization, encryption etc., to achieve this and keep the connection secure. There are various use cases and implementations of VPN and how it operates, but in this chapter our main focus is on its use to stay anonymous.

VPN-based anonymity works similar to the proxy-based anonymity, the only major difference is the connection to the server is made using a VPN which adds an extra layer of security, though we should not forget that here we are trusting the VPN service provider to be secure.

There are various such services available online and most of them are paid. Here we are listing two services which provide a free version, but they do come with their own restrictions such as limited time, speed etc.

### cyberghostvpn.com

CyberGhost is one of the best VPN-based anonymity providers. It provides both free and paid service. To use the service we need to download the client from the website http://www.cyberghostvpn.com. Once the client is downloaded we can simply install it and start the application.

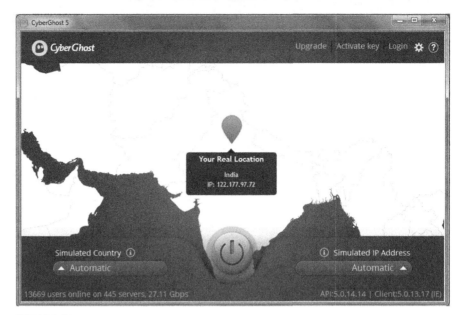

**FIGURE 8.14**

CyberGhost interface.

The interface of the application is pretty simple. We can make the configuration changes and also upgrade to a paid account from it. On the home screen the application will display our current IP address with the location in map. To start using the service we simply need to click on the power button icon. Once we click on it CyberGhost will initiate a connection to one of the servers and will display a new location once the connection is made.

**FIGURE 8.15**

CyberGhost in action.

In the settings menu of CyberGhost we can also make changes such as Privacy Control and Proxy which further allows us to hide our identity while connected online.

### Hideman

Similar to CyberGhost, Hideman is another application which allows us to conceal our identity. The client for the application can be downloaded from https://www.hi deman.net/. Like CyberGhost, in Hideman also we don't need to make much configuration changes before using it, simply install the application and we are good to go. Once the application is installed, it provides a small graphical interface, which displays our IP and location. Below that there is an option where we can choose the country of connection, which is set to "Automatically" by default. Once this is done we simply need to click on the Connect button and the connection will be initiated. Currently Hideman provides free usage for 5 hours a week.

**FIGURE 8.16**

Hideman interface.

Apart from the mentioned services there are also many other ways to utilize VPN for anonymity. Some service providers provide VPN credentials which can be configured into any VPN client and can be used, others provide their own client as well as the credentials.

## ANONYMOUS NETWORKS

An anonymous network is a bit different in the way it operates. In this the traffic is routed through a number of different users who have created a network of their own inside the internet. Usually the users of the network are the participants and they help each other to relay the traffic. The network is built in a way that the source and the destination never communicate directly to each other, but the communication is done in multiple hops through the participating nodes and hence anonymity is achieved.

### The Onion Router

Tor stands for "The Onion Router." It is one of most popular and widely used methods to stay anonymous online. It is basically a software and an open network which allows its users to access the web anonymously. It started as a US navy research project and now is run by a nonprofit organization. The user simply needs to download and install the Tor application and start it. The application starts a local SOCKS proxy which then connects to the Tor network.

Tor uses layered encryption over bidirectional tunnels. What this means is that once the user is connected to the Tor network, he/she sends out the data packet with three layers of encryption (default configuration) to the entry node of the Tor network. Now this node removes the uppermost layer of the encryption as it has the key for that only but the data packet is still encrypted, so this node knows the sender but not the data. Now the data packet moves to second node which similarly removes the current uppermost encryption layer as it has the key for that only, but this node does not know the data as well as the original sender. The packet further moves to the next node of the Tor network, which removes the last encryption layer using the key which works for that layer only. Now this last node, also called the exit node has the data packet in its raw form (no encryption) so it knows what the data is, but it is not aware who the actual sender of the data is. This raw data packet is then further sent to public internet to the desired receiver, without revealing the original sender. As already stated this is bidirectional so the sender can also receive the response in similar fashion. One thing that needs to be mentioned here is that the nodes of the Tor network between which the data packet hops are choosen randomly, once the user wants to access another site, the Tor client will choose another random path between the nodes in the Tor network. This complete process is termed as onion routing.

So Tor is pretty good at what it does and we just learned how it works. But as we need to use different nodes (relay points) and there is also cryptographic functions involved, which makes it pretty slow. Apart from this we are also trusting the exit nodes with the data (they can see the raw packet).

Tor is available in many different forms, as a browser bundle, as a complete OS package etc. The browser bundle is the recommended one as it is completely preconfigured, very easy to use, and comes with additional settings which helps to keep the user safe and anonymous. The browser bundle is basically a portable Firefox browser with Tor configured. It also contains some additional addons such as HTTPS Everywhere, NoScript. Tor browser can be downloaded from https://www.torproj ect.org/download/download-easy.html.en. Once it is downloaded we simply need to execute the exe file and it will extract it in the mentioned directory. After this has been completed we simply need to execute the "Start Tor Browser" application, which is a portable Firefox browser with Tor configured. It will present us with the choice to connect directly to the Tor network or configure it before going forward. General users simply need to click on the Connect button, in case the network we are connected to requires proxy or other advanced settings, we can click on the Config-ure button to make these settings first. Once we are good to go, we can connect to the network and the Tor browser will open up as soon as the connection is made. Apart from this other packages which allow us to run bridge, relay, and exit nodes can be downloaded from https://www.torproject.org/download/download.html.en.

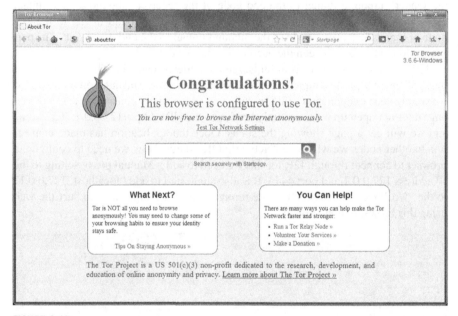

**FIGURE 8.17**

Tor Browser.

Apart from allowing users to surf the web anonymously, Tor also provides another interesting service, about which we will learn in next chapter.

### Invisible Internet Project

I2P stands for Invisible Internet Project. Similar to Tor, I2P is also an anonymous network. Like any network there are multiple nodes in this network, which are used to pass the data packets. As opposed to Tor, I2P is more focused on internal services.

What this means is that Tor's main focus is to allow people to access the clear web (explained in next chapter, for now let's just say the part of web accessible without any restrictions) anonymously, whereas I2P focuses more on allowing people to use the web anonymously but in the context of the applications/features available in it, such as e-mail services, IRCs, Torrents, etc.

Unlike Tor, I2P uses layered encryption over unidirectional connections. Each I2P client application has I2P routers, which builds inbound and outbound tunnels. So each client has different incoming and outgoing points. When a client needs to send a message to another client, it sends it to its outbound tunnel with specifying the target. Depending upon the configuration this message will hop through a number of clients and eventually will reach the inbound node of the target and then the target. To receive the message in reverse order the same process will be followed but the nodes involved will be different as the inbound and outbound tunnels are separated from each other for each node. Any content that is passed over I2P is passed using layered encryption. The layers are garlic encryption, which is between the starting node of the sender outbound tunnel to the end node of the receiver inbound tunnel; tunnel encryption, which is between the starting node of the outbound tunnel to the end node of it and the starting node of the inbound tunnel to the end node of it; transport encryption, which is between the each node and its next hop.

I2P can be downloaded from https://geti2p.net/en/download. The installation of the application is pretty simple and straightforward. Once the installation is completed we simply need to open "Start I2P," it will open up the router console. In case the web page does not open up we can simply browse to the URL http://127.0.0.1:7657/home and we will get a page showing the status. Once the application has made connection to other nodes we will get a "Network: OK" status. Now we need to configure a browser to connect through I2P, for this we need to add a Manual proxy setting to the IP address 127.0.0.1 and port 4444. It is also suggested to add "localhost, 127.0.0.1" to the "No Proxy for" box. Once the proxy settings are done we can surf the web using this browser anonymously.

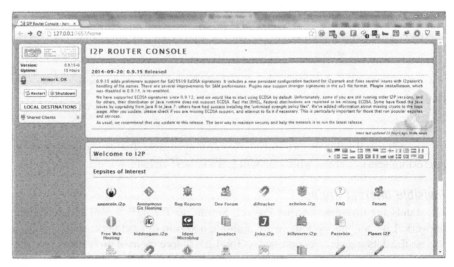

**FIGURE 8.18**

Invisible Internet Project. Network: OK.

Similar to Tor, I2P also provides other services which we will discuss in next chapter.

Browser addons like FoxyProxy (http://getfoxyproxy.org/) can be used to make the proxy changes easily in the browser.

The individual techniques we have discussed in this chapter can also be chained together to make it more difficult to get traced. For example, we can connect to a VPN-based proxy server, further configure it to connect to another proxy server in another country, and then use a web-based proxy to access a website. In this case the web server will get the IP address of the web-based proxy server used to connect to it, and it will get the IP address of the proxy server we connected through the VPN; we can also increase the length of this chain by connecting one proxy to another. There is also a technique called proxy bouncing or hopping in which the user keeps on jumping from one proxy to another using an automated tool or custom script with a list of proxies, in this way the user keeps on changing his/her identity after a short period of time and hence makes it very difficult to be traced. This can also be implemented at server side.

---

Some scenarios in which people still get caught after using these tools/techniques:
- The user of a specific network (e.g., University) is known, and it is also known that which one of them was connected to a specific proxy server/Tor around a specific time.
- Rogue entry and exit points. In an anonymous network like Tor if the entry point and the exit point can correlate the data packet based on its size or some other signature, they can identify who the real sender might be.
- DNS leak. Sometimes even when we are connected to an anonymous network our machines might send out the DNS requests to the default DNS server instead of the DNS server of the anonymous network. It means that the default DNS server now may have a log that this specific address resolution was requested by this IP at this point of time.
- Leaked personal information. Sometimes people who are anonymous to the internet leak some information which can be used to directly link it to them such as phone numbers, same forum handles which is used by them when they are not anonymous, unique ids etc.
- Metadata. As discussed in the last chapter there is so much hidden data in the files that we use and it might also be used to track down a person.
- Hacking. There can be security holes in any IT product which can be abused to identify the real identity of the people using it.
- Basic correlation. As shown in the first scenario, correlation can be used to pinpoint someone based on various factors such as timing, location, restricted usage, and other factors.

---

Some of the suggestions/warnings for using Tor are listed at https://www.tor project.org/download/download-easy.html.en#warning. These should be followed with every tool/technique discussed above, where applicable. Also use a separate browser for anonymous usage only and do not install addons/plugins which are not necessary.

So we learned about various ways to stay anonymous online, but as stated earlier 100% anonymity cannot be guaranteed online. What we can do is to try to leak as little information about ourselves as possible. The methods discussed in this chapter are some of the most popular and effective ways to do this. Online anonymity can have various use cases such as privacy, protest, accessing what is restricted by the authority, business related, law enforcement, journalism but it can also be used by people to perform illegal activities like malicious hacking, illegal online trade, money laundering, selling drugs etc. We need to be very careful what we do with the knowledge we acquire.

Moving on, in the next chapter we will extend the topic and deal with the darknet and other associated terms. We will learn more about the tools like Tor and I2P and see what parts of the internet we haven't touched yet, how to access/create it, and what we can expect to find there.

# Deepweb: Exploring the Darkest Corners of the Internet

## INFORMATION IN THIS CHAPTER

- Clearweb
- Darkweb
- Deepweb
- Why to use it
- Why not to use it
- Deepweb: Tor, I2P, Freenet

## INTRODUCTION

In this chapter we will start from where we left in the previous one. We learned about various tools and techniques related to how to stay anonymous online and also discussed about some of the ways in which people still get caught. Here we will deal with the terms like darknet and deepweb and understand some of the fundamental differences.

One of the most efficient ways discussed to stay anonymous was connecting to the anonymous networks like Tor and I2P. We will take this topic further and see what else we can do with it and how it relates to the topic of interest for this chapter.

Until recent past terms like darknet and deepweb were not too popular. They were mostly a topic of interest for people who want to stay anonymous and related to IT (especially information security). Recently there has been some news stories related to these topics, which have made people interested in them and understanding what they are, how they operate, what to expect there, etc. We will cover all those things here and see if there is anything of interest for us.

Before going any further with the technical details, let's understand the basic definitions of the terms we will be dealing with in this chapter

## CLEARWEB

We have already discussed in previous chapters about how the search engines work. Simply stated, it works by following the links on a web page and then on the next one and so on. So the part of the web which can be accessed by a search engine is called clearweb. What this means is that anything that we get as a result of a search engine query is part of the clearweb.

## DARKWEB

As a user we have clicked on different links on a webpage, but that is not the only way we interact with a website. Sometimes we have to submit some text to get the desired page (e.g., search box), sometimes we have to authenticate before accessing a specific page (e.g., social network website login), sometimes there are things like CAPTCHA which need to be entered before moving further.

So apart from the web that is accessed by search engines there is still a huge amount of data that exists in pages not touched by web spiders/crawlers. This part of the web is known as darkweb or darknet.

## DEEPWEB

Now we have a clear separation of the web into two parts, clearweb and darkweb, based upon their accessibility to the search engine. Now we will move a little deeper.

The darkweb comprises of a huge part of the overall web. Inside this darkweb there exists another section which is called as deepweb. This deepweb is also not accessible to the search engines but it also cannot be accessed directly by standard browsers we daily use. This portion of the web is hidden deep inside the web and requires special applications and configurations to be accessed and hence is called deepweb.

Now we have a clear understanding of what is darkweb and deepweb. We are well aware of how to access the regular darkweb and do it on a regular basis. Pages like social media profile which require login, search result page in a website, pages generated dynamically are some of the examples. However if we need to access the deepweb, we need to make special arrangements. Before getting into those details let's understand a bit more about the deepweb.

As stated earlier deepweb is a part of darkweb. Now the question arises that how come it exists inside darkweb but is still not directly accessible. The answer is that because it exists in the form of a network inside the internet, which in itself is a huge network, which means is that darkweb is created as a part of the internet but to access this specific network we need to have the right tools so that a connection could be made to it. Once we have the means to connect to it we can access it.

In this fancy land of deepweb we can find all sorts of things like illegal drugs, weapons, art, and all sorts of black market things. On the other hand it is also used by people to speak freely, exchange ideas, etc.

## WHY TO USE IT?

If we are whistleblower, cyber investigator, cyber journalist, government intelligence agent, cyberspace researcher then this is the place for us. This will help us understand how the underground cyberspace works. It will give us ideas about the private days, targets, and attack pattern of cyber-crime, etc. It will help us predict the next attack pattern by understanding the underground community mind-set through the technology they use most frequently.

It also provides freedom of speech, so if you want to protest for a good cause this is the place for you. For investigation of a cyber-crime this can be a popular place. As most of the underground community works here there is a chance of getting ample amount of proof from this place. This can be also used to keep track of online activities of a person or group.

There are dedicated services for optimized use of deepweb such as secure file uploading facilities where activists or whistleblowers can anonymously upload documents. There are services related to people spreading a word that other should know, sharing what's happening all around them, etc. There are online forums to discuss technology, politics, and much more; so if we have these kind of specific requirements or similar then we can use deepweb.

## WHY NOT TO USE IT?

Apart from utilizing this space for ethical motives some people also use it to perform many illegal activities. There are many places in this area where we can find people selling drugs, fake ids, money laundering, hackers for hire, etc. Some websites even say that they provide assassins for hire. Apart from this it might also contain websites which provide many disturbing things. One must be very careful while accessing or downloading any content from such places at it might be illegal to access or have it on our computers.

## DARKNET SERVICES
### TOR

One of the most popular portion of the deepweb is the *.onion domains. In the last chapter we learned about Tor, how it works and also how to use to stay anonymous. The same Tor also allows us to create and access one of the largest portions of the deepweb. We are already aware about how to use Tor browser bundle to access the regular web, now that same tool can be used to access places which are not directly touched.

We simply need to download the Tor browser bundle, extract it, and run the Tor browser. Once the connection to the Tor network is made we are good to go. Apart from accessing the regular websites Tor allows to create and access *.onion websites. These websites if tried to access through a regular browser without Tor configured, will simply display a "The Webpage is not available" message, some kind of error or redirect message; whereas will open up like a regular website through the Tor browser or a browser configured to access the internet through Tor as a proxy.

Let's start exploring these Tor-based domains. One of the most common places to start with is "The Hidden Wiki." The address of this wiki is http://zqktlwi4fecvo6ri.onion/wiki/index.php/Main_Page. Notice that this URL does not contain a .com, .net, .org, or other familiar domain names, but is .onion. Firstly try to open this URL into a regular browser, does it open up? Now open this URL into our Tor browser. We will get a webpage which contains a wiki page with a huge list of other .onion domains divided category wise. The categories listed are financial services, anonymity and security, whistleblowing, P2P file sharing, etc. We can explore this wiki further and check out some of the interesting links listed in it.

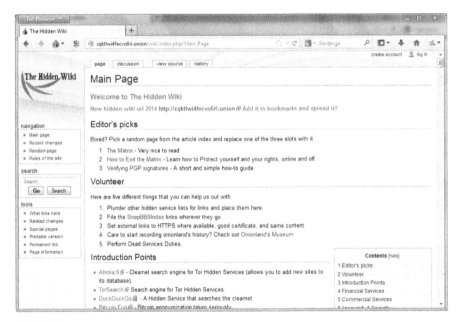

**FIGURE 9.1**

The Hidden Wiki.

Similarly there is another wiki, 'Tor Wiki' which lists a huge list of .onion domains. It also contains various categories in a neater way. This wiki makes it easier to explore the listed domains by marking them as verified, caution, or scam.

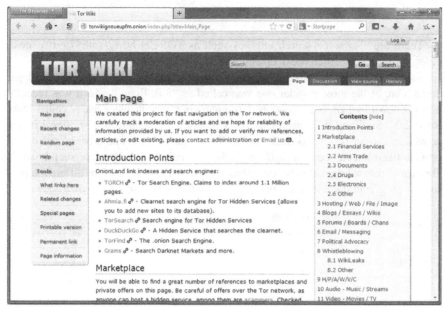

**FIGURE 9.2**

TOR Wiki.

The search engine DuckDuckGo that we discussed in a previous chapter, also has a .onion address, http://3g2upl4pq6kufc4m.onion/. Using this we can search the clearweb from a Tor domain.

**FIGURE 9.3**

DuckDuckGo Search Engine (.onion domain).

There are also some search engines such as TORCH http://xmh57jrzrnw6insl. onion/ available to search the deepweb, but they seldom work properly.

As we can see in the wikis list there are various market places which sell illegal drugs. One of the most popular one was called as "Silk Road'" which was recently brought down by FBI, but a new one has come up to take its place and is called "Silk Road 2.0." Similarly there are many other places which claim to have illegal items, as well as various forums, boards, internet relay chats (IRCs) and other places which provide like-minded people a platform to discuss and learn things. One such board is Torchan http://zw3crggtadila2sg.onion/imageboard/. There are various different topics such as programming, literature, privacy etc., on which people discuss their views.

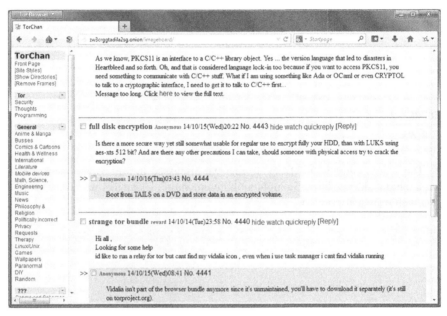

**FIGURE 9.4**

TorChan.

Till now we have seen how to access .onion domain websites, now let's see how to create these. To create a .onion site first we need to have a local web server. XAMPP is one such option which uses Apache as a server. Once the server is installed and configured to host a local website, we need to modify the "torrc" file. This file can be found at the location "Tor Browser\Data\Tor". Open this file in an editor and add the following lines to it:

HiddenServiceDir C:\Tor\Tor_Browser\hid
HiddenServicePort 80 127.0.0.1:80

The path in front of "HiddenServiceDir" is the path where Tor will create files to store information related to the hidden service we are creating. The part in front of

'HiddenServicePort' contains the port using which the Tor users will think they are using to connect to the service and the next portion is the localhost with the port at which the service is actually running locally.

Once this information has been added to the file simply save it and restart Tor. Once it starts, two files will be created in the above mentioned folder: hostname and private_key. The file hostname contains the name which can be used to access our webpage through Tor, under a .onion domain. The content of the file private_key must be kept secret so that no one else can impersonate our service.

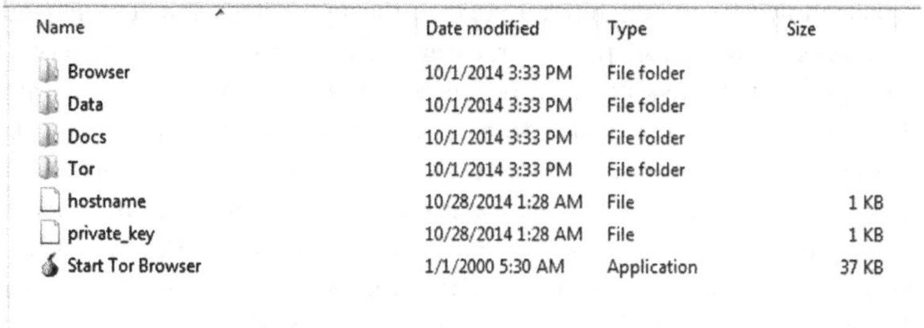

| Name | Date modified | Type | Size |
|---|---|---|---|
| Browser | 10/1/2014 3:33 PM | File folder | |
| Data | 10/1/2014 3:33 PM | File folder | |
| Docs | 10/1/2014 3:33 PM | File folder | |
| Tor | 10/1/2014 3:33 PM | File folder | |
| hostname | 10/28/2014 1:28 AM | File | 1 KB |
| private_key | 10/28/2014 1:28 AM | File | 1 KB |
| Start Tor Browser | 1/1/2000 5:30 AM | Application | 37 KB |

**FIGURE 9.5**

Files created.

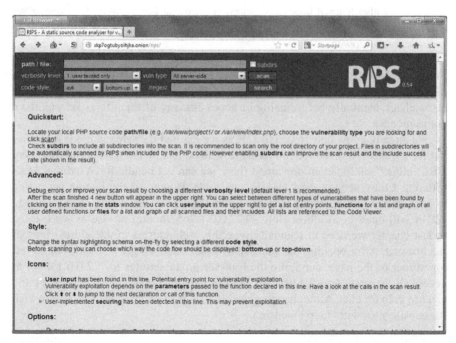

**FIGURE 9.6**

TOR hidden service.

We have seen how to create a Tor hidden service, but for it to be safe and anonymous we need to take various steps as followed:

- Configure the server to not leak any information (e.g., Server Banner, error messages).
- Do not run any service on that machine which might make it vulnerable to any attack, or might reveal the identity.
- Check the security of the web application hosted.

Tor also allows us to run hidden service through relays but it is not advised. Relays are nodes which take part in transferring the traffic of the tor network and act as routers for it. Relays are of different kinds: middle relays—which are starting and middle nodes in the packet transfer chain; exit relays—which are the final node in the chain and connect directly to the receiver; bridges—which are the relays that are not publicly listed as tor relays. Bridges are helpful when we are connecting to the internet through a monitored/managed network (e.g., college network) as it would make it difficult to identify if the user is connected to Tor using that network. These applications to run these services can be downloaded from the page https://www.torproject.org/download/download.html.en

## I2P

Like Tor we also learned how to be anonymous using I2P. Now in this chapter we will not focus on the anonymity part again but will focus on how I2P will help us to access/create deepweb.

Though we will find number of places where we will get lots of market places of hidden services related to I2P or can be accessible by I2P and in most places sites will claim the authenticity of the services provided, it's better to cross check manually before using or accessing any of them to avoid unknown consequences.

We already know how to install I2P, as we learned the same in the last chapter but for a quick reference we can easily download and install it from the following URL: https://geti2p.net/en/download (here we can get bundle for Windows, Mac, different Linux version, and also for android). Download the bundle according to your device and operating system and install. After installation once you open I2P, it will open in localhost (http://127.0.0.1:7657/home) or else as we learned in last chapter we need to manually type this web address in the address bars of the browser. After opening the same in browser once we get Network OK in left top corner of the page, configure the browser proxy settings to 127.0.0.1:4444 to access all the sites. And for IRC we can use localhost:6668 in our IRC client and can use #i2p for chat. After changing the browser proxy setting we will able to visit the eepsite sites with *.i2p extension.

**FIGURE 9.7**

I2P home.

Some of the sites are listed in the router homepage as shown in the figure.

E.g., Anonymous git hosting: http://git.repo.i2p/

Here though we need to provide some details to push the respiratory, the identity is provided by us will not link to our real IP address, in this way we can use git anonymously.

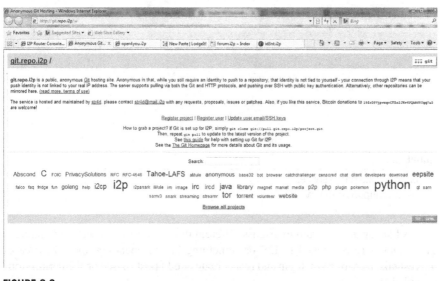

**FIGURE 9.8**

I2P git.

Free web hosting: http://open4you.i2p/

Here we can get details of how to use the free web hosting service. There are other details that can be found in the forum maintained in the following URL: http://open4you.i2p/index.php

If we want to host any kind of website in the deepweb, this can be helpful.

Pastebin: http://pastethis.i2p/

It is a website generally to save text online for a period of time for personal use. But popularly it is used as a source to provide credentials, latest cyber news, deface site details, cyber-attack target details, etc. Though in the normal pastebin we need to provide certain details to paste something, here no details required.

We can also find all the paste details from the following URL: http://pastethis.i2p/all/.

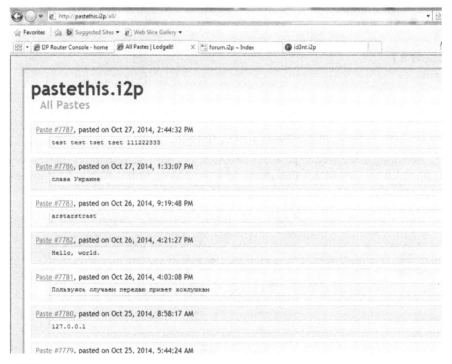

**FIGURE 9.9**

I2P based Paste data service.
  Forum: http://forum.i2p/

It's like a general forum to discuss different things in different section of threads. The topics may be related to I2P or something else. Depending upon the area of interest take membership, login and read, create or edit posts based on the permissions provided by the site.

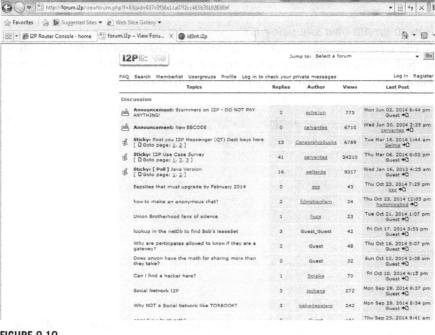

**FIGURE 9.10**

I2P based forum.

Microblog: http://id3nt.i2p/

Id3nt is a microblogging site like twitter. Here we can post whatever we want, we can share our views, discuss on a particular topic, reply to some post of our interest. It's quite similar to the normal microblogging site.

**FIGURE 9.11**

Id3nt.

### How to create own site using I2P:

To create our own anonymous I2P web server we need to edit files from the following path. In case of windows machine the path is %APPDATA%\I2P\eepsite\docroot\ and in case of Linux machine the path is ~/.i2p/eepsite/docroot/.

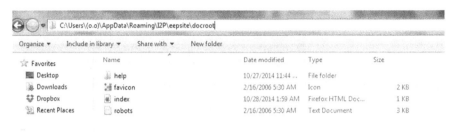

**FIGURE 9.12**

Eepsite files.

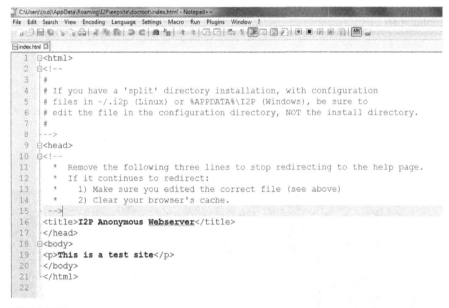

**FIGURE 9.13**

Edit file.

After completing all the edits we need to set up server configuration details from the following URL: http://127.0.0.1:7657/i2ptunnel/edit.jsp?tunnel=3

The options are shown in below figure

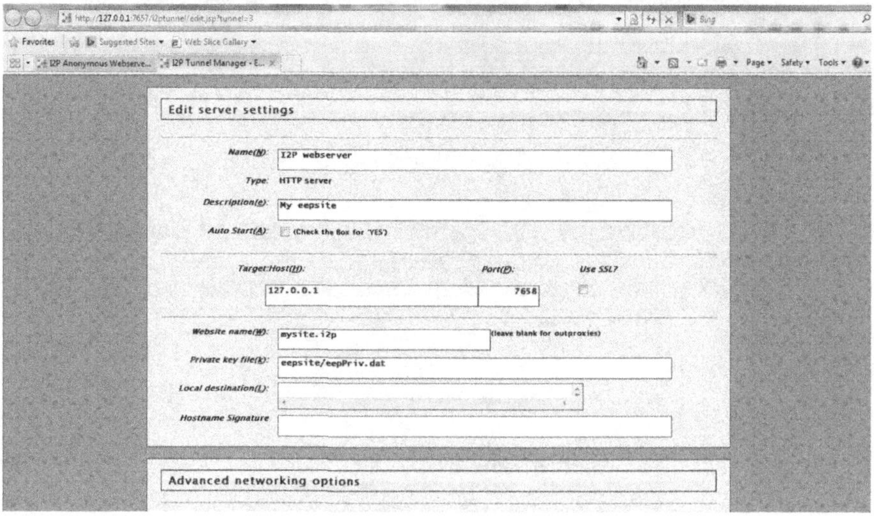

**FIGURE 9.14**

Edit server settings.

By default the site created can be accessible locally from the following path http://127.0.0.1:7658.

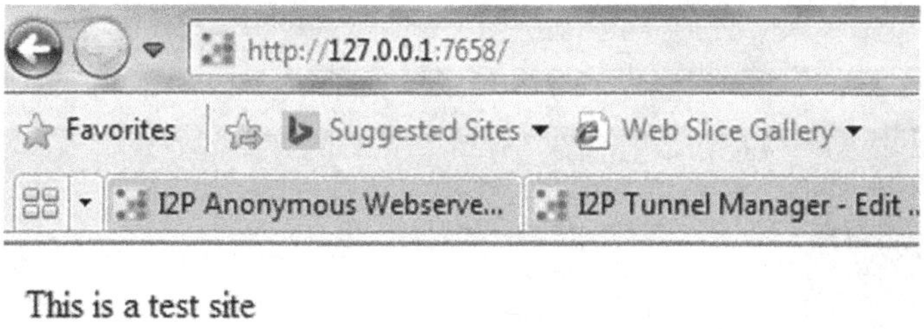

This is a test site

**FIGURE 9.15**

Local site.

Though we can edit the same from the server settings, additionally we can use setup name, description, protocol, IP and port number, as well as the domain name from the above server edit page. There are certain advance options. But the options are quite straightforward so we can easily configure our web server and anyone can access the same using the provided domain name.

Once completing all the configurations save the details. We will get the page where we need to start the web services we just configured shown in below figure.

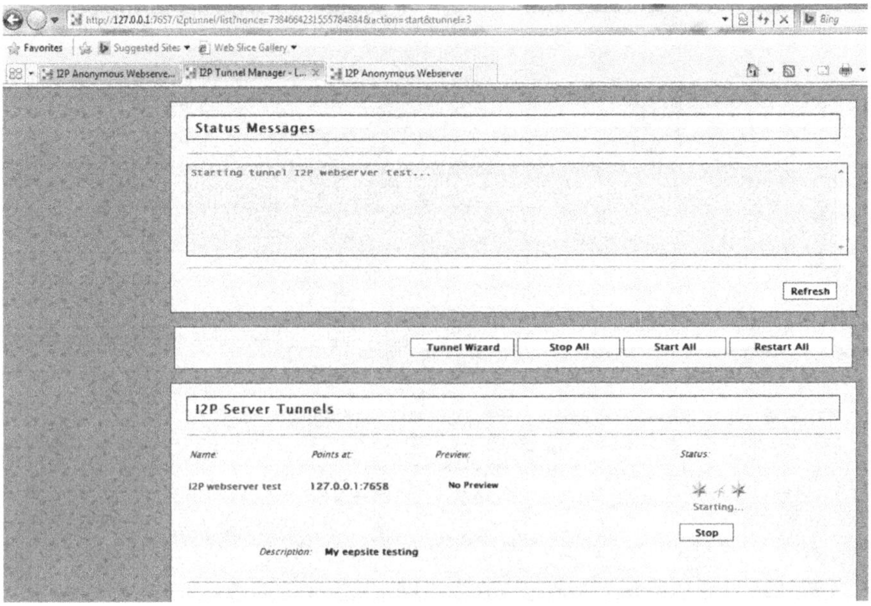

**FIGURE 9.16**

Starting the service.

Sometime we need to add the domain name and a long base64 key generated by the page in the router address book to access the site as shown in below image.

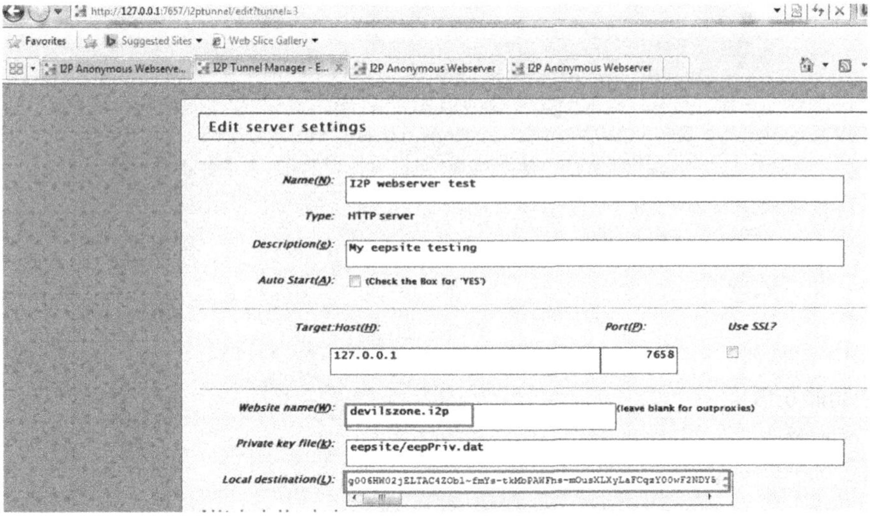

**FIGURE 9.17**

Adding the name.

Now we can access the page by the domain name. In my case as from the above figure it's quite clear that the name is http://devilszone.i2p/.

Here is the figure showing the same using the domain name in the browser.

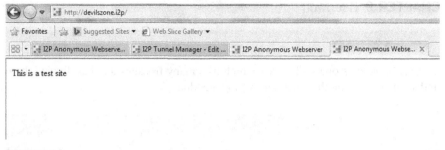

**FIGURE 9.18**

Service running.

Here we learned how to get different internal sites from the internet with *.i2p extension, how to access them using I2P, how to create our own I2P site for providing services. This will help us to understand the deepweb quite easily.

## FREENET

Similar to Tor and I2P there is yet another anonymous network, freenet. It is one of the oldest networks around and is known for P2P file sharing capabilities. The applications can be downloaded from https://freenetproject.org/download.html. Once downloaded, simply install the application and run it.

Freenet will open up a browser once it is run. The webpage displayed will provide us a series of choices to determine the security and data usage limit we desire to have and then perform the setup accordingly. Once this setup is complete, we will be presented with the freenet homepage. This page contains links to indexes of freenet websites (called freesites) similar to the Tor wikis and documentation related to other associated softwares and HOW TO guides. In the homepage there is also a search box which allows to search through freesites. Using certain plugins such as freetalk and freemail we can also use freenet to have communication over freenet.

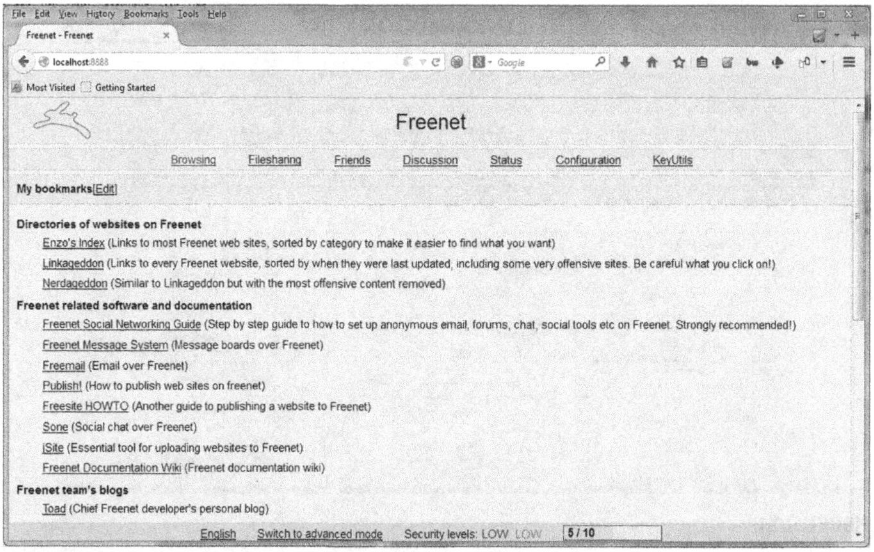

**FIGURE 9.19**

Freenet homepage.

Enzo's index is one such index which lists many freesites and has divided them under categories. Another such list is Linkageddon.

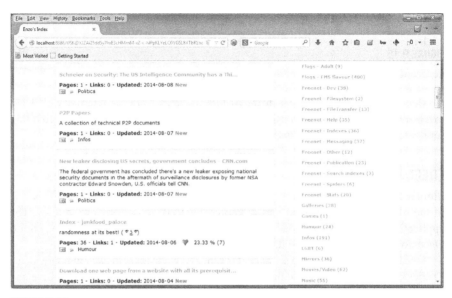

**FIGURE 9.20**

Freenet Enzo's Index.

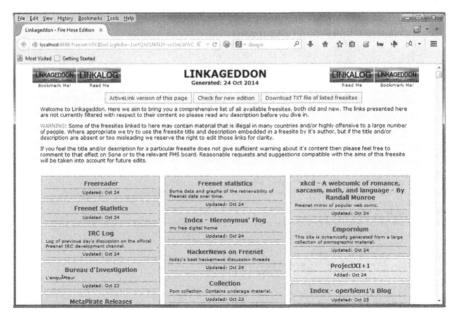

**FIGURE 9.21**

Freenet Linkageddon.

Freenet also allows us to connect with people whom we already know and are using freenet under the URL http://localhost:8888/friends/. For this we simply need to exchange a file called as noderefs with them and provide this file on the mentioned page and simply click on the add button at the bottom. Under the URL http://localhost:8888/downloads/ we can perform file sharing operations. Similar to other networks discussed, freenet also allows to create and share our websites in their network. Freenet maintains its own wiki https://wiki.freenetproject.org which lists information related to different features of it and about how to perform different operations including freesites setup.

Apart from these mentioned networks there are also some other networks which provide similar functionalities, but Tor, I2P, and freenet are the most popular ones.

In this chapter we moved on from exploring the regular internet and learned about some less explored regions of it. We discussed in detail about the deepweb, how to access it, how to create it, and what to expect there. We also learned about its uses and also how it is misused. We have also shared some associated resources which would help to explore them further, but be warned you never know what you might find there so act with your own discretion.

Till now we have learned about various tools, techniques, and sources of information which might help us to utilize the internet in a better and efficient way. Moving ahead we will learn about some tools and their utility in managing, visualizing, and analyzing all the collected data so that we can better understand and utilize the raw data to get actionable intelligence.

## DISCLAIMER

The part of the internet that will be discussed in this chapter might also contain illegal and/or disturbing things. Readers are advised to use their discretion and act accordingly.

# Data Management and Visualization

## 10

## INFORMATION IN THIS CHAPTER

- Data
- Information
- Intelligence
- Data management
- Data visualization

## INTRODUCTION

Till now we have learned about gathering data using different methods. Generally people think that open source intelligence OSINT means collecting data from different internet-based open source options. But it's not limited to that because if the data we collected from different sources are not categorized properly or we cannot find relations between one another it can be just a huge amount of random data that is of no use. We will discuss later the need of managing data and analyzing its worth, but for the time being let's refresh what we learned so far and how to collect different data using different sources.

From the very beginning we have focused on data extraction using different methods. We started with search engines, where generally a normal user gets answers for all the questions, and we also discussed how that is just a minute part of the web as popular conventional search engines have only a limited amount of internet indexed in their databases. So we learned how to use other specific search engines to get specific data. Some popular features of mainstream search engines that make them unique as compared with other. Further we learned about some interesting tools and techniques to find out data which is openly available. Later we moved on to power searching and learned how to get desired information from the web effectively. Then we moved to metadata and how it can be helpful. We learned how to get all the metadata information and how can we use it for different purposes and last but not the least we covered Deep Web, the part of web which is not directly indexed by conventional search engines. We learned how to access it to get more information.

So for the time being we can say that we learned how to collect data from different sources directly using some well-known solutions and also using some unconventional tools that open even more doors to collect data. Before going any further, let's discuss a bit about what is data, information, and intelligence and how they differ from one another.

## DATA

"Data" is one of the most commonly used terms in any domain, especially IT. If we describe data in simple words it means the RAW form of entities. It is the depiction of facts in a basic form. For example, if we get a text file that consists of some kind of names abc.inc, xyz.com, john, 28, info@xyz.com, CTO, etc. We can see there are certain entities we found but have no meaning. This is the raw form. In its original form, data do not have much worth.

## INFORMATION

The systematic form of data is called information. When data is categorized based on the characteristics it can be called as information. We can say that aggregated and organized form of data is information. Hence to achieve information we need to process data. Let's take the same example abc.inc is a company name. xyz.com is a domain, john is a username, 28 is age, info@xyz.com is an email address registered with xyz.com, and CTO is a position.

## INTELLIGENCE

When we relate different information based on their relations with one another and derive a meaning out of that, then what we get is called intelligence. So we analyze and interpret the information at hand according to the context to achieve Intelligence. From same example we can derive that xyz.com and info@xyz.com belong to same domain. It is quite possible as john is 28 year old and is the CTO of abc.inc. These are primary predictions they may be false positives also, so we need to validate the same later but for the time being the information that we have looks like relative so we can conclude that. John who is 28 years old is the CTO of abc.inc and the domain name of the same company is xyz.com and email id to communicate is info@xyz.com.

To validate we will need to extract information from other sources and we might get to know that the name of the CTO of abc.inc is someone named John and there is a John who works at abc.inc whose email is info@xyz.com and similar information which might correlate to prove our theory right or wrong. Now let's say we are a salesperson and our job is to contact management of different companies, then the validation of this information being right allows us to contact John and craft an email depending upon his age group and other information about him that we might have extracted.

The definition of intelligence may differ from different people. This is our own definition based on our experience, but the bottom line is it's about the usefulness of the information. Unlike data, which states raw facts, actionable Intelligence allows us to take informed decisions.

As we discussed earlier also, data is the raw form which just contains the entities. Entity means anything tangible or intangible. It may be name, place, character, or anything. If it is just a data it is worthless for us. We do not know what it is about. We can get lots of random data but for using that we must understand what that data is all about. Let's again take another example, we got 1000 random strings, but what to do with that. But if we come to know that those are some usernames or passwords then that 1000 random strings are worth a lot. We can use that as dictionary attack or brute force etc.

It's not the data that is always valuable, it's the information about the data or the information itself that is worth a lot.

Managing data is very important. Managed data can be quickly used to find relationships. Let's say we have got lots of data and we know that the data consists of name, email id, mobile number etc. If we will not manage that systematically in rows and columns, we will lose track of that and later when we need a particular set of data, let's say name, it will be difficult for us to differentiate and fetch from large amount of unmanaged data.

So it's always important to manage the data by its types in a categorized manner so that later we can use the same quite easily. As seen in previous chapters there are various sources of information. Every source is unique in its own way. When all the data from different sources comes together it creates the complete picture and allows us to look at it from a wider perspective.

As we covered Maltego earlier, we have seen how it collects data from different sources, but even then there are many other sources. The thing to focus here is that it's not about running a tool and collecting all the data. It's about running transformations one by one to get desired final result. To extract data from different sources, correlate it and interpret it according to our needs. it's not possible in most cases that we will be able to get all the data we want from a single source. So we need to collect different data from multiple sources to complete the picture.

For example, let's take a condition that we need to collect all the data about a person called John. How to do that? As John is quite common name, it is very difficult to get all the information. Let's start with some primary information. If we can identify the picture of John then we might start with a simple Google search to check the images, we might or might not get his picture, if we get the picture visit the page from where Google fetched this picture to get to know more about John but if not then simply try social networking sites like Facebook or LinkedIn, there is a chance that we can get the picture as well as the profile of John in one of the social network sites or all. If we get the profile then we can get more further information like his email id, company name, position, social status, current city, permanent residence.

After getting those details we can use the email id to check what other places it is used, such as any other sites, blogs, forums etc. There are different online sources which can help us get these details and we have discussed some in previous chapters. Then we can manually visit those sites to gather more information. This is just an example how to collect different data from different steps by taking one output as another step input and collect all the data to complete the picture.

As from the above example it is clear that the enumeration or data collection process is a stepwise process which includes number of different sources and also the result of one process is generally used as the point of enumeration for other process. So the relationship between the data enumerated or collected is very difficult to track, if we won't work on it from the very beginning. If we are looking for some specific data flow without sorting it in a structural manner it will be very difficult to search for relations among the data. Then it will be worthless to get all the required data about a single entity without knowing what are those all about. So hence we need to manage data in structural manner.

There are different ways to structure the data collected but the best way is to sort them according to parent and child entities. Let's say we found email from name, then name will be parent entity and email is it's child. If we get something from email, like domain name then that email will become parent entity, likewise we can organize the whole data collected.

Data can be structured using rows and columns in a spreadsheet quite easily but the tracking process will become little difficult. For getting the every parent node we need to search for the shell number. And the text form of data is not that easy to remember. That is the only reason there are graphs, flowcharts, smart arts used to define complex processes or statistics so that it will be easy to remember as well as understand. And this is also a major reason why Maltego is popular in its segment. As Maltego provides easy to understand visualized output, it proves the importance of visualized data that can help in easy analysis of the relations and crystal clear about the established relations between entities.

## DATA MANAGEMENT AND ANALYSIS TOOLS
### EXCEL SHEET

Before jumping into data analysis and visualization let's not avoid the fact that there are other simpler ways to categorize the data and are used in industry for a long time. One of such tools is excel sheet. Some also call it as spreadsheet. The easy user interface differentiating rows and columns in a tabular way is a great way to categorize the data. It's also very handy when we just have static values for different entities such as a user detail. Let's say we want to manage data that consists of username, email id, organization, and position. For every user in a row we will add all the details in columns. And for this type of job, excel or spreadsheet is the best feasible option.

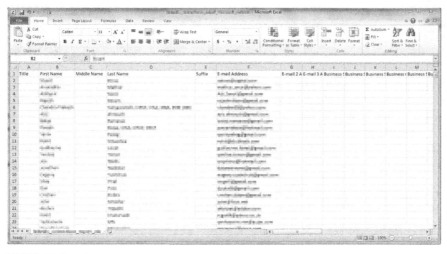

**FIGURE 10.1**

A sample excel sheet.

Excel has great formatting features where we can apply formulas, filter data, add comment, create dropdown buttons, and many more. The final thing is that excel is a great tool to categorize the data if we are categorizing all for a primary entity, but we might face problem when we have more than one primary entity. In that case either we need to create different tables in a single sheet or have to go for a new sheet for another table. Then we have to manually track down the relationships between data by switching the tables or sheets. This is definitely a problem for huge amount of data which contains more than one primary entity.

## SQL DATABASES

SQL also known as structured query language designed for managing data. Using SQL databases we can store data in tabular format in a system. It allows us to insert, query, delete, and update database elements. Though it's not just what it looks like. SQL databases have great features of data management and are widely used in industry to store lots and lots of data. The only reason it is being popular in the industry is that using simple queries we can able to manage the database.

We discussed about the problem in above paragraph that when there are multiple tables then it's very difficult to relate and manually fetch data for a particular entity. Here SQL comes as a savior. In SQL by writing simple queries we can fetch data of a particular entity from multiple tables quite easily. There are lots of DBMS or database management softwares are available. Some are open source and some are not, but some popular DBMS are MySQL, MSSQL, SQL Server, Oracle etc. Apart from the SQL-based databases there are also some NoSQL databases which allow to store more than just text.

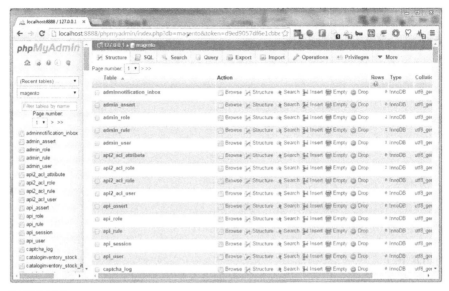

**FIGURE 10.2**

A sample MySQL database accessed through phpMyAdmin.

The only disadvantage is that, it cannot be used by an average user. Though it is not very difficult to install and configure yet it requires a bit of technical knowledge and also SQL query knowledge to manage the database properly. Though there are certain tools and frameworks available which provide features like command auto-complete, syntax correction etc., for providing ease of use to the user who just do not want to open a dark black screen whether that is a terminal or a command prompt or any kind of console but still the understanding of language limits its use to corporate sector. They are actually designed to hold and work with large amount of data and hence are not much used by people for their normal data storage needs.

## FLOWCHARTS

As excel sheet and SQL databases store data in text form or we can say just text form which only categorizes the data, but flowchart adds graphics to the data. There are certain chart symbols available for different types of data and it allows a user to not only manage data graphically but also providing feature to easily show their relations by different symbols and arrows.

It is a type of diagram that represents a set of data, workflow, or process, showing the steps as boxes of various kinds, and their relations by connecting them with arrows. This graphical representation can be very helpful as we discussed earlier for ease of understanding and keeping things remembered. Flowcharts are used to analyze and manage different data and it has special boxes for different purposes. Some examples are given below.

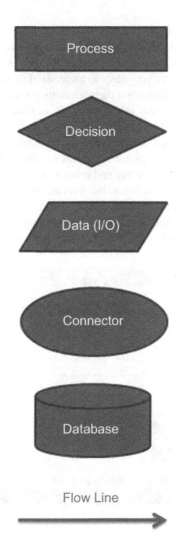

**FIGURE 10.3**

Some commonly used flowchart symbols.

We discussed a bit about the methods which are usually used for data storage and/ or management. Now let's move on to learn about something different than the usual stuff and see what other great options are available out there which can help us with our data management and analysis needs.

## MALTEGO

Any open source assessment is not complete without the use of Maltego. It's an integral part of OSINT. We already discussed a lot about this tool earlier and discussed how to utilize it to extract data using it. The reason Maltego is very popular and widely used is not just it's cool features but also its data representation. Maltego has different set of views such as main view, bubble view, and entity view. And we can also change the type of view. The result looks very easy to understand as different types of icons are used for different types of entities and their relations are well expressed by the arrows.

Maltego represents all the information is a nice and easy to understand entity–relationship model. Apart from extracting data using various transforms and machines we can also take the data we have found from other sources and include it into the graph to create a bigger picture. For that we simply need to take the appropriate entity type from the left entity bar and bring it into the graph, then insert the data we have found and simply connect it to the relevant entity or entities. If we don't find the appropriate entity for the datatype, Maltego allows us to create a new entity and use it according to our needs. This makes it very easy to take the advantage of the data mining feature and further extend it for data analysis purpose.

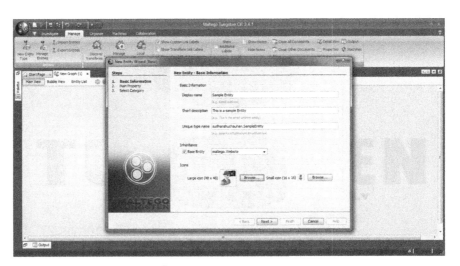

**FIGURE 10.4**

Maltego entity creation.

## CASEFILE

CaseFile is another great tool from Paterva which can be found on https://www.paterva.com/web6/products/casefile.php. Similar to an original CaseFile used by investigators to collect all the information related to any case at one place, Maltego CaseFile also helps us to build an information map which connects all this information in one place along with the connection between them. It provides us simple interface to add, link, and analyze data quickly and effectively. The motive behind creating this tool is to provide offline data analysis. There are certain jobs which include lots of field work and real-life information gathering such as investigators etc. So to help them which something as cool as Maltego visualized data representation, Paterva came up with this tool which is worth using.

As it is focused for offline data analysis, it contains lots of daily life entities that can be found mostly during information gathering exercise. Some of the entity categories are devices, locations, tracking, weapons, infrastructure etc. It also provides user the freedom to add customized entities. Another exciting feature of CaseFile is that it can be used to visualize data stored in excel sheets or CSV files, which make it easier to make sense of the data we have acquired in those forms.

The interface is very similar to the Maltego and as it is very popular in OSINT segment and widely used, if any Maltego user wants to try CaseFile he/she can use it without any problem. The options to create visualizations are also quite the same.

Similar to Maltego, to create a new graph in CaseFile we need to take all the entities we have information about, or add new entities and input relevant data into them, then further make the connections among those entities to create a complete picture. Though CaseFile does not have any data extraction feature yet its data visualization feature proves to be very helpful when we have data from a variety of sources and needs to be connected together to make sense out of it.

CaseFile contains of three tabs placed at the top of the interface named Investigate, Manage, and Organize. Under the Investigate tab there are functions like cut, copy, paste, entity selection, and graph zooming. It allows to quickly work with the graph and play with the entities around. Another tab is the Manage tab which allows to add new entities and to manage existing ones. We can also add notes and work with features related to the CaseFile window. The last tab is the Organize tab which provides features like managing the layout of the graph into different structures and also performs the alignment according to the requirement.

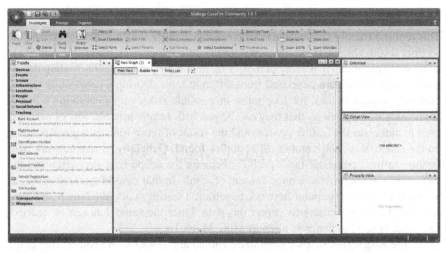

**FIGURE 10.5**

CaseFile entity palette.

So this is all about Maltego CaseFile that we can use for different purposes starting from investigation to data analysis. Like Maltego, CaseFile also comes in two forms, one is community or the free version and another is the commercial version. Both the versions can be found on https://www.paterva.com/web6/products/download2.php. It also supports operating systems like Windows, Mac, and Linux. The installation process is quite easy and similar to Maltego.

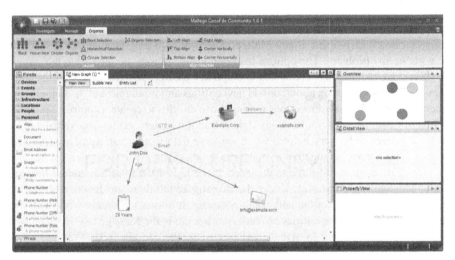

**FIGURE 10.6**

A sample CaseFile graph.

## MagicTree

This tool is basically for pentesters who need to manage the data they get during the security testing. MagicTree http://www.gremwell.com/what_is_magictree is made to solve some problems that every pentester faces in their job and that is finding details from a large set of data generated from different tools. During a penetration testing exercise, pentesters look for loopholes, or possible risks, or vulnerabilities in any application or network so that they can be patched. In this process, lots of tools are used to automate the testing process and the result of those tools is huge depending on the scope, size, and number of loopholes found. Generally in any network penetration testing, pentester faces problem because the scope is always large and the tools used always provide a huge amount of result. In that case MagicTree comes as a savior. It supports popular network penetration testing tools like Nmap and Nessus, and it allows its users to import this data. Later the same data can be queried, analyzed, or used to generate a report using MagicTree.

To use MagicTree first we need to download and install it. We can download the same from following URL: http://www.gremwell.com/download. This is a jar file so can be used in any operating system but with java installed. So to start working with

MagicTree simply open it, add some network address or host address to the scope so that MagicTree will able to build a data tree for the same. The advantage of storing data in tree form is that if later we want to add some other data it will not affect the tree, we just need to create a new tree. It stores the data in tabular or list form and uses XPath expression to extract data. There are many report templates that can be customized and used for report generation.

The only limiting feature of this tool is that it only supports import option for xml. So we cannot add tools which generate text output. Although it is limitation but still this tool is pretty helpful for workflow automation for data retrieval from any tool, and also highly recommended for pentesters.

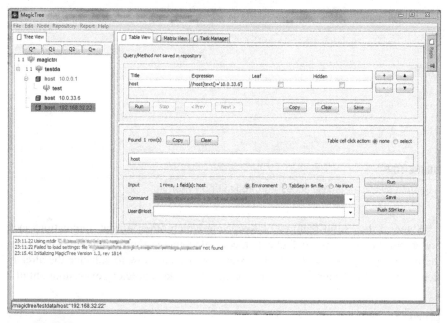

**FIGURE 10.7**

MagicTree interface.

## KeepNote

As the name suggests KeepNote is a note taking application. It is a cross-platform application which can be downloaded from http://keepnote.org/. Unlike traditional tools for note making such as Notepad, KeepNote contains of various features which make note taking more efficient and allows to include multiple media into it.

To start note taking using KeepNote we need to first create a new notebook from the File option. Once a notebook has been created we can add new pages and sub-pages into the notebook. Now in these pages we can keep our notes and keep them categorized. We can simply write the text into the bottom right part of the interface.

Apart from that we can also include different supporting media such as images to make our notes more informative.

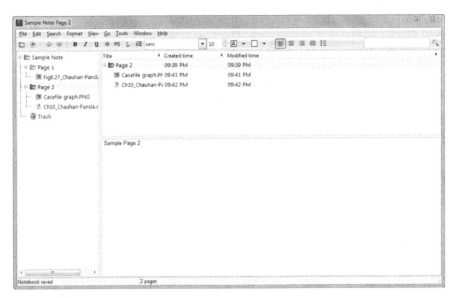

**FIGURE 10.8**

A Sample MySQL database accessed through phpMyAdmin.

Some of the useful features of KeepNote which other similar applications lack are organized hierarchy, spell check, media attachment, interlinking etc. Apart from these the application also has many extensions which allow to enhance the already rich features of it. Extensions can be found at http://keepnote.org/extensions.shtml.

## LUMIFY

One of the best options available for data visualization and analysis in the open source domain is Lumify. As Lumify is open source, its code is available at https://github.com/lumifyio/lumify. There is an easier way to use and test Lumify and that is through the preconfigured virtual machines, which can be found at https://github.com/lumifyio/lumify/blob/master/docs/prebuilt-vm.md.

Lumify presents us with an easy to use web-based interface. Based on the graph-based model we can aggregate our data into the interface and perform analytical operations over it. There are several entities with data field which we can use to represent the information we have. Apart from this, it also provides advanced features like Map integration, using which we can represent the data over world map; live shared workspace, which allows to share information with other team members in real time and work in a collaborative manner; customization, which makes it easier to create own data model etc.

The wide range of features and ease of use makes Lumify a great choice for our data visualization and analysis requirements. Some good examples of Lumify usage can be found at their homepage http://lumify.io/.

**FIGURE 10.9**

Lumify interface.

## Xmind

We have seen some tools to organize data for better understanding. There is actually a term used for visually organizing information and it is called as mind map. As the name suggests a mind map is map of our ideas or thoughts about any topic. Usually a mind map is started around a central idea and then expanded from it further. The central idea remains the theme of the diagram and all the information revolves around it. It is actually chain of associated ideas and information spreading in different directions. Using branches the subcategories are created out of the main branches and similarly expanded further. Mind maps include different forms to represent the information or idea such as images, text, colors, shapes etc.

One of the most famous and efficient tools to create mind maps is Xmind. The download link can be found at http://www.xmind.net/download/. Once we open up the interface of Xmind, it provides us with a huge list of templates and themes from which we can choose the one which best suits our needs. Once we have made the selection, we can start by editing the data fields, changing or adding new ones. Xmind allows us to insert information in the form of text, image, marker, summary, attachment, audio notes etc. The variety of data types allowed by Xmind makes it very easy and effective to create a mind map which can actually translate our ideas into a visual representation. We can create mind maps to create diagrams for project management, planning, decision making etc.

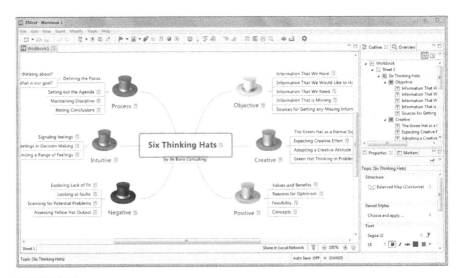

**FIGURE 10.10**

Xmind sample template.

Though the free version of Xmind has some limitations as compared to the pro version, yet it provides ample ways to visualize our ideas in a creative and effective manner.

There are various models and methodologies which are used in different domains for data analysis process. Some are generic and some only fit to certain industries. Here we are giving a basic approach which applies generically and can be modified according to the specific needs:

- Objective: Decide what is the question that needs to be answered.
- Identify sources: Identify and list down the sources which can provide data related to our objective.
- Collection: Collect data using different methods from all the possible sources.
- Cleaning: From the data collected, anything that is irrelevant needs to be removed and the gaps present need to be filled.
- Data organization: The cleaned data needs to be organized into a manner which allows easy and fast access.
- Data modeling: Performing the modeling using different techniques such as visualization, statistical analysis, and other data analysis methods.
- Putting in context: After we have performed the analysis of data we need to interpret it according to the context and then take decision based on it.

Unlike other chapters where we focused on data gathering, here we focused around data management and visualization. Collecting data is important but managing it and representing it into a form which makes the process of analysis easy is quite important. As we learned earlier in this chapter that raw data is not of much use, and we need to organize it and analyze it to convert it into a form which is actionable, the tools mentioned in this chapter assist in that process. Once we have analyzed the data and put it in context, we will achieve intelligence which helps us to take decisions.

Moving forward in the next chapter we will discuss about online security. Day by day cyberspace is becoming more insecure. New malwares keep on surfacing every now and then, attack techniques are advancing, scammers are developing new techniques to trick people etc. With all this around there is so much that we need to safeguard ourselves from. We will discuss about tools and techniques to shrink this gap in our security and will learn how to minimize our risk.

# Online Security

## 11

## INFORMATION IN THIS CHAPTER

- Security
- Online security
- Common online threats
- Identify threats
- Safety precautions

## INTRODUCTION

In the previous chapters we have fiddled a lot with the internet. We have used a variety of tools to access it in different forms, we have also been to some of the lesser touched areas of it and also learned about how to stay anonymous while doing so. We also learned about some tools which would help us during the analysis of all the data we have collected from this massive information source. In this chapter we are going to touch upon a topic which has become very relevant in today's digital age and it is online security. Internet is a great place where we can learn different things, share it with others and much more. Today internet is available worldwide, and accessing it is pretty easy. We have devices which allow us to stay connected even on the move.

Today we rely on the internet for our many needs such as shopping, paying our bills, registering for an event, or simply stay social. Even our businesses rely on the internet for their day to day operations. We as a user of internet use different platforms, click on various buttons, visit various links on a daily basis. For an average user, it may seem pretty simple but involves huge amount of technical implementation at the backend.

Similar to our physical world this virtual world also has security issues. It's no big news that daily people are becoming victim of cyber-crimes. There are a variety of threats which we face in this digital world and sometimes we don't even recognize them. For example, we all get that spam message stating that we have won a huge amount of money in some lottery and we need to share some details to receive it. Although most of us simply ignore such messages, some people do respond and are victimized. Similarly we have already seen how the information we share online might reveal something about us that we don't intend to. This kind of information in wrong hands can be used against us. Recently there have been many cases which involved hackers attacking an employee's machine to gain access to the corporate data. The main reason behind the success of such attacks is the lack of security awareness among the users. Though understanding the technical aspects of cyber security can become a bit complex for a nontechnical person but understanding how some of the common attacks work, learning how to identify them, and finally how to mitigate them is a necessity for every user. One question that is mostly asked by people is that why would someone try to hack us though we don't have any sensitive/financial information on our computers. Instead of answering this question right away let's learn about some of the attack methods and then discuss why someone would attack an average user.

We are in a world where we love to spend more time online than in social. The reason may be anything starting from shopping, e-mails, social online hangout, chats, messages, or online recharge or banking. We may use internet for our professional use such as it may be part of our day to day job or for personal use to browse or surf. Anyways the motive behind discussing is that internet is now an integral part of life, and it's quite difficult to avoid it.

Earlier we came across about only one aspect that is internet privacy: how to maintain privacy using different online solutions, browser setting, or anonymity applications. What about the other aspect that we missed. That is security. So we need to also put some light on the security aspects of the internet.

When we say security aspect it's not just about using secure applications or visiting secure sites, or having security implementation on our system such as updated antivirus and firewall. In this case security also means about data security or to be precise internet data security.

Securing not only the data of an organization will make it secure but also the users' data that's also quite important. So in case of data security we need to focus on both organizational data as well as users' data. For example, let's say an organization implements proper security mechanism to secure its data. All kinds of security softwares starting from antivirus, firewall, intrusion detection system, intrusion prevention system, and all other security tools implemented or installed in a system but if the security question of the HR's (Human Resource) e-mail id is what is your favorite color and the answer is pink then all these security implementations will go vain. So it's both the users' data as well as organizational data that are important and we need to take care of both.

As an organization we discussed a little bit on how the metadata can disclose certain information and how DLP (data leakage/loss prevention) can be helpful to secure all those. But from a user perspective it is also quite important not to share details in public that can be used against us or our security, for simple example, do not disclose information in public that can be used to know more about our way of thinking or about our certain area of interests. Let's say we disclose information that can be used to recover our password such as the answers related to any security questions, e.g., who is our favorite teacher, what place we like the most, what is mother's maiden name etc. These are common security questions which we generally find in different online applications that can be used as an additional verification to recover passwords. If we will disclose these information in public, let's say in any social networking site, blog, or anywhere else, that can be a threat to our security. So think twice before disclosing any such information in the internet. The other way around is to select a wrong answer to such security questions. For example, for the question what is your favorite color, if we provide an answer such as pit bull, it will be quite difficult for someone to guess this answer and recover your account. Password reset is one of the examples for such an act, there are many other ways where information provided by us can be used against us such as social engineering attack, simple phishing attack, etc. Let's take another example such as if we tag ourselves in a particular place in a particular date most of the time then our present can be expected there and any ill-minded person can use it to exploit us. Other example can be if we show a particular hardware information or show off about a latest gadget then also that can be used against us. For example, if we disclose that we use iPhone and that too a jailbroken then there are certain jailbroken iPhone-related vulnerabilities that can be used against us such as the default openSSH credentials alpine/alpine. An attacker just has to be in the same wireless network where we use our jailbroken iPhone and he just needs to guess the IP address to start an SSH connection and we know that the default credentials can be used there to compromise our device. It's quite common now a days and people getting hacked everyday for these silly mistakes or unintentional information leakage. The only way to secure online user data is most of the time awareness. Be aware and avoid such information leakage and surf safely.

It's not any certain type of information we provide that can be used against us. The information can be anything. So it's better to avoid disclosing any specific information in public internet. And precaution is better than cure so share your data accordingly.

If we are in the security field then we must know the importance of information gathering. There is a great saying that "if you want to win a battle then you should know your enemy first." The more information we get about a person or organization the more way we can find weakness in them and later that can be exploited. Now we will discuss the common threats and their exploitation.

## MALWARES

Malware is a word which came from the combination of two words, malicious and software. The simple definition that can be derived from this is that any software that performs malicious activity can be considered as malware. There are different types of malwares based on their behavior. Different malwares have different functionalities and different modes of spreading the infection. If we think of infecting a targeted audience or person then collecting information related to him/her can help a lot. If we know our victim personally then we can provide him/her software of his/her interest infected with malware directly in any storage device or by sending him/her a download link remotely. If we need to execute it first time, then collecting information about the operating system and security implementation on that will help a lot. So as a user if we get any link from a known person or any stranger, do not install it directly. Think twice before installation or else you can be a victim of malware. Most of the malwares come from online where we try to access certain restricted sites such as adult sites, free music, or software hosting sites etc. So as a user, verify the source before downloading anything. There are various classifications of malware, some of which are defined below.

## VIRUS

Virus or Vital Information Resources Under Seize is a term taken from the normal virus that affects person and can be the reason for different diseases. Similarly the computer virus is a malicious code that when executes in a system, infects the system and performs malicious activity like deleting data, memory corruption, adding random temporal data etc. The only weakness of the virus is, it needs a trigger for execution. If our system contains a malicious software that is affected by virus until and unless we install that in our system there is nothing to fear. To avoid a virus infection use genuine updated antivirus.

## TROJAN

Trojan is quite interesting malware, it generally comes as a gift such as if we visit restricted sites then we will get some advertisements such as we won an iPhone, click here to apply and all, or in popular paid games as free, then once user is lured to that and installs that after downloading then the application will create a backdoor and provide all user actions to the attacker. So to spread a Trojan, if the attacker will choose a popular demanding paid app, game, movie or song then the chances of getting more people are quite a lot.

Trojans are nonself-replicating but hide behind another program. It is recommended that do not install any paid thing that comes as free. You never know what is hidden inside that application and also use antimalware in system for better safety.

## RANSOMWARE

As the name suggests, it is quite interesting malware which after infecting the system blocks some popular and important resources of our computer system and then demand ransom money to give back the access. Usually ransomwares use encryption technologies to hold our data as captive. The recommendation will be the same as mentioned above.

## KEYLOGGER

Keylogger is a piece of malware that collects all the keystrokes and sends the same to the attacker. So when user inserts any credential for any site, the credential can be recorded and sent back to the attacker and that can be later used by the attacker for account takeover. The recommendation for this is if you are typing credentials for any transaction-related site or value-related to any critical information, always use on-screen keyboard.

## PHISHING

It is one of the oldest and still popular attacks which are also used in many corporate attacks. It is a simple attack where attacker tricks the user by sending a fake link that contains a page that looks quite similar to the original site page that user needs to log in. Once user will login in that site the credentials will be sent to the attacker and user can be redirected to the genuine site. The major weakness in this attack is the site address. If a user will verify the site address properly then there is very less chance of getting a victim of phishing attack.

The information needed here is which site the target is having account on and which site the target generally visits quite often. So that later attacker can create a fake page of that and trick the user.

There are many new ways of phishing attack techniques available now. Some are desktop phishing where the host entry of the victim's system will be changed such as it will add an entry on the host file with the sites' original domain name with the address where the fake page is installed. So when a user types the IP address or domain name in the browser it will search for host entry. The host entry will redirect and call the fake page server, and the fake page will be loaded instead of the real page.

Another such popular phishing attack is tabnabbing. In tabnabbing when user opens a new tab the original page will be changed into fake page by URL redirection. There are also other popular phishing attacks such as spear phishing.

## ONLINE SCAMS AND FRAUDS

One of the most widely faced issues online is the spam mails and scams. Most email user receives such mails on a daily basis. These mails usually attempt to trick users into sending their personal information and ultimately skim their money. Sometimes it is a huge lottery prize that we have won, or a relative in some foreign country who left us huge amount of money.

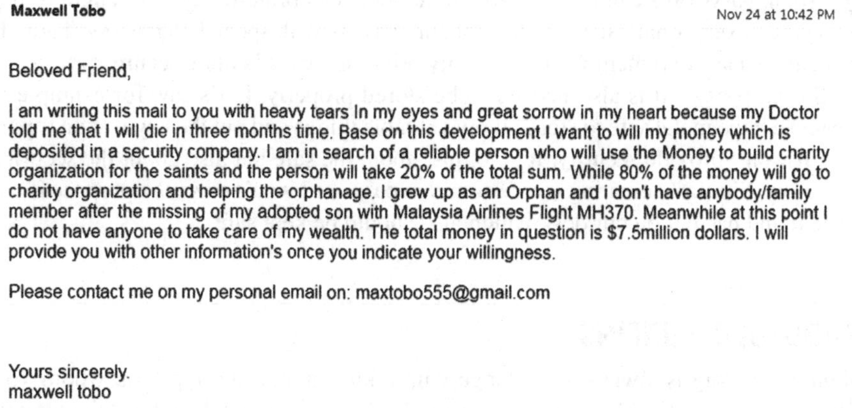

**Maxwell Tobo**                                                                 Nov 24 at 10:42 PM

Beloved Friend,

I am writing this mail to you with heavy tears In my eyes and great sorrow in my heart because my Doctor told me that I will die in three months time. Base on this development I want to will my money which is deposited in a security company. I am in search of a reliable person who will use the Money to build charity organization for the saints and the person will take 20% of the total sum. While 80% of the money will go to charity organization and helping the orphanage. I grew up as an Orphan and i don't have anybody/family member after the missing of my adopted son with Malaysia Airlines Flight MH370. Meanwhile at this point I do not have anyone to take care of my wealth. The total money in question is $7.5million dollars. I will provide you with other information's once you indicate your willingness.

Please contact me on my personal email on: maxtobo555@gmail.com

Yours sincerely.
maxwell tobo

**FIGURE 11.1**

A sample spam mail.

Scammers also try to exploit human nature of kindness by writing stories that someone is stuck on a foreign land and needs our help and other such incidents. Sometimes attackers also pose as an authority figure asking for some critical information or as the e-mail service provider asking to reset the password. There are various Ponzi schemes which are used by scammers with ultimate purpose of taking away our hard earned cash.

## HACKING ATTEMPTS

There are cases where we found that users with updated operating systems, antivirus, and firewall also face some issues and being victim of the hacking attack. The reason of those is certain popular application flaws that can be found in any operating system. Some such applications are Adobe Acrobat Reader or simply the web browsers. These kind of applications are targeted widely which covers almost all the operating systems and also widely used. So targeting these applications allows an attacker to hack as many as users possible. They either create browser plugins or addons that can help user to complete a process or to automate a process and the same in the backend can be used for malicious intention,i.e., collecting all the user's actions performed in the browser.

## WEAK PASSWORD

Weak passwords always play a major role in any hack. For the ease of user, sometime applications do not enforce password complexity and as a result of that users use simple passwords such as password, password123, Password@123, 12345, god, own mobile number etc. Weak password does not always mean length and the characters used, it also means the guessability. Name@12345, it looks quite complex password but can be guessable. So do not use password related to name, place, or mobile number. Weak passwords can be guessable or attacker can bruteforce if the length of the password is very small, so try to use random strings with special characters. Though that can be hard to remember as a security point of view it's quite secure.

Strong password is also needed to be stored properly. Let's say, for example, I created a huge metal safe to store all my valuable things and put the key just on top of that. It won't provide security. It's not just about the safe but also about the security of the key. Similarly creating a very complex password won't serve the purpose if we write it and paste it on our desk which also should be kept safe.

## SHOULDER SURFING

Shoulder surfing is always a challenge with a known attacker, a person whom you know and you work with. If he/she wants to hack your account then it is quite easy to do it while you are typing the password. The only way to make it difficult is that type some correct password characters then write some wrong characters then remove the wrong characters and complete the password or else do not enter your password when someone around.

## SOCIAL ENGINEERING

The first thing comes to our mind when we read social engineering is "there is no patch for human stupidity" or human is the weakest link in the security chain. This is a kind of attack which is done against the trust of the user. In this attack, first attacker wins the trust of the victim then collects all the information that is needed to execute one of the attacks we discussed above or any other attack. The only way to prevent from being a victim is trust no one, you never know when your boyfriend/girlfriend will hack your account. Jokes apart, do not disclose any information that has a possible significance with security to anyone.

So these were some of the security-related challenges that we face everyday, but we have only covered the problems. Let's move on to see what are the solutions.

## ANTIVIRUS

As we discussed that there are various kinds of malwares out there and each one has unique attack method and goal. There is a huge variety of these and most of the computer users have faced this problem at least some point of time.

Antiviruses are one of the security products which are widely used by organizations as well as individuals. An antivirus is basically a software package which detects malwares present on our computer machines and tries to disinfect it. What antiviruses have is a signature and heuristics for malwares, and based upon these they identify the malicious code which could cause any digital harm. As the new malwares are identified, new signatures and heuristics are created and updated into the software to maintain the security from the new threat.

Many antiviruses have been infamous for slowing down the system and making it difficult to use, also the frequent updates have also annoyed people a lot. Recently antiviruses have also evolved and become less annoying and more efficient. Many solutions also provide additional features such as spam control and other online security solutions along with antivirus. The regular update is not just for the features but also to keep the database updated to maintain security. There are various choices in the market for antivirus solutions free as well as commercial, but it all comes down to which one is the most updated one because new malwares keep on surfacing everyday. One more thing that needs to be kept in mind is that there are also some malwares posing as antivirus solutions and hence we need to be very careful when making a choice for an antivirus solution and should download only from trusted sources.

## IDENTIFY PHISHING/SCAMS

We encounter a huge number of scam and phishing mails on daily basis. Today e-mail services have evolved to automatically identify these and put them in the spam section, but still some of these manage to bypass. Here are some tips to identify these online frauds:

- Poor language and grammar: Usually the body of such mails is written in poor language and incorrect grammar.
- Incredibly long URL and strange domain: The URLs mentioned in such e-mails or the URLs of the phishing page can be checked by simply hovering the mouse over the link. Usually such URLs are very long and the actual domains are strange. This is used to hide the original domain and show the domain of the page that is being phished in the browser address bar.
- Poor arrangement of the page: The arrangement of the text and images is generally poor as many attackers use tools to create such e-mails, also sometimes the alignment changes because of the change in resolution.
- E-mail address: The original email should be checked to verify the sender.
- Missing HTTPS: If the page is usually an HTTPS one and is missing this time then this is an alarming sign.
- Request for personal/sensitive information: Usually no organization asks for personal or sensitive information over e-mail. In case such email is received it is better to verify by calling the organization before sending any such information.
- Suspicious attachments: Sometimes these kinds of e-mails also contain an attachment file in the name of form or document usually with strange extensions such as xyz.doc.exe to hide the original file type. Unless trusted and verified, these attachments should not be opened. In case the attachment needs to be opened it should be done in a controlled environment such as a virtual machine with no connection.

## UPDATE OPERATING SYSTEM AND OTHER APPLICATIONS

One of the major methods used by attackers to gain access to our machines is to hack through the applications running on the system. The operating system we use or the applications running over it contain flaws in the form of vulnerabilities. Attackers use exploit codes to attack specific vulnerabilities and get a connection to computer systems. New vulnerabilities are discovered on regular basis and hence the risk keeps on increasing. On the other hand patches for these vulnerabilities are also released by the vendors. Keeping our machine's softwares updated is an effective method to minimize our risk of being attacked.

Almost all operating systems come with mechanisms which allow it to update with the recent patches available. They also allow us to manually check for updates and install if available. Apart from this other applications that we use such as multimedia players, document readers etc., also have patches and some of them are updated automatically while some need to be downloaded separately and installed.

Secunia PSI is a Windows-based application which helps us to identify outdated software and is also capable of automating the process of updating it. It can simply run in the background and identify the applications that need to be updated. User can download the appropriate patch and also install it. In case it is unable to do so it notifies the user and also provides useful instructions.

## ADDONS FOR SECURITY

Web browsers are one of the most widely used applications on any platform and also the medium for most of the attacks. Let's learn about some easy-to-use addons which can help us to stay secure online.

### WEB OF TRUST (WOT)

WOT is a service which reviews website reputation based upon crowdsourced method. Based on the review of the crowd the addon allows us to know how it is rated on the scale of trustworthiness and child safety. Similarly users can also rate a website and hence contribute to make the web a safer place. Details and comments about the website you are visiting can also be viewed which help users to make an informed decision. Using the applications is pretty simple, visit the website and click on the WOT addon in the browser bar and it will display the details related to it. The addon is available at https://www.mywot.com/en/download for different browsers.

**FIGURE 11.2**

Web of trust (WOT) in action.

## HTTPS EVERYWHERE

HTTPS Everywhere is yet another security-focused browser addon. Some websites have HTTP as well as HTTPS pages but don't use HTTPS by default or sometimes provide limited HTTPS support. HTTPS Everywhere allows to enforce the usage of HTTPS over such platforms and hence helps to make the data transmission more secure between the client and server. The addon is available at https://www.eff.org/HTTPS-EVERYWHERE.

### NoScript

NoScript is a browser addon which allows us to manage the execution of JavaScript and similar active content technologies on websites. We can simply whitelist the applications we trust and block execution on others. This allows us to protect ourselves from Cross-site Scripting (XSS) and Clickjacking which are the most widely discovered and exploited web application vulnerabilities. NoScript is available for Firefox-based browsers and can be found at https://noscript.net/. The chrome alternative is ScriptSafe (https://chrome.google.com/webstore/detail/scriptsafe/oiigbmnaad bkfbmpbfijlflahbdbdgdf?hl=en).

## TOOLS FOR SECURITY

Though not all of us have the technical understanding of running a full-fledged vulnerability scan and making a sense out of it, there are some simple tools available which allow us to perform a scan and identify the basic flaws in our machine.

For Windows-based machines we have Microsoft Baseline Security Analyzer (MBSA). MBSA is an application provided by Microsoft which helps us to test the baseline security of Windows and associated services. It basically looks out for missing software patches and common misconfigurations so that they can be patched. Apart from the base operating system it also checks for flaws in other Microsoft services and applications.

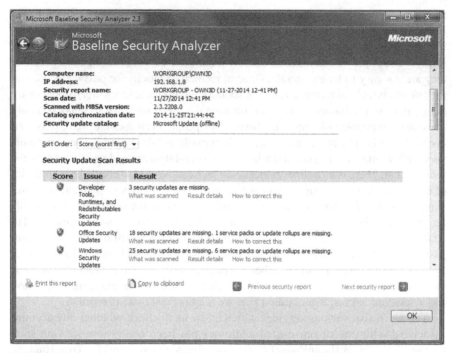

**FIGURE 11.3**

Microsoft Baseline Security Analyzer scan result.

Similarly there is Linux Basic Security Audit (LBSA). This is a script which aims at making the Linux-based systems more safe and secure, though the setting should be applied depending upon the requirements and might not be suitable for all scenarios. More details about it can be found at http://wiki.metawerx.net/wiki/LBSA.

Using such free and easy to use utilities we can certainly identify the gaps in our security and take appropriate steps to patch them.

# PASSWORD POLICY

As we use keys to maintain the authentication in real world similarly we use passwords in the digital world. Passwords are combinations of characters from different sets of alphabets, digits, special characters which we provide to access and prove that we are the rightful owner of the specific data/service. Using passwords we access our computers, our social profiles, and even bank accounts. Though passwords are of such relevance most of us choose to have a weak password. The reason behind it is that as humans we have a tendency to choose things which are easy to remember. Attacker exploits this human weakness and try to access our valuable information through different techniques. Without going into the technical details of such attacks some of them are guessing, trying our name, our parents/siblings/spouse name, our date of birth etc.; bruteforcing, trying every possible combination using automated tools/scripts; exploiting web application flaws such as SQL Injection. We cannot have control to mitigate all these issues yet we can make an effort to make our passwords strong enough so that they are not easy to be enumerate. General recommendations for passwords are that they should be at least 8 characters long, should contain characters(lower + upper case), digits, and special characters. This combination should be such that it cannot be easily guessed even people who know us. Sometimes people even create a weak password even after following these rules, one such example is "Pa$$w0rd." There are tools which allow attackers to generate a list of such combinations and use it to attack the user account. There is an online application which can be used to check the complexity of our password and tells us how much time will it take to crack it: https://howsecurei smypassword.net/. Apart from this we should also not use that same password for different accounts because in case one account gets hacked it could also be further used to compromise our other accounts. This brings us to the problem of remembering many passwords, it can be solved by using a password manager such as LastPass (https:// lastpass.com/). There are many other alternatives also available. Also choose your security questions wisely. We often forget what we have set as the security question and if someone asks us that question later we might reveal that information.

There are also various services which allow us to check whether any account associated with one of our e-mail addresses has been compromised. One such free service is HaveIBeenPwned (http://haveibeenpwned.com/) by Troy Hunt.

**FIGURE 11.4**

HaveIBeenPwned result.

# PRECAUTIONS AGAINST SOCIAL ENGINEERING

One of the main techniques used by hackers to extract sensitive information from the victims is social engineering. We as humans are naturally inclined to help others, answer to authority, and reciprocate. Using these and other similar weaknesses (in context of security) of human nature, we are exploited by attacker to make us reveal something sensitive or take an action which might not be in our favor. People simply pose as the tech. guy and ask for the current password or tell that they are the CTO of the company speaking and ask the receptionist to forward some details. To safeguard against such attacks, security awareness is very important. People need to understand what information is sensitive in nature. For example, it might seem that there is no harm in telling someone the browser version we are using at the enterprise but this information is very crucial for an attacker. Also one may trust but must verify. People should ask for proof of identity and also cross-verify it to check if the person is actually who he/she is saying he/she is. In case of doubt it is better to ask someone higher in authority to make the decision than to simply do as told.

# DATA ENCRYPTION

At the end the motive behind most of the attacks is to access data. One step to stop this from happening is to use a disk encryption software. What it does is that it will encrypt the specified files in our machine with a strong encryption method and make it password protected. In case even if the machine is compromised it would make it very difficult for the attacker to get the data. There are many such solutions available which provide this functionality such as BitLocker, TrueCrypt. It is advised to check if the software being used has no publicly known vulnerability in itself. Similarly it is advised to store and send all sensitive online data in encrypted format.

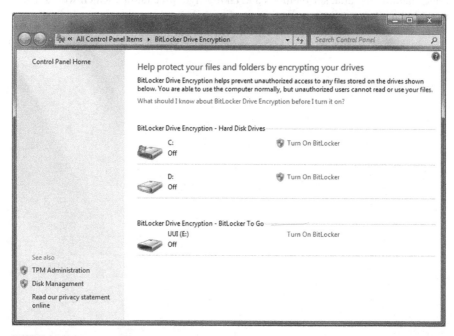

**FIGURE 11.5**

BitLocker Drive Encryption.

Some generic methods which would help us maintain our security online and keep our data safe:

- Don't open URLs that you don't trust.
- Try to understand what it means before clicking on "I accept."
- Don't download from untrusted sources.
- Don't ignore abnormal behavior (regular system restart, crash, hard disk filling up without any reason etc.).
- Backup important data on regular basis.

There are multiple motives behind such attacks and unlike popular beliefs they are not just targeted on big corporations. As already discussed most of the attacks being a spam mail or phishing are simply used to directly take the money of the victim, but some attacks have a bigger reason behind. Some of the attacks are made to extract information which could be leveraged to gain further confidential information, for example, attacking an employee's personal computer to extract information which could allow access into the corporate network. Similarly some attackers simply need to have a connection to victim machines so that they can use them later for different purposes such as Bitcoin mining, as a proxy to attack others, as part of a botnet for sale etc.

So we learned about some of the common methods used by the attackers and also how to identify them and safeguard from them. The virtual world is pretty insecure though there are various products and services out there which could help to minimize our risk none of which can guarantee security. Humans being the weakest link in the security chain are the easiest target for attackers. It is only by our awareness, understanding the attacker methods and taking right precautions which would make us digital life safer.

# Basics of Social Networks Analysis

## 12

## INFORMATION IN THIS CHAPTER

- Social network analysis
- Gephi
- Components
- Analysis
- Application of SNA

## INTRODUCTION

In one of the recent chapters we have discussed about the importance of data management and analysis. We also learned about certain tools which could be useful in the process. In this chapter we will deal with an associated topic, which is social network analysis (SNA). SNA is widely used in Information Science to learn various concepts. This is wide topic and has applications in many fields and in this chapter we will attempt to cover the important aspects of the topic and the tools required for it so that the readers can further utilize it depending according to personal needs.

As the name suggests, social network analysis is basically the analysis of social networks. The social network we are talking about is a structure which consists of different social elements and the relationship between them. It contains nodes which represent the entities and edges representing relationships. What this means is that, using SNA we can measure and map the relationships between various entities, these entities usually being people, computers, a collection of them, or other associated terms. SNA utilizes visual representations of the network for the purpose of better understanding it and implements mathematical theories to derive results. There are various tools that can be used to perform SNA and we will deal with them as and when required.

Let's deal with some basic concepts.

## NODES

Nodes are used to represent entities. Entities are an essential part of social network as the whole analysis revolves around them. They are mostly depicted with a round shape.

## EDGES

Edges are used to represent the relationships. Relationships are required to establish how one node connects to another. This relationship is very significant as it helps to perform various analyses such as how information will flow across the network etc. The number of edges connected to a node defines its degree. If a node has three links to other entities, it has degree 3.

## NETWORK

The network is visually represented and contains nodes and edges. Different parameters of nodes and edges such as size, color etc., may vary depending upon the analysis that needs to be performed.

Networks can be directed or undirected, which means that the edges might be represented as simple lines or as directed arrows. This primarily depends upon the relationships between the edges. For example, in a network of mutual connection such as friends, can have an undirected network but for a network of relations such as who likes whom can have directed network.

Now we have a basic idea of SNA. Let's get familiar with one of the most utilized tools for it.

## GEPHI

Gephi is a simple yet efficient tool used for the purpose of SNA. The tool can be downloaded from http://gephi.github.io/ and the installation process is pretty straightforward. Once installed, the tool is ready to be used. The interface is simple and is divided into different sections. There are three tabs present at the top left corner which allow working with the network in different manner. These three tabs are Overview, Data Laboratory, and Preview.

## OVERVIEW

The Overview tab provides the basic information about the network and displays the network visualization. It is primarily divided into three sections which further have subsections. The left-hand side panel consists of sections which allow partitioning and ranking of nodes and edges, performing different layouts for the network based on different algorithms. The middle section consists of the space where the network is visualized and the tools to work with the visualization. The right-hand sections contain information about the network such as number of nodes and edges and operations such as calculating the degree, density, and other network statistics.

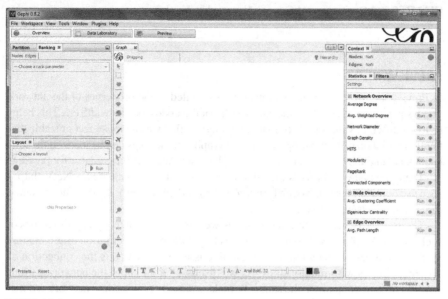

**FIGURE 12.1**

Gephi Overview.

## DATA LABORATORY

Under the Data Laboratory tab we can play with the data in its raw form. In this tab, the entities and their relationships are displayed in the form of a spreadsheet. Here we can add new nodes and edges, search for existing ones, import and export data, and much more. We can also work on columns and delete them, copy them, duplicate them etc. The data present can also be sorted depending upon different parameters by simply clicking on the row names.

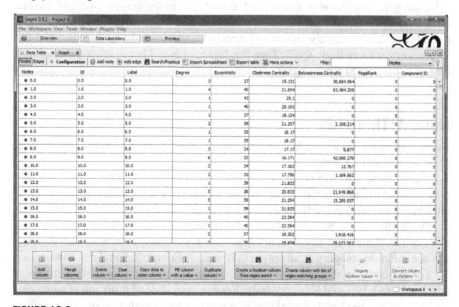

**FIGURE 12.2**

Gephi Data Laboratory.

## PREVIEW

In Preview tab we can change various settings related to the properties of the network graph such as the thickness of the edges, color of the nodes, border width etc. This helps us to set different values for different parameters so that we can make recognizable distinction based on different properties of the graph. The settings can be made in the left-hand panel and the changes are reflected in the rest of the section available for preview.

There are many other tools available for SNA, some of which are SocNetV (http://socnetv.sourceforge.net/), NodeXL (http://nodexl.codeplex.com/), EgoNet (http://source forge.net/projects/egonet/) etc.

The term network is quite the same as we use in computers or any other aspect such as math or physics. The terminologies to get the proper definition might change in different areas of study but the bottom line is network which is the connection of different entities with relationships. As we discussed a bit about the network earlier, now it's time to dig a bit on the same. To make a simpler approach to network we will use term "NODE" for entities and term "EDGE" for the relationship.

To create a meaningful and easy to understand network or graphical representation of a network, we must need to focus on certain areas such as highlight the widely used and important nodes and edges, remove nodes with no data or edges, remove redundant data, group similar nodes based on geographical location, community, or anything that broadly relates those. These are the basic practices or points to be remembered while creating a meaningful and easy to understand network.

The components of a network such as the edge and the node have certain attributes based on that we can create a network. Those attributes play a vital role in understanding a network and its components better. Let's start with a node.

As discussed earlier, node has a property called degree. Degree can be used for calculating the likelihood of that node. It is nothing but the number of edges that are connected to the node. Though it also matters is that whether the edges are directed or undirected. Let's say the number of directed edges toward a node X is 5 and the directed edges away from X is 2. Then the degree of X is 7 because it's the combination of in-degree (5) + out-degree (2).

## NODE ATTRIBUTES

Every node in a network can have a range of attributes that can be used to distinguish some properties of a node.

The attribute can be in binary form to explain in simple true/false, yes/no, online/offline, or married/unmarried. This is one of the easy representations of an node attribute where we have only choose one out of the two choices.

The attributes can be set categorical based on if options available are more than two such as if we want to set an attribute to a node called as relationship then we can use different category as an option to it, e.g., 1. Friend, 2. Family, 3. Colleague.

The attribute can also be set as continuous such as based on some of the information that cannot be same for every node. For example, date of birth, job position etc. We can also use the same as attributes of a node to distinguish as node quite easily.

# EDGE ATTRIBUTES
## DIRECTION
Based on direction, two major types of edges can be found.

1. Directed edges
2. Undirected edges

### Directed edges
Directed edges are the edges with unidirectional relationship. The best example of a directed edge is $X \rightarrow Y$. Here X is unidirectional related with Y. We can say that Y is a child of X or X loves Y or any such one-sided relationships.

### Undirected edges
It can be used for establishing mutual relationships, such as $X \leftarrow \rightarrow Y$ or $X - Y$. The relationship can be anything like X and Y are friends or classmates or colleagues.

## TYPE
It can be the type of relationship that put an edge in a group. Let's say that there are different nodes and edges but if some of the edges are similar by the type let say a group then we can distinguish them quite easily. Type can be anything such as starting from friends, close friends, colleague, relative etc. And it has a significant role in differentiating different edges.

## WEIGHT
It can be the number of connection that two nodes can have. For example, if $X \leftarrow \rightarrow Y$ shares more than one mutual/undirected or directed edge to each other then the weight of that edge is that number. For example, X relates with Y in five ways then the weight of that edge is 5. We can simply draw five edges between those two nodes or we can draw a deeper edge between them to make it easy to understand that these two nodes contain a higher weighted edge.

Weight can be also of two types:

1. Positive
2. Negative

### Positive weight
It's based on the likelihood of a relationship. For easy understanding let's talk about a politician. There are many people who like a particular politician. So the relationship they establish with the same will be the positive weight.

### Negative weight
Similarly as we came across, the negativity or the hate or the unlikelihood can be also a factor in a relationship. That can be measured by the negative weight.

## RANKING

Based on the priorities of the relationship established between two nodes, edges can have different rankings. Such as X's favorite subject is Math, X's second favorite subject is Physics. So to differentiate between these priorities ranking comes in to existence for easy understanding in a network.

## BETWEENNESS

There are certain scenarios where we can see that there are two different group of nodes connected to each other by an edge. So those kind of edges perceive a unique quality to combine two different groups or set of nodes and that can be called as betweenness. There are many other attributes that can be found situational. For the time being we can say that we have basic knowledge of network, its components, and its attributes so that if in future we get a chance to create a network or understand a given network then we can understand at least the basics of it properly.

The core basics of the network and about its components are covered above but still we haven't covered the main topic that is SNA.

As discussed earlier in the chapter, SNA is about mapping and measuring of relationships between different entities. These entities can be people, groups, organizations, systems, applications, and other connected entities. The nodes in the network are usually people but it can be anything based on what network we are looking at, while the links represent relationships or flows between the nodes. SNA provides both mathematical as well as graphical analysis of relationships using which an analyzer can deduce number of conclusions such as who is a hub in the network, how different entities connected to each other, and why they connected to each other with a proper logical and data-driven answer. The factors that come into act such as degree, betweenness, and others are already covered.

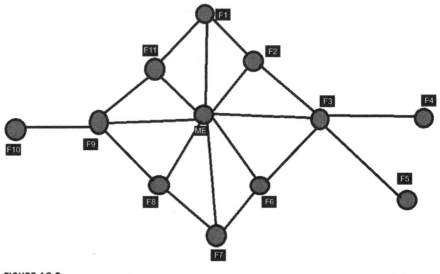

**FIGURE 12.3**

A small sample network to understand different components.

This is a sample network of friends where the edges define the level of communication shared between each one of them. It is a simple network to understand different aspects of SNA about how to find different important information by just looking at a network.

The first thing we can find quite easily is that the active node in the network. An active node or a hub is that node that has highest degree of edges. In this case as it is quite clear that node "me" has the highest degree of edges, and the degree is 8, we can conclude that node "me" is the most active node and connects almost all the other nodes. In any personal network generally it is said that the greater the number of friends the better the network, but it is not always true. Another thing we can conclude that node "me" connects to only those who have a common friend at least. These are some of the assumptions that can be derived from the network.

There are two nodes that play a vital role in the network. Node "F3" and "F9." These two nodes connect some nodes to the "me" node cluster. These "F3" and "F9" are the single points of contact in terms of connecting "F4"and "F5," and "F10" respectively. These two nodes decide what information to send in to the cluster and what information to send out according to the location that makes these two nodes extremely powerful in this network. We came across a term betweenness. Now it's time to use it. The node with high betweenness has the greater influence on the data flow through that. So in our case as the node "F3" has the highest betweenness, and that is 2, it will influence the most and can be considered as the most powerful node in this network. And in other words it can be the one point of failure for rest of the nodes that is not directly connected in the cluster. In this way we can conclude that location plays a vital role in a network. It is the location that can make a node important as we have just seen in this case. These nodes can also be called as boundary spanners. As these nodes having ideas and information from both part of the network such as the cluster and the extended part, these nodes can be innovators that can think of new ideas and services by combining ideas from both part of the network.

If we look at the network centralities, then we can understand the network structure quite easily. It allows us to understand individual locations and its importance. If a network is very much centralized and has a single point of failure then the network can be easily fragmented by deactivating that node. So it's always better not to have a centralized network. In our case, it is a less centralized network. Though we have a hub and two nodes with betweenness, it's good to have a network like this because the deactivation of the hub will not affect the network directly because there are still paths to pass on information from one node to another. Though the failure of node "F3" and "F9" will create a sub network, the major part of this network or the "me" node cluster will still be unaffected.

Network reach is also a topic to discuss here. Network reach is nothing but using the shortest path that is generally one hop or two hop difference whether a node is able to communicate with any other node or not. This can be easily understood in live example of one of the popular social networking sites that is LinkedIn. It uses the same concept to look for the network reach. What it does, if we want to connect with a particular person then it will show the number of first, second, and third degree connections so that we can use any of them to get introduced. As in LinkedIn it is always better to use the first degree connection to get introduced because it is the shortest path to reach to a connection, so it makes all our direct connections important in LinkedIn. Similarly in case of this network, it's always good to have a hub as a neighbor node. Because it's the neighbor node that plays a vital role in communication. If your neighbor node is a hub and connected to everyone then in a way we are also connected to everyone by him and it expands our network reach. Here in this network apart from node "F4," "F5," and "F10" rest of the nodes that come under "me" node cluster has very good network reach because of "me" node.

To get information from different sources differently, we have to be in a position where we have alternative shortest paths for a single node as this will allow us to get same information with different perspective in a network. This basically depends on the network integration but in our case it is very poor. Whatever information will flow, it must flow through the hub "me" node. So it will be very difficult to get different perspective on the information. If the nodes F1, F2, F3, F6, F7, F8, F9, F11 would have connected to each other like mesh topology then most of the nodes would have different alternative shortest paths and that opens an option to get same information flows from different paths adding different flavors to it.

Most of the time we don't value the extended network such as in our case node F4, F5, and F10. These nodes are not the part of the cluster and the same makes them very important. They are the one who will get very low information from the network cluster but for the network point of view they are the point of fresh ideas. They can provide outside valuable information into the cluster. For this network they might be foreign but for some network they must have been local and that information can be passed on to this "me" cluster using them. These kinds of nodes also called as peripheral nodes.

A network is never a result or report. It's more like a mirror which reflects a number of things about a network not necessarily good always. So try to understand the key components, key players of a network to understand the behavior of a network.

According to the position of a node, a node works in a specific way or vice versa. We can say that according to the role of a node we can find its position in a specific place in a network. So either way a position based on role or role based on location is quite important to understand a network. Now let's look into some of the roles and then try to figure it out how many roles were there in the previous network.

Roles based on location of the node.

### Star/Hub

Star is an entity that is highly central. Previously we have used the term hub for the node that contains major number of connections, this is the same. So we can use term start or hub and from the previous example, we can see that we have a star node and that is "me."

### Gatekeeper/Boundary spanners

An entity who mediates or we can say controls the flow between one portion of the network with another, earlier we named it different, we used boundary spanner for it. These are just different keywords with same definitions or are the same. In our previous example, "F9" and "F3" are the gatekeepers.

### Bridge

It is the only edge which links/belongs to two or more groups. In the previous example, there are three bridges, (1) F9 → F10, (2) F3 → F4, (3) F3 → F5.

### Liaison

An entity which has links to two or more groups that would otherwise not be linked, but is not a member of either group. In our previous example, it does not have any such node that was in a position of Liaison.

### Isolate

As the name suggests, isolate is an entity which has no links to other entities; generally a linkless or edgeless node. In our previous example, we do not have any isolate nodes.

So there are certain roles that are not present in our example, so here is a new network that contains all the roles and highlighted properly for easy understanding.

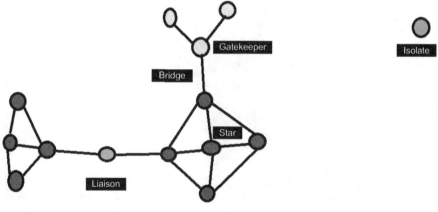

**FIGURE 12.4**

Network highlighting different roles.

SNA can be helpful in many ways to understand the information flow, we can use the same in variety of situations such as predict exit poll results from the verdict of online users or identify how and to what extent an information will flow in a network of friends, understand an organizational culture, or even find the loopholes in a process.

For a simpler example, to use it in generic scenario we can create a network of Twitter users of a community or organization and see who is following whom and who is being followed. This would help us to understand who the key players are in that structure and create the most influence. Similarly we can also understand, who is more follower type and who are leaders. In a network of professionals in an organization, it can be used to identify the people who create a hierarchy and how path would be better if one professional needs to connect to another one who is not a direct connection.

Similarly it can be used to analyze a network of connected people to identify how a communicable disease would spread in the network and which links need to be broken before the whole network gets infected. Another example could be in a network of market leaders of an industry to identify who is the hub in that network and needs to be targeted to be influenced for a decision to be taken.

Most of the attributes and functions that we have discussed in the chapter can be automatically calculated using Gephi, it also has many algorithms which can be utilized to perform the layout, identify key elements, implement filters, and perform various other operations. It can also be extended utilizing various plugins option which is present under the tools button.

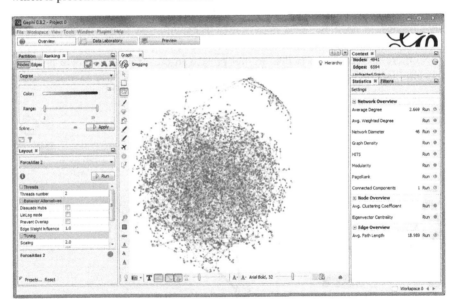

**FIGURE 12.5**

Sample network in Gephi with different values calculated.

SNA is used by various social network platforms and organizations which deal with connection between people; similarly it has application in many domains which depend on information science to flourish their market.

We learned something new in this chapter and can use the same in future for easy understanding of any complex system by creating a simpler network for that. Here we have covered the very basics of the concept of SNA. This topic has very wide applications in different fields. Our aim here has been to introduce the topic so that readers can get familiar with it and understand its importance and hence explore it further for practical usage.

Moving on in the next chapter we will be learning about Python basics. Though programming basics will be covered, it is a good idea to brush up basic concepts before moving onto it.

# Quick and Dirty Python

## INFORMATION IN THIS CHAPTER

- Introduction to programming
- Python intro
- Python components
- Examples and Samples
- Creating tools and transforms

## INTRODUCTION

After covering many interesting topics related to utilizing different automated tools, in this chapter we will be learning to create some. Sometimes there is a need to perform some specific task for which we are not able to find any tools which suits the requirements, this is when we have some basic programming knowledge so that we can quickly create some code to perform the desired operation. This chapter will touch upon the basics of Python programming language. We will understand why and how to use Python, what are the basic entities and then we will move on to create some simple but useful code snippets. It is advised to have some programming knowledge before moving on with this chapter as we will be covering the basic essentials related to the language and jump straight into the code. Though the examples used would be simple yet having some programming experience would be helpful.

Anyone who has some interest in computer science is familiar with the concept of programming. In simple terms it is the process of creating a program to solve a problem. To create this program we require to have a language using which we can write instructions for computer to understand and perform the task. The simple objective of a computer program is to automate a series of instructions so that they need not to be provided one by one manually.

## PROGRAMMING VERSUS SCRIPTING

The language we are going to be discussing in this chapter is Python, which is commonly termed as a scripting language, so before moving further let's understand what that means. Usually the code written in a programming language is compiled to machine code using a program called compiler to make it executable. For example, code written in C++ language is compiled to create an exe file which can be executed in a Windows platform.

There is another program called as an interpreter which allows running a language code without being compiled. So if the execution environment for a piece of code is an interpreter it is a script. Usually Python is executed in such environment and hence is commonly called a scripting language. This does not mean that a scripting language cannot be compiled, it simply is not usual. All scripting languages are programming languages.

## INTRODUCTION TO PYTHON

Python is a high-level programming language created by Guido Van Rossum, which emphases on the readability of code. Python is very fast and allows solving problem with minimum amount of code and hence is very popular among people who need to create quick scripts on the go, such as pentesters. There are various versions of Python but we will be focusing on the 2.7 version in this chapter. Though the latest version as of now is 3.4, yet most of the Python tools and libraries available online are based on the 2.7 version and the 3.x version is not backward compatible and hence we will not be using it. There are some changes in 3.x version but once we get comfortable with 2.7 it won't require much effort to move to it, if required.

The main agenda behind this chapter is not to create a course on Python that would require a separate book in itself. Here we will be covering the basics quickly and then move on to creating small and useful scripts for general requirements. The aim is to understand Python, write quick snippets, customize existing tools, and create own tools as per requirements. This chapter strives to introduce the possibilities of creating efficient programs in a limited period of time, provide the means to achieve it, and then further extend it as required.

There are other alternatives to Python available, mainly Ruby and Perl. Perl is one of the oldest scripting languages and Ruby is being widely used for web development (Ruby on Rails) yet Python is one of the easiest and simplest language when it comes to rapidly creating something with efficiency. Python is also being used for web development (Django).

## INSTALLATION

Installing Python in Windows is pretty straight forward, simply download the 2.7 version from https://www.python.org/downloads/ and go forward with the installer. Linux and other similar environments mostly come preinstalled with Python.

Though, it is not mandatory yet highly recommended to install Setuptools and Pip for easy installation and management of Python packages. Details related to Setuptools and Pip can be found at https://pypi.python.org/pypi/setuptools and https://pypi.python.org/pypi/pip respectively.

## MODES

We can run Python basically in two ways, one is to directly interact with the interpreter, where we provide the commands through direct interaction and see the output of it (if any) and other one is through scripts, where we write the code into a file, save it as filename.py and execute it using the interpreter. Though writing the script is a better way of writing a code which could be used and modified later yet the interactive mode is also very helpful. We can quickly check how a command works, what are its attributes, we can quickly try something that we want to write and see the results, and we can test and debug our code easily and also get help related to any command quickly. It is also a good practice to start with the interpreter to learn about the different aspects of the language and then utilize them to create the script by combining the blocks.

## HELLO WORLD PROGRAM

So for the customary "Hello World" program, we can simply go ahead into the Python interpreter by typing "Python" and write the code.

```
print "Hello World"
```

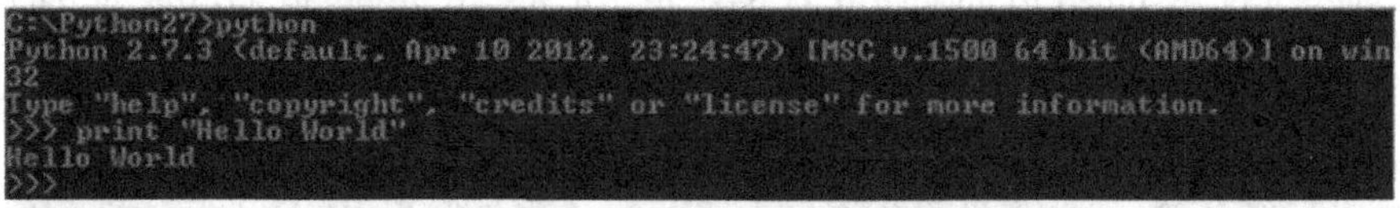

```
C:\Python27>python
Python 2.7.3 (default, Apr 10 2012, 23:24:47) [MSC v.1500 64 bit (AMD64)] on win32
Type "help", "copyright", "credits" or "license" for more information.
>>> print "Hello World"
Hello World
>>>
```

**FIGURE 13.1**

Hello World example.

This prints "Hello World" into the interpreter and it can't get simpler than this. If we want this in a script form then we can write the same code in a text file and save it as helloworld.py. Now to execute it we need to call this file through Python.

```
python helloworld.py
```

In Windows we can also call the script file simply from the command prompt to run our script or by double clicking on the script file. In Linux environment we can execute this script directly using the dot slash notation, but for that first we need to make the file executable using the command "chmod."

```
chmod 755 helloworld.py
./helloworld.py
```

Though it is not mandatory it is a good practice to specify Python environment into the script file itself through shebang notation. For this we simply need to include the following line at the starting of the script file.

```
#!/usr/bin/python
```

It simply specifies where is the interpreter required to execute this file. This is only supported in Linux environment but including it into the code does not have any change in Windows environment so it is better to include it so that the same code can execute in both the environments. If multiple interpreters are installed in Linux then we can simply change the environment path to the one suitable for our code, for example, if both Python 3.0 and 2.7 are installed we can write #!/usr/bin/Python2.7 to use the 2.7 interpreter to execute our code.

## IDENTIFIERS

In programming, identifiers are the names used to identify any variable, function, class, and other similar objects used in a program. In Python, they can start with an alphabet or an underscore followed by alphabets, digits, and underscore. They can contain a single character also. So we can create identifiers accordingly, except certain words which are reserved for special purposes, for example, "for," "if," "try," etc. Python is also case sensitive which means "test" and "Test" are different.

## DATA TYPES

Python has different variable types, but is decided by the value passed to it and does not require to be stated explicitly. Actually the data type is not associated with the variable name but the value object and the variable simply references to it. So a variable can be assigned to another data type after it already refers to a different data type.

**FIGURE 13.2**

Value assignment.

Commonly used data types are:

- Numbers
- String
- Lists
- Tuples
- Dictionaries

To define a number simply assign a variable with a number value, for example,

```
>>>samplenum=10
```

Just to know there are various types of numerical such as float, long, etc.

To define a string we can use the help of quotes (both single and double), for example,

```
>>>samplestr="This is a string"
>>>samplestr2='This is another string'
```

We can also utilize both the types of quotes in a nested form. To create multiline strings we can use triple quotes.

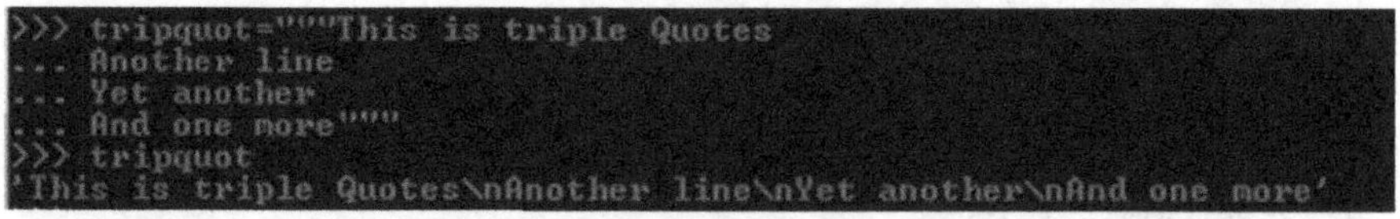

```
>>> tripquot="""This is triple Quotes
... Another line
... Yet another
... And one more"""
>>> tripquot
'This is triple Quotes\nAnother line\nYet another\nAnd one more'
```

**FIGURE 13.3**

Triple quotes.

We can also utilize the % operator for strings to include different data types. The values are passed in a tuple (discussed later) and %d is for integers, %s is for strings, %f for float.

### *Example code*

```
>>>sample_str="There are total %d number of floors in the %s
   building"%(4,'xyz')
>>>sample_str
```

There are total 4 number of floors in the xyz building

Python provides an interesting data type called list and according to its name it is a list of variables of different types. To create a list we can utilize square brackets and separate the variables with commas.

```
>>>samplelist=[123, "str", 'xyz', 321, 21.22]
>>>samplelist
[123, "str", 'xyz', 321, 21.22]
>>>samplelist[1]
'str'
```

Tuples are similar to lists but are immutable and are created using parentheses.

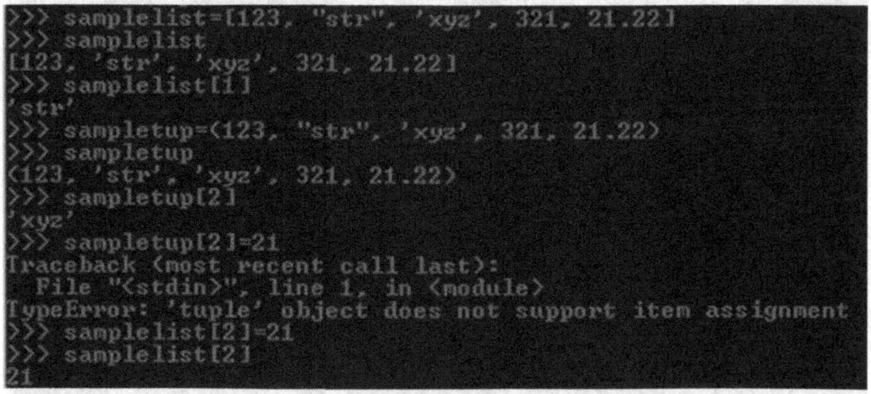

```
>>> samplelist=[123, "str", 'xyz', 321, 21.22]
>>> samplelist
[123, 'str', 'xyz', 321, 21.22]
>>> samplelist[1]
'str'
>>> sampletup=(123, "str", 'xyz', 321, 21.22)
>>> sampletup
(123, 'str', 'xyz', 321, 21.22)
>>> sampletup[2]
'xyz'
>>> sampletup[2]=21
Traceback (most recent call last):
  File "<stdin>", line 1, in <module>
TypeError: 'tuple' object does not support item assignment
>>> samplelist[2]=21
>>> samplelist[2]
21
```

**FIGURE 13.4**

List and tuples.

Dictionary is another interesting data type which consists of items with values associated with them. In these key-value pairs the key needs to be unique whereas the value can change.

```
>>>sampledict={'test1':'123','test2':'234','test3':'345'}
>>>sampledict['test1']
'123'
>>>sampledict['test4']='456'
>>>sampledict['test3']='333'
>>>sampledict
{'test1': '123', 'test2': '234', 'test3': '333', 'test4': '456'}
```

There are also various functions provided by different object which can be of great help at times, instead of writing whole new set of code to perform it. To find out these we can get help from Python functions "dir" and "help".

```
>>>dir(sampledict)
>>>help(sampledict)
```

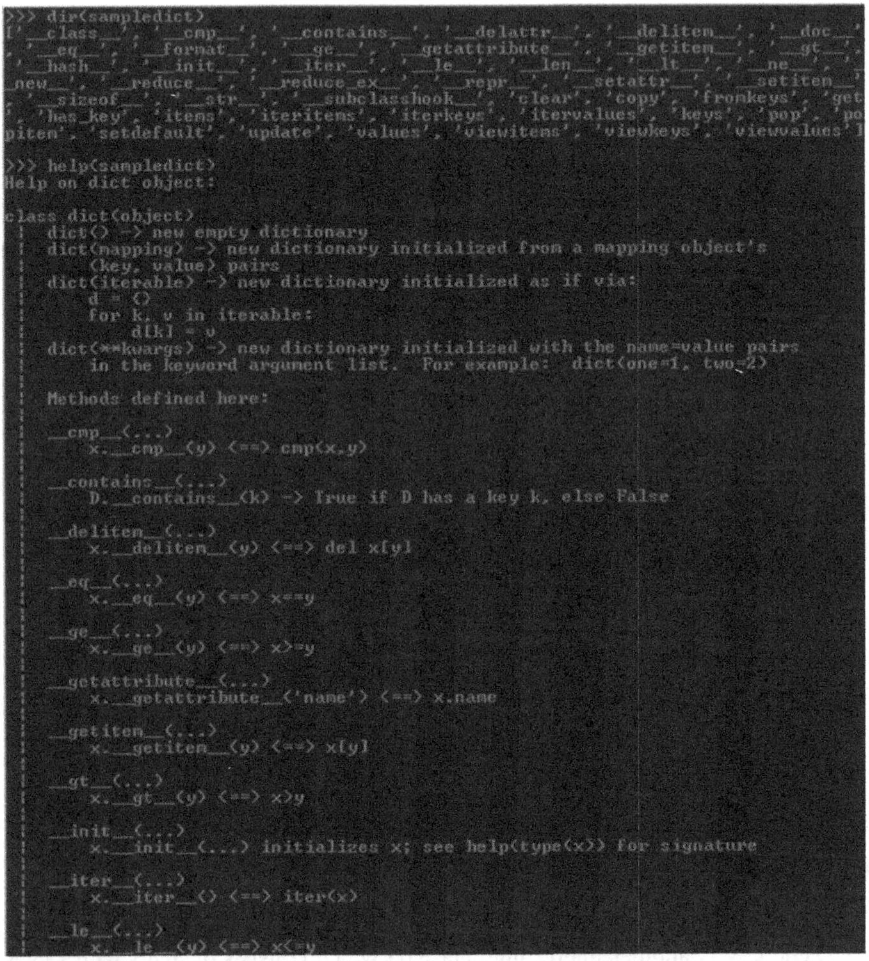

**FIGURE 13.5**

Using Python help.

We have demonstrated some basics of data types but there is much more operations which can be performed on these data types. Some basic examples are shown below:

```
>>>a=12
>>>b=2
>>>a*b
24
>>>a="test"
>>>b="next"
>>>a+b
'test next'
>>>lt1=['1','2','3']
>>>lt2=['4','5','6']
>>>lt1+lt2
['1', '2', '3', '4', '5', '6']
```

We can perform various operations on these elements. Some examples are shown below.

```
>>>a=1
>>>b=2
>>>a+b
3
>>>a="test"
>>>b="string"
>>>a+b
'teststring'
>>>a.upper()
'TEST'
>>>c="This is a string"
>>>c.find('ring')
12
>>>c.find('xyz')
-1
>>>sample_list=['qw','er','ty',123]
>>>sample_list.append(456)
>>>sample_list
['qw', 'er', 'ty', 123, 456]
```

## INDENTATION

Before moving further let's clear up on one import concept of Python. Python supports code readability. Unlike other languages such as C++ it does not use brackets to specify the code blocks, whereas uses indentation. So when creating a block of code we need to provide whitespaces to indicate the structure. One important point is that we can have variable number of spaces for indentation but within a block all the statements should have the same amount. Some people use spaces for indentation and some use the tab feature, it is better to stick with one and not mix up both in a single code. The examples shown in the following chapter will work on this concept and we will be using spaces.

Basic terms (class, function, conditional statements, loops, etc.)
Now let's move forward with conditional statements.

The most basic conditional statement is "if." The logic is simple, if the provided condition is it will execute the statement, else it will move on. Basic structure of "if" and associated conditions is shown below.

```
if condition:
  then_this_statement
elif condition:
  then_this_statement
else:
  this_condition
```

### Example code

```
#!/usr/bin/python
a=10
b=12
c=15
if (a==b):
  print "a=b"
elif (b==c):
  print "b=c"
elif (c==a):
  print "c=a"
else:
  print "none"
```

Write this in a notepad file and save it as if_con.py. This code will result in the response "none," when executed in Python. The "elif" and "else" conditions are not mandatory when using "if" statement and we can have multiple "elif" statements. Similarly we can also have nested "if" conditions where there will be if statements within another if statement, just proper indentation needs to be kept in mind.

```
if condition:
  then_this_statement
  if nested_condition:
   then_this_nested_statement
  else nested-else_condition:
   then_this_nested-else_statement
```

The "while" loop is next in line. Here we will provide the condition and the loop will run until that condition is true . Structure of "while" is shown below.

```
while this_condition_statement_is-true:
  run_this_statement
```

### Example code

```
#!/usr/bin/python
a=10
c=15
while (a<c):
  print a
  a=a+1
```

### Output

```
10
11
12
13
14
```

We can also utilize "break" and "continue" statement to control the flow of the loop. The "break" statement is used to break out of the current loop and the "continue" statement is used to pass the control back to the starting of the loop. There is one more interesting statement called "pass" which does nothing, in particular is used just as a placeholder.

Another useful conditional statement is "for" loop. Using it we can iterate through the items present within an object such as a tuple or list.

### Example code

```
#!/usr/bin/python
sample_tup=('23','test',12,'w2')
for items in sample_tup:
print items
```

### Output

```
123
test
12
w2
```

We are simply passing the individual values in the tuple sample_tup and putting them inside the variable items one by one and printing them.

### Example code

```
#!/usr/bin/python
str="String"
for items in str:
  print items
```

### Output

```
S
t
r
i
n
g
```

We can also utilize the attributes of the objects (find through "dir" and "help") for the iteration purpose. Similar to "while" we can also use "break" and "continue" statements in "for" loop as well.

Now we are done with the conditional statements and move forward with other structures.

## MODULES

Sometimes there is a need to reuse the code or manage it depending upon our requirement, this is where modules come into picture. Say there are multiple components of an object and these components are also required in some other object, so instead of creating these components again and again we can simply create and store them separately and call them into the object as and when required. For example, creating a program for an entity car and another for truck, both will have common components such as brakes, accelerator, etc., so we will code these components once and simply call them into the program according to the requirement, instead of creating them again and again. This is very helpful in organizing and managing the code.

Modules can define variables, functions, and classes, we will discuss about these shortly. Once we create these and save them in separate files, we can import them into our code and use their functionalities.

### Example code

```
#!/usr/bin/python
y="Module String"
```

Save this as x.py. Create another file called mod.py and save the following code into it:

```
#!/usr/bin/python
import x
print x.y
```

### output

```
Module String
```

So we simply created a module with just a variable, called it into another code and used its variable. Utilizing modules we can create complex programs without cluttering all the code into a single file. We can also import a module using the call "from module_name import desired_portion".

Let's learn about functions and classes.

## FUNCTIONS

Functions help to group a set of code as a single functionality, which is useful in code with large number of lines of code. Function start with the keyword "def" followed by the function name and then the parenthesis inside which the arguments are placed and then the colon. Functions also contain a return statement to terminate it and pass back values (can be null). To call a function we can use its name along with the values to be passed (inside the parenthesis).

### *Example code*

```
#!/usr/bin/python
def simplefunc(atr_arg):
  print "Print me first"
  print atr_arg
  return
str="Sample String"
simplefunc(str)
```

### *Output*

```
Print me first
Sample String
```

## CLASSES

Using classes we can group different operations together. To create a class we simply need to start with the keyword class followed by a name for the class and then a colon.

### *Example code*

```
#!/usr/bin/python
class sample_class:
  def __init__(self, classarg):
    self.cla=classarg
  def firstfunc(self):
    print "First Function"
    return self.cla+" Return"
  def secfunc(self):
    print "Second Function"
    return self.cla+" Return"
classobj=sample_class("Argument")
print classobj.firstfunc()
print classobj.secfunc()
```

### Output

```
First Function
Argument Return
Second Function
Argument Return
```

Here the function __init__ is the constructor of the class and is the first function which runs in the class. The variable "classobj" is the object for the class "sample_class" and using it we can communicate with the objects inside the class. As discussed earlier we can also create this as a module and call it inside another program.

As discussed earlier, let's take another example of importing modules.

### Example code

```
#!/usr/bin/python
class sample_class:
  def __init__(self, classarg):
    self.cla=classarg
  def firstfunc(self):
    print "First Function"
    return self.cla+" Return"
  def secfunc(self):
    print "Second Function"
    return self.cla+" Return"
classobj=sample_class("Argument")
```

This file is being saved as mod.py and another file calls this as a module with the code:

```
#!/usr/bin/python
from mod import *
print classobj.firstfunc()
```

### Output

```
First Function
Argument
```

In Python we can also create directory of modules for better organization through packages. They are hierarchical structures and can contain modules and subpackages.

## WORKING WITH FILES

Sometimes there is a need to save or retrieve data from files for this we will learn how to deal with files in Python.

First of all, to open a file we need to create an object for it using the function open and provide the mode operation.

```
>>>sample_file=open('text.txt',"w")
```

Here the name sample_file is the object and using open function we are opening the file text.txt. If the file with this name does not already exists it will be created and if already exists it will be overwritten. The last portion inside the parenthesis describes the mode, here it is w which means write mode. Some other commonly used modes are "r" for reading, "a" for append, "r+" for both read and write without overwriting, and "w+" for read and write with overwriting.

Now we have created an object so let's go ahead and write some data to our file.

```
>>>sample_file("test data")
```

Once we are done with writing data to the file we can simply close it.

```
>>>sample_file.close()
```

Now to read a file we can do the following:

```
>>>sample_file=open('text.txt',"r")
>>>sample_file.read()
'test data'
>>>sample_file.close()
```

Similarly we can also append data to files using "a" mode and write() function.

Python has various inbuilt as well as third party modules and packages which are very useful. In case we encounter a specific problem that we need to solve using Python code it is better to look for an existing module first. This saves a lot of time figuring out the steps and writing huge amount of code through simply importing the modules and utilizing the existing functions. Let's check some of these.

## *Sys*

As stated in its help file this module provides access to some objects used and maintained by interpreter and functions that strongly interact with it.

To use it we import it into our program.

```
import sys
```

Some of the useful features provided by it are argv, stdin, stdout, version, exit(), etc.

## *Re*

Many times we need to perform pattern matching to extract relevant data from a large amount of it. This is when regular expressions are helpful. Python provides "re" module to perform such operations.

```
import re
```

## *Os*

The "os" module in Python allows to perform operating system-dependent functionalities.

```
import os
```

Some sample usages are to create directories using mkdir function, rename a file using rename function, kill a process using kill function and display list of entries in a directory using listdir function.

### Urllib2

This module allows to perform URL-related operations such as open a web page. It is very helpful when working with web applications.

```
import urllib2
```

There are many other useful modules such as Scapy (network), Scrapy (web scraping), nose (testing), mechanize (stateful web browsing), and others which provide huge amount of functionalities in their domain. Some modules are inbuilt and some need to be installed separately. There is still much more to explore in this topic but here we will be stopping with these points and move on to the next topic.

## USER INPUT

Certain problems require to take user input. Here are two methods to do so:

Using Sys module we can take user input from command line argument.

### Example code

```
#!/usr/bin/python
import sys
a=sys.argv[1]
print a
print a*4
a=int(a)
print a
print a*4
```

Save this as usrinp.py and pass the command line argument.

C:\Python27>usrinp.py 2

### Output

```
2
2222
2
8
```

argv is a list that takes command line arguments where the index 0 is reserved for filename. We can also pass multiple values and iterate by changing the index value of argv. Here we have also demonstrated a simple type conversion (string to integer).

Another method is to get input at run time, this can be done using raw_input.

### Example code

```
#!/usr/bin/python
import sys
a=raw_input("Enter something: ")
print a*4
```

When executing this code, it will prompt the message "Enter something", once we input the value it will generate the response accordingly. For an input value "a" it will generate the output "aaaa".

## COMMON MISTAKES

Some common issues faced during the execution of Python code are as follows.

### Indentation

As shown in examples above, Python uses indentations for grouping the code. Some people use spaces for this and some use tabs. When running the code written by some person or modifying it we sometimes face the indentation error. To resolve this error, check the code for proper indentation and correct the instances; also make sure to not mess up by using tabs as well as spaces in the same code as it creates confusion for the person looking at the code.

### Libraries

Sometimes people have a completely correct code, yet it fails to execute with a library error. The reason is missing of a library that is being called in the code. Though it is a novice mistake, sometimes experienced people also don't read the exact error and start looking for errors in the code. The simple solution is to install the required library.

### Interpreter version

Sometimes the code is written for a specific version of the language and when being executed in a different environment, it breaks. To correct this, install the required version and specify it in the code as shown earlier in this chapter or execute the code using the specific interpreter. Sometimes there are multiple codes which require different versions; to solve this problem we can use virtualenv, which allows us to create an isolated virtual environment where we can include all the dependencies to run our code.

### Permission

Sometimes the file permissions are not set properly to execute the code so make the changes accordingly using chmod.

### Quotes

When copying code from some resources such as documents and websites there is a conversion between single quote (') and grave accent (`) which causes errors. Identify such conversions and make the changes to the code accordingly.

So we have covered basics about the language let's see some examples which can help us to understand the concepts and understand their practical usage and also get introduced to some topics not discussed above.

Similar to shodan, discussed in a previous chapter there is another service called zoomeye. In this example we will be creating a script using which will query zoomeye and extract the IP address from the result page. We have to pass the query term from command line.

For this we will first create the URL for this by combining the base URL and the search term passed through command line. Then we will send the request to this URL using the function urlopen from the module urllib2. Further we will be parsing the response page and extract the IP addresses from it using BeautifulSoup.

```python
#!/usr/bin/python
import sys
import urllib2
from bs4 import BeautifulSoup
url="http://www.zoomeye.org/search?q="
term=sys.argv[1]
comurl=url+term
response=urllib2.urlopen(comurl)
soup = BeautifulSoup(response)
for item in soup.findAll("a",{'class':'ip'}):
  print item.string
```

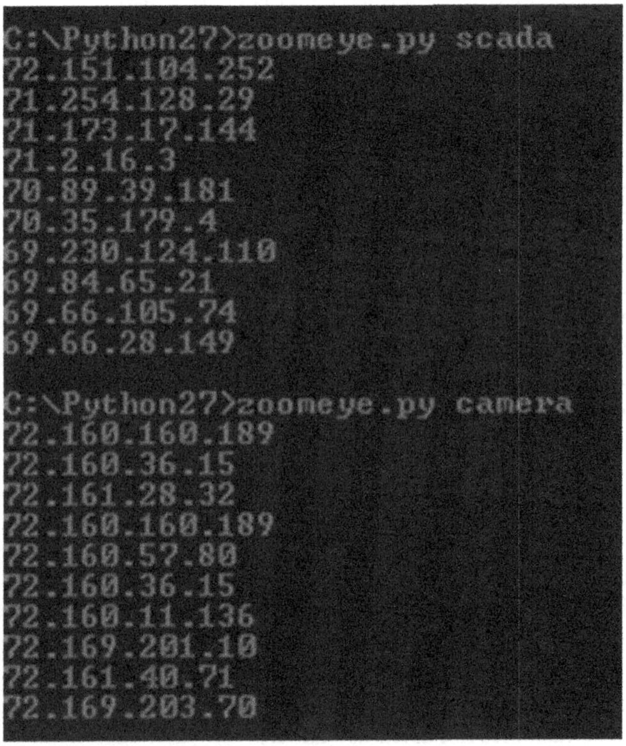

**FIGURE 13.6**

Zoomeye script result.

For our next example we will create an extension for Burp Suite. Burp Suite is an application proxy which is used for web application security assessment. It allows to create extensions through which we can extend its functionalities. For our extension we will simply extract the host name of the target.

```python
#! /usr/bin/python

# A sample burp extension in python (needs jython) which extracts
hostname from the request (Target Tab).
from burp import IBurpExtender
from burp import IMenuItemHandler
import re
import urllib2
class BurpExtender(IBurpExtender):
  def registerExtenderCallbacks(self, callbacks):
    self.mCallBacks = callbacks
    self.mCallBacks.registerMenuItem("Sample Extension",
hostnamefunc())

class hostnamefunc(IMenuItemHandler):
  def menuItemClicked(self, menuItemCaption, messageInfo):
    print "--- Hostname Extract ---"

    if messageInfo:

      request1=HttpRequest(messageInfo[0].getRequest())
      req=request1.request
      host=req[1]
      print host
      print "DONE"
class HttpRequest:
  def __init__(self, request):
    self.request=request.tostring().splitlines()
```

To make this extension run, first we need to install Jython and configure it under the options tab within extender. Once this is done we can add our extension under the Extensions tab within extender. To use our extension we simply need to right click on a target domain under the target tab and click on the "Sample Extension" on the right click menu, the result will be shown in the Extensions in extender tab. The example is simply to demonstrate an extension using Python we can further enhance it by performing other operations on the host name.

## MALTEGO TRANSFORMS

In a previous chapter we discussed about Maltego, a simple and effective open source intelligence (OSINT) tool. We learned how to use it, what all features it provided, what are its elements, etc. Let's take this a step further and utilizing the knowledge of Python we have just acquired to extend this framework. As mentioned in a previous chapter, the power of Maltego lies in its transforms. For quick recall a transform is basically a piece of code which takes an entity (or a group of entities) as an input and extracts data in the form of entity (or entities) based upon the relationship. Maltego has a lot of inbuilt transforms and keeps on updating the framework with new ones, but it also allows to create new ones and use them, this can be very helpful when we need something custom according to our needs.

Before we move any further we need the "MaltegoTransform" Python library by Andrew MacPherson, which is very helpful in local transform development. It can be downloaded from the page https://www.paterva.com/web6/documentation/develo per-local.php. Some basic examples of local transforms created using the library are also present at the bottom of the page. Once we have the library in our directory we are ready to go and create our own first transforms.

To create any program first we need to have a problem statement. Here we need to create a transform so let's first identify something that would be helpful during our OSINT exercise. There is a service called as HaveIBeenPwned (https://haveibee npwned.com) created by Troy Hunt which allows users to check if their account has been compromised in a breach. It also provides an application programming interface (API) using which we can perform the same function. We will be using the v1 of the API (https://haveibeenpwned.com/API/v1) and provide an e-mail address to check if our supplied e-mail has any account associated.

To utilize the API we simply need to send a GET request to the service in the form shown below and it will provide a JSON response to show the website names.

https://haveibeenpwned.com/api/breachedaccount/{account}

Let's first specify the path of the interpreter

```
#!/usr/bin/python
```

Now we need to import the library MaltegoTransform

from MaltegoTransform import *

Once we have the main library we need to import some other libraries that will be required. Library "sys" is to take user input and urllib2 to make the GET request.

```
import sys
import urllib2
```

Once we have imported all the required libraries, we need to assign the function MaltegoTransform() to a variable and pass the user input (e-mail address) from Maltego interface to it.

```
mt = MaltegoTransform()
mt.parseArguments(sys.argv)
```

Now we can pass the e-mail value to a variable so that we can use it to create the URL required to send the GET request.

```
email=mt.getValue()
```

Let's create a variable and save the base URL in it.

```
hibp="https://haveibeenpwned.com/api/breachedaccount/"
```

As we have both the parts of the complete URL, now we can simply combine them to create the complete URL.

```
getrequrl=hibp+email
```

Let's send the GET request using the function urlopen in the library urllib2 and store the response in a variable, but while handling the exception. Now we need to run a for loop to go through the values being stored in the variable (response) and add these values to the variable for the transform.

```
try:
  response = urllib2.urlopen(getrequrl)
  for rep in response:
    mt.addEntity("maltego.Phrase","Pwned at " + rep)
except:
  print ""
```

In this last step we need to return the output of the variable.

```
mt.returnoutput()
```

Now simply save this as emailhibp.py.

### Complete code

```
#!/usr/bin/python
from MaltegoTransform import *
import sys
import urllib2
mt = MaltegoTransform()
mt.parseArguments(sys.argv)
email=mt.getValue()
hibp="https://haveibeenpwned.com/api/breachedaccount/"
getrequrl=hibp+email
try:
  response = urllib2.urlopen(getrequrl)
  for rep in response:
    mt.addEntity("maltego.Phrase","Pwned at " + rep)
except:
  print ""
mt.returnoutput()
```

Now to check if our code is running properly we simply need to execute this program in the terminal and pass an e-mail address as a command line argument.

### Example

```
./emailhibp.py foo@bar.com
```

or

```
python ./emailhibp.py foo@bar.com
```

```
C:\Python27>emailhibp.py foo@bar.com
<MaltegoMessage>
<MaltegoTransformResponseMessage>
<Entities>
<Entity Type="maltego.Phrase">
<Value>Pwned at ["Adobe","Gawker","Stratfor"]</Value>
<Weight>100</Weight>
</Entity>
</Entities>
<UIMessages>
</UIMessages>
</MaltegoTransformResponseMessage>
</MaltegoMessage>
```

**FIGURE 13.7**

Transform output.

We can see that the response is a XML styled output and contains the string "Pwned at ["Adobe","Gawker","Stratfor"]". This means our code is working properly and we can use this as a transform. Maltego takes this XML result and parses it to create an output. Now our next step is to configure this as a transform in Maltego.

Under the manage tab go to Local Transform button to start the Local Transform Setup Wizard. This wizard will help us to configure our transform and include it into our Maltego instance.

In the Display name field provide the name for the transform and press tab, it will generate a Transform ID automatically. Now write a small description for the transform in the Description field and the name of the Author in the Author field. Next we have to select what would be the entity type that this transform takes as input, in this case it would be Email Address. Once the input entity type is selected we can choose the transform set under which our transform would appear which can also be none.

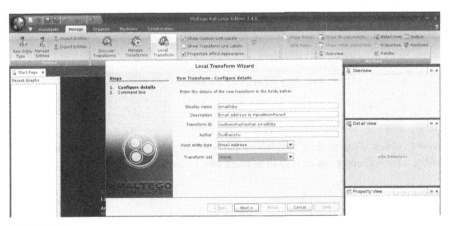

**FIGURE 13.8**

Transform setup wizard.

Now click on next and move to the second phase of the wizard. Here under the command field we need to provide the path to the programming environment we are going to use to run the transform code. In our case it would be

```
/usr/bin/python (for Linux)
```

C:\Python27/python.exe (for Windows)

Once the environment is set we can move to the parameters field, here we will provide the path to our transform script. For example,

```
/root/Desktop/transforms/emailhibp.py (for Linux)
```

C:\Python27\transforms\emailhibp.py (for Windows)

One point to keep in mind here is that if we select the transform file using the browse button provided in front of the "Parameters" field, then it will simply take the file name in the field, but we need absolute path of the transform to execute it so provide the path accordingly.

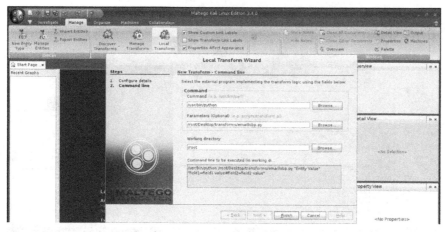

**FIGURE 13.9**

Transform setup wizard.

After all the information is filled into the place we simply need to finish the wizard and our transform is ready to run. To verify this, simply take an e-mail address entity and select the transform from the right click menu.

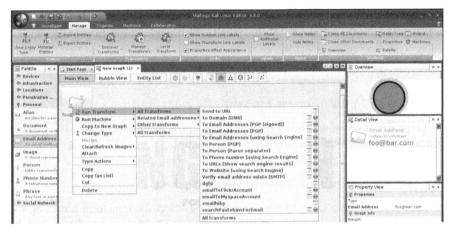

**FIGURE 13.10**

Select transform.

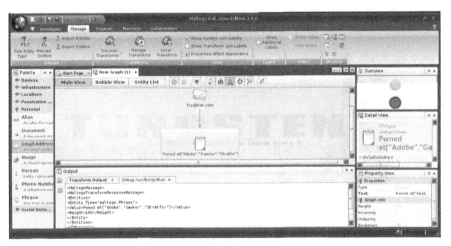

**FIGURE 13.11**

Transform execution.

Now we have created our first transform and also learned how to configure it in Maltego. Let's create another simple transform. For this example we will be using the website http://www.my-ip-neighbors.com/. It allows to perform a reverse IP domain lookup, simply said the domains sharing the same IP address as the one of the provided domain. As in the previous transform we provided an e-mail address as the input here we require a domain name, but this website provides no API service and hence we will have send the raw GET request and extract the domains out of the web page using regular expressions through the library "re".

```
#!/usr/bin/python
from MaltegoTransform import *
import sys
import urllib2
import re
mt = MaltegoTransform()
mt.parseArguments(sys.argv)
url=mt.getValue()
mt = MaltegoTransform()
opencnam="http://www.my-ip-neighbors.com/?domain="
getrequrl=opencnam+url
header={'User-Agent':'Mozilla'}
req=urllib2.Request(getrequrl,None,header)
response=urllib2.urlopen(req)
domains=re.findall("((?:[0-9]*[a-z][a-z\\.\\d\\-]+)\\.(?:
[0-9]*[a-z][a-z\\-]+))(?![\\w\\.])",response.read())
for domain in domains:
  mt.addEntity("maltego.Domain", domain)
mt.returnoutput()
```

*http://txt2re.com/ can be used to create regular expressions.

Similarly we can create lot of transforms which utilize online services, local tools (e.g., Nmap scan), and much more using Python. The examples shown above and some more can be found at https://github.com/SudhanshuC/Maltego-Transforms. Some other interesting transforms can be found at https://github.com/cmlh, else they are just a quick Github search away (https://github.com/search?utf8=%E2%9C%93 &q=maltego+transform).

There is also a Python-based framework available, which allows creating Maltego tranforms easily called as Canari (http://www.canariproject.com/).

There are various topics which we have not covered but the scope is limited and topic is very vast. Some of these are exception handling, multiprocessing, and multithreading. Below there are some resources which can be helpful in this quest of learning Python.

## RESOURCE

https://github.com/dloss/python-pentest-tools

A great resource to learn more about Python and its usage is the Python docs itself https://docs.python.org/2/. Another great list of Python-based tools with focus on pentesting is present at https://github.com/dloss/python-pentest-tools. It would be great to create something interesting and useful by modifying, combining, and adding to the mentioned resources. The list is divided into different sections based on the functionality provided by the tool mentioned.

So we have covered some basics of Python language and also learned how to extend Maltego framework through it. Through this chapter we have made an attempt to learn about creating own custom tools and modify existing ones in a quick fashion.

This chapter is just an introduction of how we can simply create tools with minimum amount of coding. There is certainly room for improvement in the snippets we have shown in functional as well as structural terms, but our aim is to perform the task as quickly as possible.

Though we have tried to cover as much ground as possible yet there is so much more to learn when it comes to Python scripting. Python comes with a large set of useful resources and is very powerful; and by using it one can create power tool-set, recon-ng (https://bitbucket.org/LaNMaSteR53/recon-ng) is great example of it. We have discussed about this Reconnaissance framework in a previous chapter. One great way to take this learning further would be to practice more and create such tools which could be helpful for the community and contribute to the existing ones such as recon-ng.

Slowly we are moving toward the end of this journey of learning. We have been through different aspects of intelligence gathering in different manners. Moving on we will be learning about some examples and scenarios related to our endeavor, where we can utilize the knowledge we have gained in a combined form.

# Case Studies and Examples

## INFORMATION IN THIS CHAPTER

- Introduction
- Case studies
- Example scenarios
- Maltego machines

## INTRODUCTION

After working with so many tools and techniques and going through so many processes of information gathering and analysis, now it's time to see some scenarios and examples where all this comes together for practical usage. In this chapter we will include some real scenarios in which we or people we know have used OSINT (open source intelligence) to collect the required information from very limited information. So without wasting any time let's directly jump into case study 1.

## CASE STUDIES

### CASE STUDY 1: THE BLACKHAT MASHUP

One of our friends returned from Black Hat US conference and he was very happy about the meetings and all. Our friend works for a leading security company and takes care of US sales. He was very excited about a particular lead he got there. The person he met there was in senior position of a gaming company and interested in the services offered by our friend's company. They had a very good networking session in the lounge while having drinks and in excitement he forgot to exchange the cards. So he had to find the person and send him the proposal that he committed.

- Problem No. 1: He forgot his full name but remembers his company name and location.
- Problem No. 2: While discussion the other person said that as many people approach him for such proposals, he uses a different name on LinkedIn.
- Problem No. 3: We know the position of the other person, but it is not a unique position such as CEO or CTO.

When he came to us with this case we had a gut feeling that we can find him. We have some sort of information about the person though that does not include any primary information such as e-mail address or full name.

These are the steps we followed.

The first thing we asked him was that whether he can recognize the person's picture or he forgot that also, to our good luck he said "yes." So the major point in our case was that if we will find some profiles of persons he can validate and confirm the right person.

Step 1:

As usual we first started with a simple Google query with the first name, his position, and company name. Let's say his position is senior manager and company name is abc.inc. The query we used is

Senior manager abc.inc

Step 2:

We tried the same in Facebook to get a profile equivalent to that but never the less no leads.

Step 3:

We went to LinkedIn tried that simply and failed.

Step 4:

We went to that company profile page and tried to visit all the employees' profiles but we found that there are more than 7000 registered employees therein LinkedIn and it's really a tough task to find anyone from there.

Step 5:

As we covered in Chapter 2 LinkedIn provides an advanced search feature and we have some of the direct data for the fields. So we have decided to use that.

https://www.linkedin.com/vsearch/p?trk=advsrch&adv=true

We filled data in the fields such as title, company, and location as our friend has these information. In result we got many equivalent profiles but this time we got far less results which we went through one by one and finally found the person in twenty-first result as he had shared that he has recently been to the conference. After visiting his profile we got a bit more details about that person and our friend confirmed that we got what we were looking for.

What could have been done after this?

We might get his primary e-mail id, company e-mail id, and other details using different sources such as Maltego or simple Google. Using the image we might go for a reverse image search to get related image and the sources. We might get the blogs or websites created by that person and many more. There were endless possibilities but we stopped there because for the time being that was out of our scope. We sent the link to our friend, who then sent him connection request and later got the deal and so we got a small treat.

## CASE STUDY 2: A DEMO THAT CHANGED AUDIENCE VIEW

We can't forget that demo because it changed many audiences' view on security. We were working on a project with a client who wanted to become partner with our organization. We were told that we need to provide some quality reports and all and then have to provide a report walkthrough to our prospective client. Later we were informed that some delegates including the operational manager and a senior consultant will visit us. We requested our management to let them sit in our internal knowledge sharing program where we were giving a demo on OSINT and how it can help in penetration testing and after that we can have report discussion. Our management agreed on that so we prepared a special OSINT demo.

We had the names of the delegates so the first thing we did was that quickly visited their profile to understand their background to know more about them. LinkedIn helped us a lot in this. We got bit understanding on their likes, dislikes, and technical background. We found that both were having a very good technical background in security so we planned the demo accordingly.

We started the demo with basics such as what is OSINT, why it is more important now a days, and so on. We moved on to talk about its importance in pentesting. Then we moved to how to collect different data about an organization or an application (web application without sending a single packet).

- Problem: We cannot demonstrate anything that requires access to their environment for which we don't have authorization.

We decided to start with the website of our client and then will jump to something interesting.

Following are the steps we followed:

Step 1:

We opened Maltego and added the domain name of our client. There is an option in Maltego to add a domain as an entity and we did the same and then ran some transforms to get different data such as Name server records and many more.

Step 2:

Running the buildwith transform on some of their domains displayed the technologies being used. They were happy seeing it in a graphical and organized way. Other transforms helped us to discover some other related domains/subdomains.

Step 3:

In one of the domains, we found that a very older version of php is being used. So what we did was simply opened the application in a browser where Shodan and Punk Spider plugins were enabled and running. The moment we opened that application in browser Shodan showed that application is vulnerable to Heartbleed and some sensitive ports opened while the punk spider provided that there were two blind SQL injections and some cross-site scripting vulnerabilities present previously.

Running an advanced Google search for the same parameters (vulnerable to SQLI and XSS) on their other domains (discovered in previous step) provided some URLs. This suggests that they might also be vulnerable to the same vulnerabilities.

```
site:example.com inurl:vulnpar
```

They were amazed by the results. They told us that it was a very older site they used to use and due to some technicality they forgot to bring that down. But we found some interesting facts about that application and we were happy.

Step 4:

Then we again opened Maltego where we ran the transform "Domain to Email address" other similar ones, where we collected some of the e-mail addresses.

Step 5:

Then we showed them the local transform written by us, HaveIBeenPwned. It's based on the API provided by Troy Hunt. In the previous chapter, we just covered about its working but just for the information it checks in the database of the popular sites where there is an account breach. If the e-mail id of any person has been breached there then it would have popped up an alert. After running this transformation in all the e-mail ids that we got from the domain name luckily we found two of their colleagues' accounts have been breached in a popular product-based company site.

It was something new for our clients and they immediately informed their colleagues about this. Though we got their attention, yet we wanted to demonstrate the impact of such information. We could have simply explained that there were sites to get particular passwords related to these e-mail ids such as pastebin, but we tried to show the bigger picture.

Step 6:

Then we selected those two e-mail ids and ran another transform written by us that is "Email-Rapportive." It is based on the service Rapportive: http://www.rapportive.com/ (based on the code of Jordan Wright). What it does exactly is that finds information about the person based on his e-mail address and provides us result. The result contains LinkedIn, Facebook, twitter profile links along with the name and job title of the person.

So basically it helps us to get the person's social existence and some important primary details such as full name.

Step 7:

After that we ran a Maltego machine on the e-mail generated in a previous step. A machine is nothing but a collection of one or more transforms to run in a collective fashion. We discussed a bit about this in Chapter 6 and will discuss more later in this chapter. So this machine discovers other e-mail addresses of similar pattern on e-mail services such as Gmail, Yahoo, Outlook etc. We got many results and explained them that there are people who use same password for different e-mail ids. So if someone can collect a password associated with a breached e-mail id and can find all other e-mail ids and registered website details, then there is a possibility that attacker might compromise some or all the accounts of the victim based on the information he collected.

We found our delegates understanding the risk associated with this scenario and they were happy that we presented it in a live demo to them. The only question from their side was that though IDS/IPS and Firewalls installed in their infrastructure if someone tries to do the same, will they get the IP address from the log?

The answer to which is that we used all openly available information to show how we can break into the security. The tools used such do not send any malicious packet to the original infrastructure, which makes it almost impossible to identify who is performing such enumeration. Apart from this there are various anonymity techniques such as Tor and proxy which we can hop through to conceal our identity.

It changed their perception about security. Security is not just to secure your network or infrastructure. It's also associated with what we were sharing on the internet. We won't discuss the after effects of the demo but as expected it resulted in a positive outcome.

## CASE STUDY 3: AN EPIC INTERVIEW

One of our friends was looking for a change in security domain. One fine morning he got a call from a resource consulting firm about an opening in one of the leading security companies. The first discussion went well as everything was in his favor. The salary expectation, location, and the notice period everything but the only problem was that the profile was a bit different. Our friend was into pentesting earlier but this profile consists a bit of pentesting and more on security monitoring. He got some personal experience based on his own interest on this domain but was not fully into it or in other words he was not having any hands on experience in this. So he was a bit worried about the interview. He wanted to crack this one badly. After two days he again got a call from the same firm stating that you were selected for the technical round and could expect a call from Mr. John Doe within a day or so.

The first thing he discussed with us was, "I just want to get a bit detail about this person so that it will help me understand what kind of questions he may ask, understand his experience and hence expectation." We three decided to jump into OSINT and collect as much as information about Mr. John Doe.

- Problem 1: We just have his name but not his position details.
- Problem 2: Time frame is not fixed, we don't know exactly when to expect the call.

So we suggested him to visit the website of the company to understand the services offered and go through other details such as vision and all. Meanwhile we started digging more information about the person Mr. John Doe.

Step 1:

As we had the name of the person and company name we directly searched the person in LinkedIn. We found his profile and the profile consists of many information such as his current and previous work experience. We found that the person is one of the technical leads of that company. The LinkedIn profile also consists of some of his articles and latest achievements. The person recently got OSCP (Offensive Security Certified Professional). We also found the GitHub account link from the LinkedIn profile. We visited each of his articles, and most of the articles were about how he found some of the bugs in many major sites which consist of some of the zero-days in popular CMS system.

Step 2:

After getting these we visited his GitHub account. He wrote all his scripts to automate the testing process in Python.

Step 3:

We did a simple Google search on his name and got many links along with a slideshare account. We visited that slideshare account. There were some presentations on how to write your own IDS rules. In one of the older posts we found a comment link to his older blogs.

Step 4:

We visited that old blog of him which consists of different road trips he did with his bullet motorcycle.

Step 5:

We searched his Twitter account and found an interesting post that he was recently attending one of the popular security conferences in Goa, India.

Step 6:

We visited the conference site and found that the person Mr. John Doe had given a talk on network monitoring.

Step 7:

We searched him in Facebook and got information about his hometown, current location, educational details, and all.

Step 8:

A quick people search on Yasni provided us a link to another website of a local security community where we found his phone number as he was the chapter leader. We verified this phone number through Truecaller and it checked out right.

It almost took 25–30 min to which we stopped digging more. In the meanwhile our friend was ready with all the information he got from the company website. Based on the information we collected in different sources we concluded this.

- Save the phone number and greet him with his name in case he calls.
- First thing you need to ask him is that how his talk went in Goa.
- Read his talk abstract and tell him it was great and you are regretting that you missed the talk.
- Expect questions on IDS rule writing and can refer to the slideshare presentations for answer.
- Expect some questions on tool automation and that too in Python. So a quick Python revision was required.
- Expect some questions on network penetration testing as he recently did OSCP.
- Expect some questions on web application security, bug bounties, and zero-days as he got listed in many.
- If he asks you about hobbies, tell him your road trips and how you wanted to have a bullet motorcycle but haven't got it yet.
- If you get any question related to your vision and all tell him something related to the company's existing vision aligned with your personal thoughts.
- If he asks you where you see yourself after some years or future plans, tell him you want to go for OSCP certification and be a Red team leader. This was true anyway.

Our friend had a very good knowledge and experience in pentesting and because of his expertise and with a little homework on the company and on the background of the person, he got selected. Mr. John Doe was not only happy with his technical skills but also for the reason that he and our friend got many things in common.

So these were some interesting case studies, we have certainly added as well as subtracted some points here and there as required but all in all these are the kind of situations everyone faces. Let's learn about some basic types of information related to commonly encountered entities and how to deal with them.

It's quite easy to start with primary information such as name, e-mail id to collect all other information but there are cases where we might not have primary information but that does not mean we cannot get these primary information from secondary information. The process might be a bit difficult but it's possible. So now we will discuss in particular about a person's details. What can be collected about a person? Where and how?

Below are some of the information we might be interested to collect about a person.

**PERSON:**
- First Name
- Last Name
- Company Name
- E-mail Address (Personal)
- E-mail Address (Company)
- Phone Number (Personal)
- Phone Number (Company)
- Address (Home)
- Address (Company)
- Facebook Account URL
- LinkedIn Account URL
- Twitter Account URL
- Flickr Account URL
- Personal Blog/Website URL
- Keywords
- Miscellaneous

From above list we can start with any point and can gather most of the rest. The steps may differ from what we got as a source and how to get to others one by one but we will be using the same tools/techniques just in different order.

Whatever we take as a source, basically we need to start with simple Google search or any other popular traditional search engine search such as Yandex. If we get any relative information, use the same information to collect any of the other related information by treating it as the source.

Let's say we got simple name that contains first name and last name then we can simply use a Google query to get results. Let's say using Google we were able to get the personal blog or website.

Visit that site to search related information such as any details about the person it may be the area of interest, age, date of birth, e-mail, hometown, educational details, or any such information that can be used to get other details.

Let's say we got the educational details. Open Facebook and try to search for the name with educational details. We may get the person's profile. In Facebook we will get lots of information such as company he/she is working on, friends, pictures of him/her, and sometime other profile links along with the personal e-mail address also.

Now using the company name and person's name we can get the LinkedIn profile quite easily and can craft an e-mail address. Generally companies use a typical pattern to create e-mail addresses. Let's say the company name is abc.inc and the site is www.abc.com, and it uses the pattern, first letter of the first name and the last name without any spaces. So from the person's name and company name we can easily craft the e-mail address or we can use tool like harvester to harvest e-mail address from the company domain name and after looking at all the e-mails we can easily pick the e-mail associated with the person. In this way it is possible to get or collect information through correlation.

Collecting company details is quite easy as compared to the personal information. Most of the company information is public. So we can get it in the website itself and we can start collecting company information just by knowing the company name. It can be used as one point of source to get all the information. So if we know the company name we can get rest of the details quite easily.

Below are the list of information we generally look out for in terms of a company detail.

---

**COMPANY:**

- Company Name
- Year of Establishment
- Directors
- Website
- Registrant Name
- Phone Number
- Address
- Keywords
- Number of Employees
- Employee E-mail Samples
- HR E-mail
- Openings
- Facebook Account URL
- LinkedIn Account URL
- Twitter Account URL
- Flickr Account URL
- Other Blog/Website URL/Subdomains
- Miscellaneous

---

If we know the company name we can easily go to any search engine we want to get its registered website URL. Once we get the registered website, we can get information such as year of establishment, directors, phone number, address, HR e-mail, openings details, and, in some case, links to different social networking profiles. A simple Whois query will also result in a lot of information.

There are other places where we can get all these information. We can see these information on Glassdoor, Zoominfo, and LinkedIn. For openings we can look in job portals as well. The number of employee and employee samples can be easily found using LinkedIn or else we can simply use tool such as harvester, Maltego to get e-mail patterns. The keywords and all can be easily found in the meta part of the website source, through various SEO and SEM services such as SEMRush.

This part is a bit technical and frequently needed by technical people such as administrators, IT consultants, pentesters etc. But if you have followed the book till here even after not being a tech person, then you won't find it much difficult. In this case, for carrying out a technical audit or assessment basically analysts are provided with the domain name or the IP address, so from OSINT point of view we can consider these two information as primary information. From these or any of it, it is quite possible to get the rest of the information mentioned below.

**DOMAIN:**

- Domain
- IP Address
- Name Server
- MX server
- Person
- Website
- Subdomains
- E-mail Samples
- Files
- Miscellaneous

So as we discussed earlier let's take the domain as a primary entity and from that we want to get all other information that is mentioned above. If we wanted to simply get the IP address of that domain, we just need to run a simple ping command in command prompt or terminal based on the operating system we use.

```
ping <domain name>
```

This command will execute and will provide the IP address of the domain.

For other domain-specific information, there are domain tools freely available in the internet and from the Whois record, we will get different information such as registered company name, name server details, registered e-mail ids, IP address, location, and many more. Resources like w3dt.net can be very helpful here. Directly using domain tool we can find lots of information about a domain, or else we can use different domain specific Maltego transformations for the same.

We can also use harvester to collect subdomains, e-mail address etc., from a domain name. From the e-mail addresses we can search for the profiles of the persons in different social networking sites.

And to get subdomains and a particular file from the domain we can use search-Diggity, Google, Knock (Python tool).

To get different subdomains we can use site operator or create a Python script which will take subdomain names from our list and enumerates it along with the domain provided.

```
site:domainname
```

To get a particular type of file from the domain with a keyword we can use filetype or ext operator and can run below query,

```
site:domainname keyword filetype:ppt
```

So in this way we can get all the domain-specific information from different sources.

So these were some case studies and examples in which OSINT can be collected and be helpful in our personal and professional life.

As promised earlier in our next topic we will be learning about Maltego machines.

## MALTEGO MACHINES

We have covered various aspects of Maltego in previous chapters from understanding the interface to creating local transforms. As this chapter is more about combining the knowledge we have covered till now, so related to Maltego we will learn how to create Maltego machines. Although we have already defined what a Maltego machine is, yet for quick recall it programmatically connected a set of transforms. It allows us to take one entity type as input and move toward another type(s) which are not directly connected to it, but through a set/sequence of transforms. There are some inbuilt machines in Maltego such as Company Stalker which takes domain entity as input and runs various transform in sequential fashion to get different types of information from it such as e-mail address, files etc.

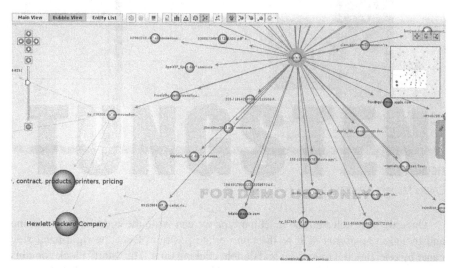

**FIGURE 14.1**

Maltego "Company Stalker" Machine

To create our own machine we need to use Maltego Scripting Language (MSL). The documentation for MSL is available as a PDF at http://www.paterva. com/MSL.pdf. The documentation is clear and simple, and anyone having basic programming skills can easily understand it. As all the terms and process are clearly described we do not need to cover them again, so straight away jump to create our own simple machine using local transforms we learned to create in a previous chapter.

Creating a Maltego machine is pretty simple, first we need to go to the Machines tab, under which we can find the New Machine option. Clicking on it will bring a window where we need to provide the name and other descriptive details related to the machine we are going to create. In the next step we need to choose type of machine we are going to create. For this we have three options:

- Macro: runs once
- Timer: runs periodically until stopped
- Blank: a blank template

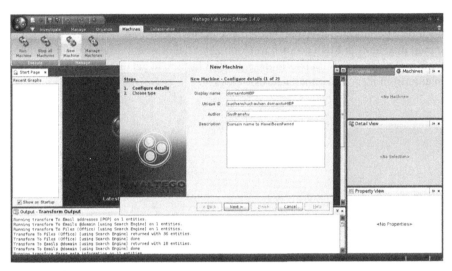

**FIGURE 14.2**

Create Maltego Machine

Once we have selected the machine type we can write the code for our machine and include transforms in it at the appropriate position, from the right-hand side panel by selecting the transform and double clicking on it. The "start" block contains the transforms and all other execution part. The "run" functions are used to execute a specific transform. To run functions in a parallel fashion we can include them inside the "paths." Inside "paths" we can create different "path" which will run in parallel with each other but the operations inside a path will run sequentially. Similarly we can provide different values, take user inputs, use filters etc.

Let's create a simple machine which extracts e-mail ids from a provided domain and further runs our HIBP local transform on these. For this we need to provide the machine name and select the macro type machine. Next we need to include the inbuilt transforms which can extract e-mails from domain such as domain to e-mail using search engine, Whois etc. Next we need to include our local HIBP transform. As we need to run these in parallel we need to create separate "path" for each e-mail extraction transform. Our final code looks like this:

```
machine("sudhanshuchauhan.domaintoHIBP",
  displayName:"domaintoHIBP",
  author:"Sudhanshu",
```

```
    description: "Domain name to HaveIBeenPwned") {

  start {

   paths{
    path{
     run("paterva.v2.DomainToEmailAddress_AtDomain_SE")
     run("sudhanshuchauhan.emailhibp")
         }
    path{
     run("paterva.v2.DomainToEmailAddress_SE")
     run("sudhanshuchauhan.emailhibp")
         }
    path{
     run("paterva.v2.DomainToEmailAddress_Whois")
     run("sudhanshuchauhan.emailhibp")
         }
    path{
     run("paterva.v2.DomainToEmailAddress_PGP")
     run("sudhanshuchauhan.emailhibp")
         }
       }
    }
  }
```

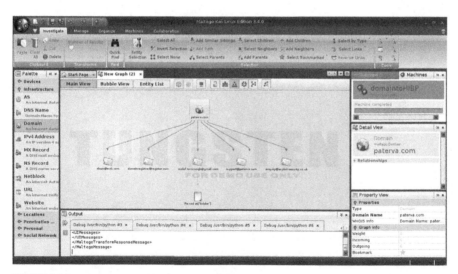

**FIGURE 14.3**

Our Maltego machine output.

Two important things that need to be kept in mind are that our local transform must be integrated into Maltego before creating the machine and the input and output data types need to be taken care of when creating a sequence.

So we learned to create Maltego machine. Though there is still much more to explore and learn related to Maltego, we have attempted to touch upon its every important aspect.

In this chapter we have learned about combining all the knowledge we gained till now and also saw some practical scenarios and examples. This is important as in real-life projects. It's not just about knowing things but also about implementing and utilizing them in an integrated manner according to the situation and generating a fruitful outcome.

In our next and last chapter we will be learning about certain general topics related to the internet which are often connected directly or indirectly to the information gathering. Having a basic understanding of these terms will be helpful for anyone utilizing internet for investigative purpose.

# Related Topics of Interest 15

## INFORMATION IN THIS CHAPTER

- Introduction
- Cryptography
- Data recovery
- IRC
- Bitcoin

## INTRODUCTION

In previous chapters we have learned about various topics which are associated to collecting and making sense out of data. We learned about social media, search engines, metadata, dark web, and much more. In this last chapter we will cover some topics briefly which are not directly related to open source intelligence (OSINT) but to the computing and internet culture and its evolution. If you practice the information provided in previous chapters it is very likely to encounter these topics somewhere.

## CRYPTOGRAPHY

There has always been a need to transfer messages from one location to another. Earlier people used to send messages through messengers who used to travel long distances to deliver them. Slowly a need to make this transmission secure came up. In situations like war, the message being intercepted by the enemy could have changed the whole situation. To tackle such scenarios people started to invent techniques to conceal the original message, so that even if the message is intercepted it cannot be understood by anyone except the desired receiver. One of the simplest examples is Caesar cipher, in which each letter is replaced by another with a fixed alphabet position difference, so if the position difference is 4 (right), then A would become D, B would become E, and so on. In modern era, technology has advanced a lot and so has the techniques to encrypt as well as break it.

## BASIC TYPES

### Symmetric key

In this type of cryptography both the parties (sender and receiver) use same key to encrypt and decrypt the message. A popular symmetric key algorithm is Data Encryption Standard (DES), there are also its modern variants such as Triple DES.

### Asymmetric key

In this type, there are two keys, public and private. As the name suggests the public key is openly distributed but the private key remains secret. The public key is used to encrypt the message whereas only private key can decrypt it. This solved a major issue with symmetric key which was the need of multiple keys for communication with different parties. RSA is a good example of asymmetric key algorithm.

Some other associated terms:

### Hashing

In simpler terms hashing is converting a character string into a fixed size value. Usually the hash is of small length. Some commonly used hashing algorithms are MD5, SHA1 etc.

### Encoding

It is simply about converting a character into another form for the purpose of data transmission, storage etc. It is simply like translating a language into another so that the other party can understand it. Commonly used encodings are UTF-8, US-ASCII etc.

The basic difference between these is that encrypted text requires a key to be converted back to plain text and it is mainly used for the confidentiality of message. In hashing, the hashed text cannot be reversed back to the original text and it is mainly used for integrity check and validation. The encoded text can be decoded back with any key.

We came across different examples, cases, scenarios where we learned how data or information plays a vital role in this digital world. Similarly any digital data stored in devices such as computer, laptop, mobile device etc., are equally important. As these are the personal devices, it consists of more personal data so should be taken care of carefully. Any hardware issue, software malfunction, device crash or theft lead to either loosing of those important data or can be in wrong hands and the consequences are much worst. So storing any important data in digital form requires a meaningful effort to make that secure. There are many solutions available both open source as well as commercial to store the data securely in these devices. Choose any of those based on the level of confidentiality of data. Apart from storing the data securely and locally in any device there are other cloud solutions available to store our data in one place so that we can retrieve and use those as per our desire. Along with the data storage and data transmission it is also recommended to use secured backup from time to time to avoid any accidental loss of data. The solutions are tightly based on what we learned above and that is cryptography or encryption. Today we frequently use cryptography on daily basis through technologies such as SSL/TLS, PGP, digital signature, disk encryption etc. So here we can conclude that encryption plays a vital role in our day to day life to secure our digital or virtual life.

With increase in computation power the ability to crack encrypted messages have also evolved. Attacks such as Brute-force, dictionary attack are easy to perform at a high speed. Also there are weaknesses in the algorithms, which make it easy to perform cryptanalysis on them. Given enough time and computation power any encrypted text can be decrypted, so today the algorithms used attempt to make it so time consuming to that the decrypted text becomes worthless in the time used to crack it.

## DATA RECOVERY/SHREDDING

Due to technological advancement now a days we prefer to store almost everything in digital form. A person who needs to send his/her documents does not want to visit a photocopy shop. He/she just wants to scan the hard copy for once and use the same soft copy number of time. This is just a simple example to understand human behavior now a days. So storing of important data in soft copy or in digital form arises some of the security risks. As we discussed above, the damage of the device, accidental delete can lead to loss of our important data. We just learned some precautions or in simple what to do with the digital data. But what if it got deleted?

There are possible ways to recover it. For a naive user, data recovery is only possible when the data is still present in trash or recycle bin, but it's not so. The capability of data recovery is way beyond that. This is just because of the very nature of data storage and deletion function implemented by the operating system. To understand this we must understand the basic fundamental of data storage or how data getting stored in different storage devices.

There are different types of storage devices such as tape drives, magnetic storage devices, optical storage devices, and chips. Tape drives are not generally used for personal use, earlier it was an integral part of the enterprise storage system, now there is a possibility that it is being deprecated so let's not talk about that. Apart from tape drive the other three are widely used. Magnetic devices are nothing but the hard disk devices we use, popularly known as HDD or hard disk drive, which stores all the data. When we delete data from our system the operating system does not delete the data from the magnetic disk but it just remove the address reference to that part, from the address table. Though the concept will be quite the same for all other media types such as DVD, but as we use these storage devices for backup and the HDDs for general storage, we will focus on HDD only. As we discussed that deleting a data from the system means removing its memory location details from the address table. So what is an address table and how it works? It's quite simple. Generally when we store the data in device it takes some memory from the HDD. The starting memory location and the ending memory location define a data in hard disk. All these memory location details are stored in a table called address table. So when we search for a particular data the system checks the address table to get the memory locations allocated for that. Once it gets that memory location it retrieves the data for us. As after deleting the data, the data is still present in the hard disk; we can recover it, unless it is overwritten by other data. Here deleting means deleting data from system as well as trash or recycle bin. So now we have some idea why data can be recovered after deletion but the major question still stands is how? Let's take a look into that as well.

There are many tools available on internet to recover deleted files from different operating systems, some are free and some are paid. The recovery process is quite easy. Install the software in the operating system and then open the application. Generally all the recovery tools come with a simple user friendly GUI or graphical user interface. Follow simple instructions and complete the wizard to recover the data successfully.

Wise Data Recovery is a good example of such tools, which can be downloaded from http://www.wisecleaner.com/wisedatarecoveryfree.html. The installation is simple and usage is pretty straightforward. Simply select the drive to be scanned for file recovery. Once the files are listed with their recoverability status we can select them and click on Recover button at the bottom right to perform the operation.

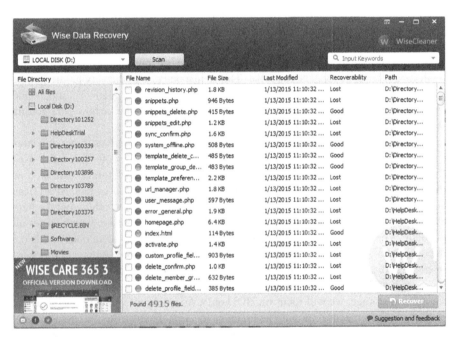

**FIGURE 15.1**

Data recovery using Wise Data.

Now as we know that sometimes it is possible to recover the data we have deleted, we should also know there are tools which can actually delete data from the disk. One such tool is FileShredder available at http://www.fileshredder.org/.

**FIGURE 15.2**

Data shredding using FileShredder.

# INTERNET RELAY CHAT

IRC or the Internet Relay Chat is like old school for many. It was developed by Jarkko Oikarinen in late 1980s. Though it was developed two decade back but the popularity of this application is still there. People still love to use IRC. The statistical data says it lost half of its users in last decade but as per a product of this old if still people are willing to use it's a great achievement.

IRC is quite same as any other chat application. It follows client server architecture and uses TCP protocol for communication. Earlier it uses plain text communication but now it also supports TLS or Transport Layer Security for encrypted communication. The major reason for its development was to use it as a group chat software and it serves the purpose quite well. As in general term we say different types of chat groups as chat room. In IRC terms it is called as channel. Unlike other chat clients it does not force a user to register but a user has to provide a nickname to start chatting. A user can chat in channel as well as directly with another user using private message option. IRC is widely used in different discussion forums and we love to use this whenever we get an opportunity to use.

Normally to use IRC we need to install an IRC client in our system. There many clients available in internet and for all kinds of operating systems. So download a client which supports the operating system being used. Once we get an IRC client installed, connect to a channel to start communicating with fellow channel member.

The chat process is also quite same as the normal chat process. It's basically line-based chat. One user will send a message in a line then the other will reply. Due to its anonymity most hackers prefer the use of IRC. The major question here is how it's going to help us in OSINT. It's quite simple as there are various channels available we can choose one based on our interest and crowdsource our question and get response from different experts. We need to be in the right place in right time to discuss what is happening in the cyber world. We can get clear scenario about what is happening all over the world and, for example, if we are lucky enough then we might get future prediction also such as which group is preparing for a distributed denial-of-service (DDOS) attack on a company, what are the possible targets, what is the current attack vectors hacktivists are using, and many more. The information we will get from here can be used to define cyberspace, trends in cyberspace and future prediction, discuss a query etc. So next time do not hesitate to use IRC, just provide a fancy name and enjoy chatting. A simple web-based IRC platform is http://webchat.freenode.net/. Simply enter a nickname and channel name, and start to explore.

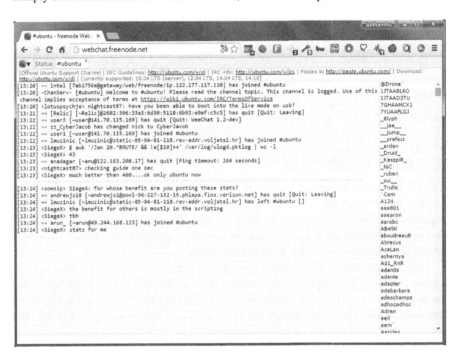

**FIGURE 15.3**

Freenode IRC.

# BITCOIN

Anyone into information security or keeping track of world media especially technical journals must have heard of the term "bitcoin." It was popular for its new concept earlier in technical field but later when the value of 1 bitcoin touched almost 1000$, it started to trend between common internet users. Many must be aware of this but still we will discuss some of the important facts about bitcoin. Bitcoin can be referred as electronic currency or digital cash developed by Satoshi Nakamoto. Unlike normal currencies it uses a decentralized concept called peer-to-peer technology for transactions. It is based on an open source cryptographic protocol in a format of SHA-256 hash in hexadecimal form. The smaller unit of a bitcoin is called as satoshis. 100 million satoshis at a time creates one bitcoin. Bitcoin can also be referred as payment system as there are no banks, organization, or individual has power to control or influence it. It's always in digital form and can be transferred within a click to any individual over the world. There are pros as well as cons for this also. Some of the pros are we can convert bitcoin into any currencies independent of country. We can transit it anonymously, hence it is quite popular in darknet. No one can fake, create, or devalue bitcoins. Similarly there a large amount of cons also such as a transaction cannot be reversed. The security of bitcoin is low as it always there in digital form. Once a bitcoin wallet is deleted it is lost forever.

Now we have a bit understanding on bitcoins. So it's important to know how to store it also. We can store bitcoin digitally only, because it's a digital data. We need a bitcoin wallet to store bitcoin. The major disadvantage of this is once accidentally we delete our wallet, we lose all the money. So take backups in proper intervals to avoid any such incident. The initial bitcoin project site is http://www.bitcoin.org/.

**FIGURE 15.4**

Bitcoin wallet.

So this is where it all ends. We had a long journey in which we explored a lot of topics, learned about many different tools, techniques, and methods to explore around. In later part we also discussed how and what to do with all this information. We also saw some related scenarios and examples. All in all hopefully we can say that it was a great learning experience at both ends. One important point that needs to be made is that in today's world "Information is Power" and with power comes great responsibility. Use the knowledge gained through this volume for ethical purposes and contribute to create a better world.

# Index

*Note*: Page numbers followed by "f" and "b" indicate figures and boxes respectively.

Printed in the United States
By Bookmasters